Municipal Dreams

Municipal Dreams

The Rise and Fall of Council Housing

John Boughton

VERSO

First published by Verso 2018
© John Boughton 2018

3 5 7 9 10 8 6 4 2

Verso
UK: 6 Meard Street, London W1F 0EG
US: 20 Jay Street, Suite 1010, Brooklyn, NY 11201
versobooks.com

Verso is the imprint of New Left Books

ISBN-13: 978-1-78478-739-4
ISBN-13: 978-1-78478-741-7 (UK EBK)
ISBN-13: 978-1-78478-742-4 (US EBK)

British Library Cataloguing in Publication Data
A catalogue record for this book is available from the British Library

Library of Congress Cataloging-in-Publication Data

Names: Bou
Title: Munic
Boughton.
Description:
references
Identifiers: I
9781784787
Subjects: LC
housing—
Britain—H
Classificatio
| DDC 36
LC record a

Typeset in Fournier by Hewer Text UK Ltd, Edinburgh
Printed and bound by CPI Group (UK) Ltd, Croydon, CR0 4YY

Contents

Introduction   1

1 'How to Provide Housing for the People': Origins   7
2 'The World of the Future': The Interwar Period   31
3 'If Only We Will': Britain Reimagined, 1940–51   61
4 'The Needs of the People': Council Housing, 1945–56   86
5 'Get These People Out of the Slums': 1956–68   108
6 'Anti-Monumental, Anti-Stylistic, and Fit
     for Ordinary People': 1968–79   139
7 'Rolling Back the Frontiers of the State': 1979–91   169
8 'Thrown-Away Places': 1991–7   196
9 'A Different Kind of Community': 1997–2010   219
10 'People Need Homes; These Homes
      Need People': 2010 to the Present   252

Acknowledgements   289
Illustration Credits   291
Notes   293
Index   319

Introduction

As I write, the charred remains of Grenfell Tower loom over North Kensington. At times, as you walk around its base among the low-rise blocks of the leafy Lancaster West Estate to which it belonged, you can almost forget the events of 14 June 2017. But then you'll see another of the ubiquitous posters of those 'missing' in the fire, or raise your eyes and see the tower: a blackened twenty-four-storey hulk — scene, now symbol, of one of Britain's worst peacetime housing disasters and funeral pyre for numbers as yet untold.

The fire at Grenfell was, above all, a personal tragedy to its residents and their friends and families. But to many more it symbolised, in devastating fashion, a crisis in social housing. It stood as an awful culmination to deeply damaging policies pursued towards council housing, and the public sector more widely, since 1979.

The lessons of Grenfell will continue to unfold and will always be disputed but some clear conclusions seem inescapable. The fire appears to condemn a very common recent form of tower block renovation. At present, dangerously combustible cladding has been found in every sample taken from similarly refurbished

blocks across the country. It seems to indict a model of social housing management, seen here as distant to residents' interests and
oblivious to the fire safety concerns they raised. It brings into
question the system of commercially driven procurement and
public–private partnership that has become near-ubiquitous in the
social housing regeneration of recent years. And, more broadly, it
challenges the cost-cutting, austerity agenda that has dominated
public policy in the past forty years. 'Neoliberalism' can seem a
'boo' word but Grenfell has exposed its reality – deregulation,
public services decimated, their underlying ethos battered, public
investment slashed and scorned, ruthless economising that saves
pennies not lives.

The universal shock and anger in the aftermath of Grenfell
has therefore been applied not only to this singular, awful event
but to current social housing policy and practice more widely.
That properly emotional response is understandable and not
unfounded. The later chapters of this book will detail the political and fiscal choices that have marginalised social housing and
its residents for four decades. But the language of 'crisis' is
double-edged. We have much to learn from Grenfell and much
to condemn but we must also defend social housing, its value
and achievements.

This book tells, first, of its *necessity* – that it was, above all, a
pragmatic response to the prevalence and persistence of slum
conditions, originating in Victorian fear of the disease-ridden
and allegedly criminal and immoral rookeries of its booming
cities and towns, but strengthened as a more democratic state
renewed its mission to end slum living, first in the 1930s and, on
a larger scale, from the 1950s. The constant was the failure of
the free market and private enterprise to provide the healthy
and affordable homes that ordinary people needed and deserved.

It reminds us that council homes — built in large numbers from the 1890s, more so after the two world wars — have been, for most of that long history, aspirational housing: the mark of an upwardly mobile working class and the visible manifestation of a state which took seriously its duty to house its people decently. The state didn't, of course, get everything right. Constraints on public investment were, nearly always, an impediment to the best of what might be achieved. Planners, sociologists and hostile politicians criticised the suburban 'cottage' estates which dominated the interwar and early post-war years just as they did the tower blocks which arose in the 1960s.

There's no value or plausibility in sugar-coating the mistakes and missteps here, of all that 'went wrong' as the conventional narrative has it. But this is a story rooted in actual estates and lived experience, and there the account is far more mixed and, generally, far more positive. Earlier chapters recount the ideals which inspired and informed the great programme of council house building which transformed our country, overwhelmingly for the better, up to the 1980s. Later chapters tell of the second transformation which has seen council housing and its community marginalised and dishonoured in the neoliberal era which followed. Before Grenfell, there was an earlier 'crisis' of council housing — a time when hostile politics and destructive economics, sometimes compounded by flaws in design and construction, often exacerbated by council neglect, troubled many estates and communities.

The image of the 'problem estate' — far more than the reality which was always more diverse, more positive — became the dominant representation of public housing at this time and a powerful force for the sweeping transformation of the sector that followed. The causes and consequences of those changes need to be better understood than the current fevered debate allows. In simple terms, it is undoubtedly the case that estates are overwhelmingly now decent places to live. I've visited many of the estates described here, and studied more – the showpieces as well as the happily ordinary – and have been struck, in nearly all cases, by their essential decency. It's hard to say that after Grenfell, but we must assert this truth against those who would use the disaster to smear public housing as a whole.

Estate regeneration, or its current practice, has been widely criticised. Some Grenfell tenants believe the block was improved to make its appearance more palatable to their affluent North Kensington neighbours. A few thought its regeneration was a prelude to privatisation. Those concerns may have been groundless but they found fertile soil in the form of regeneration taking place all around them. The very notion of the *estate* has been criticised.

'Council estates' – the term and its negative connotations are retained – have been attacked by critics as 'ghettos of the poor'. 'Mixed tenure', 'mixed communities' are the new mantra; the sell-off of council property to raise funds from profitable private development the ubiquitous means. 'Social cleansing' is an emotive term but the fact that in nearly all cases social housing stock has been reduced by regeneration and working-class tenants displaced in favour of better-off owner-occupiers and renters is undeniable.

At the same time, regeneration has benefited many estates in recent years and many thousands of social housing tenants have seen their homes and environments greatly improved.

We should also reject the bandwagon criticism of tower blocks as such. Their story is a mixed one but tower blocks have provided decent homes to many and continue to form a vital component of our social housing stock. The attack on high-rise slides easily, and sometimes explicitly, into an assault on the form and principle of social housing more generally that should be resisted. This book will look at the dynamics and ideals that led to the rise of multi-storey living (and continue to do so) as well as, of course, at the mistakes along the way.

We must be wary too of generalised criticisms of contemporary forms of social housing management where, again, the reality is mixed and often – in terms of best practice at least – much improved in recent years. Into the 1980s, a model of direct local authority ownership and administration dominated, but tenants' experiences of this (in principle) more democratic model varied. The antagonism of both Conservative and Labour governments since 1979 towards council-run housing effected a management revolution. Now most social housing – as the shifting terminology indicates – is owned and managed by so-called registered social landlords, usually housing associations. Representative, responsive and accountable governance is essential – as Grenfell has so starkly demonstrated – and tenants' voices must be strengthened as we go forward, but any large-scale reversion to direct council control is unlikely.

The outpourings of sympathy shown towards the residents of Grenfell and the fortitude of its community since the tragedy have defied common negative stereotypes. But the marginalisation of social housing and its occupants remain. In this context, the longer crisis of social housing is real and destructive. Since Mrs Thatcher's introduction of Right to Buy in 1980 and the virtual cessation of new build since then, our social housing stock has diminished drastically. The Borough of Kensington and Chelsea, in which Grenfell is situated, has built just ten new council-funded social homes since 1990.[1] In consequence, and in conjunction with well-meaning policies prioritising those in greatest need, social housing has become housing of last resort, reserved to the poorest and most vulnerable of our society even while demand for the secure and genuinely affordable homes it offers has risen sharply.

Council housing then, social housing now, arose from the duty of the state to house its people well even as the market proved unable or unwilling to do so. Grenfell Tower, at root, epitomises the dereliction of that duty, but the failure of private enterprise remains even as the state has, in recent decades, retreated from its former role. Grenfell has reminded us, in the most powerful way imaginable, how much we need the state. We need its regulation and oversight to protect us from commercially driven agendas which value profit over people. We need its investment to provide the safe, secure and affordable housing for all that the market never will. And we need its idealism – that aspiration to treat all its citizens equitably and decently which lay at the very heart of the council house building programme which improved the lives of many millions of our citizens from the 1890s.

1
'How to Provide Housing for the People': Origins

You've battled your way through the crowds and past the hipster havens of Shoreditch High Street. There's a busy road junction ahead and next to it the eighteenth-century St Leonard's Church, not quite managing the dignified aloofness its impressive Palladian styling and spiritual calling seem to merit. But take a right, along Calvert Avenue, and the mood alters. It's quieter, a wide street lined with imposing late Victorian tenement blocks and their store-front ground floors, and then, as you progress, there is an unexpected wooded green mound with what looks like a strangely displaced seaside shelter at its summit.

Climb the steps, sit down and take time to look around. Here's that little oasis of urban calm that St Leonard's church-yard can't achieve. Broad streets radiate from this central circus and carefully deployed within them is a further set of those grand tenement blocks that could look forbidding; their sturdy proportions offset by a panoply of fine decorative Arts and Crafts detailing – pitched, dormer and mansard roofs, prominent gable ends of all shapes and sizes, stone quoined windows and pedimented doorways, tall chimneys reaching for the sky, glazed terracotta tiling and, most arrestingly, quirky, colourful, streaky bacon-style banded brickwork.

The Boundary Estate, Bethnal Green

It's accomplished work, Grade II listed in fact, and good-quality housing. If you walk down nearby Brick Lane, you'll see one of the two-bed flats advertised for rent. It's expensive – £2,145 a month – but then, as the agent says, it's so 'perfect for a professional looking to be close to the City'.

This is the Boundary Estate, Britain's first council estate, opened in 1900. It remains a small working-class redoubt but around 40 per cent of its homes were purchased under Right to Buy and most of those later sold on. The defences of this little island of social housing have been breached, firstly by gentrification and, more recently, by corporate money. New battle-lines are drawn out along Calvert Avenue, between the surviving old-fashioned corner shops and community laundry on the one hand and the boutique coffee shops, organic grocery and artisan workshops on the other.

Once the area was a place the wealthier classes avoided. Boundary Passage, a narrow walkway leading off the High Street to the rear of the estate, gives just a hint of something more dangerous. In the nineteenth century it led to the Old Nichol, the most notorious of London's slum quarters. In 1863, the *Illustrated London News* had described the area as nothing 'but one painful and monotonous round of vice, filth and poverty'.[1] Later, even Charles Booth, who sought to bring detached statistical rigour to his charting of Victorian social conditions, delineated it as of the 'lowest class; vicious, semi-criminal'.

It was Arthur Morrison who most famously captured (and only lightly fictionalised) the Old Nichol in his 1896 novel, *A Child of the Jago*. Morrison's lurid opening paragraphs, describing the 'close, mingled stink – the odour of the Jago' that 'rose from foul earth and grimed walls', were surely enough to send a frisson of alarm through his middle-class readers, but, if they dared to read further, the book held other terrors too.[2] Crime: Dicky Perrott, the novel's protagonist, a pickpocket, steals the gold watch of the bishop come to celebrate the moralising efforts of his religious confrères. And death: no happy ending this time, Dicky suffers the fate ordained by his life in the Jago – he dies in a gang fight; do-goodery cannot save him.

The Old Nichol usually killed more insidiously, however, through disease and deprivation. Its death rates were over twice the London average; one in four newborns were likely to die before their first birthday. In 1891, just before its clearance, 5,719 people lived in the district, three-quarters of them in one- and two-room dwellings, in houses 'built with "billy-sweet", a mortar including street dirt which never dried out'.[3] That, as well as fetid humanity, would explain the characteristic aroma which Morrison identified.

While the Old Nichol had achieved particular notoriety, such accounts could be multiplied. The world's first Industrial Revolution had created its first urban proletariat. Taken together, they seemed to some in the upper classes to threaten the very material and spiritual foundations upon which the established order was built. Thomas Carlyle had first raised this 'Condition of England Question' in 1839 in response to the rise of Chartism. Frederick Engels had drawn the revolutionary moral more sharply (and more positively) in his book *The Condition of the Working Class in England* published six years later. Both graphically charted the ugly industrialism scarring the land and each, in their different ways, lamented its impact on our working people.

Engels, and many who followed, was a good example of another manifestation of Victorian materialism – its empiricism, the obsession with facts and measurement. Dickens satirised this in the heartless persona of Thomas Gradgrind in his 1854 novel *Hard Times* (dedicated in fact to Thomas Carlyle): 'Facts alone are wanted in life. Plant nothing else, and root out everything else.'[4]

But for every Gradgrind there was a reformer who wanted to use these data to effect progressive change. William Henry Duncan, 'an intelligent physician resident at Liverpool', gave evidence to the Commons Select Committee on the Health of Towns in 1840, and described the city's 2,400 courts which housed 86,000 people, one-third of its working population (another 38,000 lived in cellars):

Very few have an entrance wider than four feet, and that is by an arch-
way built over it; the width is from 9 to 15 feet between the rows; there
is one only six feet. The backs of the houses in one court are built against
the backs of houses in another court; at the further end there is generally
an ash pit between two privies; they are in the most abominable state of
filth.[5]

In response to further questioning (and, in further detail, in his
1844 pamphlet, *On the Physical Causes of the High Rate of
Mortality in Liverpool*), Duncan went on to calibrate precisely
the correlation between housing conditions, incidences of fever
and premature death.

The committee concluded that such conditions were 'constantly
increasing' – a testament to the breakneck speed of urbanisation
and the 'very profitable and tempting investment' they represented to slum landlords. Similar circumstances were reported in
the new industrial towns across the country. In 1889, a report by
Dr John Thresh on a particularly noisome area of Ancoats,
Manchester – the 'shock city of the Industrial Revolution' –
detailed twenty-five streets, many less than seventeen feet wide,
and housing, mostly over seventy years old. The area contained
over fifty courts; one-third of houses were back-to-back. A death
rate of over eighty per 1,000 of the population led to his dry statistical conclusion that '3,000 to 4,000 people [were] dying annually
here in Manchester from remediable causes'.[6]

The medical men and sanitary campaigners provided
evidence for a growing sense among the British upper classes
that something should be done. And although the means by
which disease was spread were little understood, the common
misapprehension of the time – that it was spread through
noxious 'bad air' (or 'miasma') – was helpful to the extent that

it persuaded the middle class of their own vulnerability to the threat that such conditions posed.

They frequently found the alleged immorality of the slums almost equally alarming. The Reverend Andrew Mearns' thirty-page pamphlet, *The Bitter Cry of Outcast London*, published in 1883, became an instant bestseller. Tellingly, Mearns' first paragraphs tell of the slum-dwellers' 'Non-Attendance at Worship'. But, having described their living quarters – 'pestilential human rookeries . . . where tens of thousands are crowded together amidst horrors which call to mind what we have heard of the middle passage of the slave ship' – he can only conclude that 'immorality is but the natural outcome of conditions like these'. He even names what was often only darkly hinted at in such sensationalist Victorian accounts: 'incest is common; and no form of vice and sensuality causes surprise or attracts attention'.[7]

William Booth, who had founded the Salvation Army on the streets of East London not far from the Old Nichol, produced the jeremiad *In Darkest England* in 1890. The title indicates his message: 'As there is a darkest Africa, is there not also a darkest England? May we not find a parallel at our own doors, and discover within a stone's throw of our cathedrals and palaces similar horrors to those which Stanley had found existing in the great Equatorial forests?'[8] Such works offered searing images and gruesome detail of the lives of Victorian society's poorest. They contributed to that mix of prurience and piety, fear and compassion, which fuelled the drive to housing reform.

In this, Liverpool led the way. The city's 1842 Sanitary Act allowed magistrates to order landlords to clean any 'filthy or unwholesome' house they owned. They also set up a council Health Committee that policed this. Four years later, the

Liverpool Sanitary Act – 'the first piece of comprehensive health legislation passed in England' – made the council responsible for drainage, paving, sewerage and cleaning. It also created the city's (and the country's) first Medical Officer of Health – Dr Duncan, no less – who set to work with a zeal, closing over 5,000 cellar dwellings declared unfit for human habitation in 1847 alone.[9]

At a time when the gods of the free market held almost unchallenged sway, national legislation dealing initially with sanitary matters followed only haltingly. The 1848 Public Health Act gave local authorities discretionary powers over drainage, water supply and the removal of nuisances. The 1866 Act sharpened responsibilities to deal with nuisance. The 1875 Public Act consolidated and extended these powers and imposed duties on the sometimes recalcitrant local bodies to enforce them.

As it touched more directly on the sacred rights of property, housing reform as such followed more slowly. The 1866 Labouring Classes Dwellings Act allowed municipalities to purchase sites and build and improve working-class homes. Unsurprisingly, Liverpool was the single authority to make use of the legislation. It built because the market wouldn't. The Corporation (as such municipal authorities were frequently termed) had even instructed the City Engineer to draw up a model scheme in the vain hope that a private builder might develop it, but speculative building profits lay in the prosperous middle-class suburbs and not the indigent inner city.

Thus, in 1869, the St Martin's Cottages, completed in Ashfield Street in Vauxhall, Liverpool, were the first council homes to be built in Britain. The 'cottages' were, in fact, tenements – 146 flats and maisonettes in two four-storey blocks, brick-built with open staircases and separate WCs placed on the half-landings; the result was so bleak that even the trade magazine *The Builder* concluded that those who built for the poor should 'mix a little philanthropy with their percentage calculations'. The blocks were finally demolished in 1977. Only a blue plaque remains to mark this inauspicious beginning to one of our greatest social revolutions.

The Builder's comment was a knowing one, as finance was key to the question of providing improved working-class housing. With hindsight, the great breakthrough of the 1866 Act was that it allowed local authorities to borrow at preferential rates from the Public Works Loan Commissioners – in effect, the first government 'subsidy' for public housing. At the time, however, the chief intended beneficiaries of this measure were the various private companies building 'model dwellings' for the working classes. The first, the Metropolitan Association for Improving the Dwellings of the Industrious Classes, was founded in 1841. Others, such as the Improved Industrial Dwellings Company and the Artizans', Labourers' and General Dwellings Company, followed and by the 1870s there were said to be twenty-eight such concerns operating in London alone. This was the so-called five per cent philanthropy, named for its financial model which, by offering that guaranteed five per cent rate of return, appealed to the pocket books as well as the hearts of Victorian investors.

This philanthropic concern with the improvement of working-class housing (and the improvement of the working classes themselves) was evidenced too in the founding of the Peabody Trust, funded from the personal fortune of the London-based American banker George Peabody. The first Peabody Trust homes were built, not far from the Old Nichol, on Commercial Street in Spitalfields in 1864. One year later, the housing and social reformer, Octavia Hill, opened the first of her schemes.

Hill, who eschewed the large block dwellings of five per cent philanthropy, nonetheless promised the same rate of return to her early investors, among them the leading Victorian art critic and social thinker John Ruskin.

Despite the hopes placed on them, most of these bodies struggled to pay their promised dividends and the sector as a whole was incapable of acting on the scale that contemporary conditions and even the modest scale of local authority slum clearance demanded. Furthermore, the 'model dwellings' themselves were unpopular, criticised for their austere, barracks-like appearance as well as the officious rules and regulations imposed on tenants. In any case, rents were too high for the slum working class in the most need. Typically, the model tenants were better-paid artisans, and even the salaried middle class.

Still, elite concern over working-class housing conditions continued and was expressed most dramatically by Tory leader Lord Salisbury in an article in the *National Review* in 1883. Salisbury's critique of existing conditions broke no new ground and, in truth, his proposals were modest – increased government loans to the model dwellings companies, tighter regulation of speculative building and a suggestion that factory owners might provide housing for their workers. However, the immediate outcome of Salisbury's article was a Royal Commission on the Housing of the Working Classes convened in 1884. Its membership was a roll call of the great and the good, including the Prince of Wales. Its published report – a record of 24,663 questions asked of 191 witnesses running to 1,300 pages – was the apogee of Victorian investigatory fact-finding.

But Salisbury's article did contain one straw in the wind of unanticipated significance. He pointed to the destruction of working-class homes in parliamentary-approved improvement

schemes for new roads and railways. Shaftesbury Avenue and
Charing Cross Road, both completed in the later 1880s and
each driven through swathes of slum housing, were notable
examples of the former. 'Under these circumstances', he
concluded, 'it is no violation even of the most scrupulous principles to ask Parliament to give what relief it can.'[10] The *Pall
Mall Gazette* applauded this as 'an unmistakable avowal that the
help of the State may be legitimately invoked in order to provide
houses for its subjects'.[11]

By 1885, Salisbury was prime minister. An 1885 Housing
Act, masterminded by his Home Secretary Sir Richard Cross
(another member of the Royal Commission) strengthened local
authorities' sanitary powers but was otherwise largely a consol-
idation of existing measures. Cross's own position had been
made clear some years earlier:

> I take it as a starting point that it is not the duty of the Government to
> provide any class of citizens with any of the necessaries of life, and
> among the necessaries of life we must of course include good and habit-
> able dwellings . . . if it did so, it would inevitably tend to make that
> class depend, not on themselves, but upon what was done for them
> elsewhere.[12]

Salisbury's 1890 Housing of the Working Classes Act apparently portended little more. It reiterated local government's
power to build 'lodging houses' (albeit generously defined to
include separate houses and cottages) but only with the express
permission of the Local Government Board, and then with the
stipulation that they be sold off within ten years. But Part I,
acting on Salisbury's words seven years earlier, required in
London – where the Royal Commission had considered

housing conditions among the most severe – that at least 50 per cent of housing demolished in clearance schemes be replaced. Part III of the Act gave the London County Council (LCC) the power to build these homes. The 1890 Act, extended in 1900 to other local authorities, provided the basis of the relative surge in council house building that followed.

Paradoxically, this seems both an unintended and inevitable consequence. It was unintended on the part of the Conservative legislators who had passed the reform. They saw it, at most, as a small shift towards increased state responsibility but retained their basic belief in the efficacy of the free market and fear (to use a later idiom) of a 'dependency culture' fostered by state provision.

But a changed context made it something more. The belief in the inevitable benevolence of an unfettered free market was in decline. Poverty, once understood (by more fortunate Victorians at least) as 'pauperism' – a product of personal improvidence – was increasingly seen as the unavoidable result of social and economic circumstance. Late Victorian politicians weren't 'all socialists now', as Sir William Harcourt claimed in 1887, but the idea of the state as a necessary reforming force in cases where private enterprise manifestly failed to serve a larger public interest had strengthened. A pragmatic collectivism sanctioning its use where the market failed – as it clearly had in the field of working-class housing – was emerging.

These subtle but significant changes in collective thinking were played out in the context of increasingly strident paternalistic fears of the threat posed by the slums. Victorian reformers feared their filth – that lack of cleanliness so far from Godliness. And they feared disease, particularly disease that failed to respect the proprieties of Victorian social divisions.

By the turn of the century, as the might of the British Empire struggled to defeat a motley crew of Afrikaner farmers in the Boer War and the economic and military threat posed by a newly united Germany seemed daily more apparent, more existential dangers were perceived. 'National Efficiency', rooted in Social Darwinist notions of racial fitness and expressed in a eugenicist ethos that crossed the political spectrum, became the watchword. British supremacy depended on a healthy (and, to some, more contentedly malleable) population.

The argument for council housing, as it emerged before the First World War, required one more component: a machinery of state with the capability and will to build it. The 1888 Local Government Act created county councils and county borough councils; a partner act confirmed a household franchise in local elections. In the capital, the new apparatus and broader electorate came together in the Progressive Party that won seventy of 118 seats in the first elections to the LCC in 1889. This Progressive majority – a mix of radical Liberals, Fabians and labour leaders – was determined to implement the large-scale reform resisted by the patchwork of ratepayer-dominated local government bodies in existence hitherto.

The formation of the LCC was a significant change in the perception of local government. As a sign of its prestige and significance, the LCC itself included 'two dukes, a viscount and thirty-seven other members of the peerage', even, briefly, a serving prime minister (the Liberal Lord Rosebery). But the hard graft was performed by a distinguished lower tier of effectively full-time councillors including Fabian socialist Sidney Webb, Liberals Arthur Hobhouse and John Benn (Tony's grandfather), and representing the labour interest John Burns and Will Crooks, both leaders of the great 1889 London docks strike.[13]

Other forces vital to the form and ethos of the Boundary Estate were emerging from more recondite quarters too. The art critic John Ruskin is readily mocked for his prudishness and apparently effete aestheticism, but he was a revered figure within the British labour movement. He was also a major influence among all those who, like him, railed against the ugliness of nineteenth-century industrialism and its mechanisation of creativity and the human spirit. Ruskin himself stated that ultimately his preference for one school of architecture over another was 'founded on a comparison of their influences on the life of the workman'.[14] In short, he proposed an aesthetic mission to tackle the problem of poverty and its material effects.

This radical sentiment was carried further by William Morris, who today is mostly remembered as a designer of pretty wallpapers and textiles. However, in his day Morris was a self-avowed revolutionary – a founder of the Marxist Socialist League and habitué of Shoreditch's left-wing International Club. Morris's views on five per cent philanthropy were characteristically trenchant: it offered only a 'miserable palliation of the evil . . . as to this matter of housing you can at the best only be housed as careful masters house their machines'.[15] Positively, his aesthetics and politics meshed seamlessly in the Arts and Crafts movement he championed as both antidote and antithesis to contemporary capitalism. Readily caricatured as rooted in unrealistic anti-industrialism and romantic medievalism that often succumbed to the very commodification it decried, it's easy to dismiss the Arts and Crafts movement, but the ideal it proclaimed – giving dignity to the life and labour of working people – was a powerful one.

A nexus of unlikely-sounding bodies emerged to give it voice. The Society for the Protection of Ancient Buildings that

Morris founded in 1877 – promoting repair and preservation rather than the vulgar 'restorations' favoured by many Victorian practitioners – paradoxically became a meeting place for many committed to a new architecture rooted in pre-industrial national traditions. The Art Workers' Guild, of which Morris became Master in 1892, joined artists, craftsmen and architects in a mission to unite the fine and applied arts and mobilise both to serve a wider public.

All this activity created a body of men – mainly men – who 'believed they had a gospel and that it was for them to propagate it'.[16] Many found a home in the LCC's Housing of the Working Classes Branch, a subset of its Architect's Department founded in 1893. Owen Fleming was one. A 'prominent student at the Architectural Association . . . with ardent Socialist convictions', a member of the Art Workers' Guild, Fleming was 'oppressed by the chain of circumstances that compelled so many of the poor to live in insanitary dwellings [and] trying to get to the bottom of things'.[17] He had begun this quest as a middle-class student at the University Hall Settlement in Russell Square (modelled on Toynbee Hall in Whitechapel). He then chose to live in the heart of the East End in model dwellings in Stepney.

He became the first of a long line of young, committed architects who brought their political ideals and architectural skills to the question of how best to house the people. In 1893, at the age of twenty-six, he was appointed architect-in-charge of the Boundary Estate scheme. Fleming and the team of nineteen he led were critical of the East End's terraced housing. 'Take a walk from Hackney to Bethnal Green, Mile End, Poplar or Bow . . . just a long row of dreary monotony, all the houses being precisely the same, without any sort of architectural feeling at all.'[18] But they were equally critical of the austere,

barracks-like 'model dwellings' erected by five per cent philanthropy. For the Boundary Estate, Fleming envisaged a 'picturesque urban village'.[19]

That mound we climbed was formed literally (but with meta-
phorical perfection) of the debris of the demolished slums. The
shelter was a bandstand; Fleming, with typical humanity, had
pictured courting couples 'strolling round the garden of a fine
summer's evening while the band played'. Together they
formed the green heart of what was envisaged as a new community, provided not only with housing – 1,069 tenements in nineteen free-standing, five-storey blocks for an estimated population of 5,524 – but with eighteen shops, two schools,
seventy-seven workshops, a central laundry with bathrooms
and two clubrooms.

A close look at the estate overall reveals variations in the
design. Some blocks are plainer than others. Different architects were responsible for different sections and Fleming details
how fluctuating costs, materials shortages and labour difficulties
all shaped the estate's evolution. But the ensemble was brought
together by a unity of purpose and ethos; its 'gospel' expressed
through the language of the Arts and Crafts movement, occasionally accented with a smattering of London School Board
Queen Anne. There was an impressive attention to design detail
– Fleming pointed out that 'every habitable room' enjoyed
plentiful light and 'nearly every room . . . a pleasant outlook'
– and build quality. As one might expect from a follower of
William Morris, Fleming also paid tribute to the 'great body of
skilled artificers who have striven to make this estate a model of
good workmanship'.[20]

In itself, the new accommodation was good, though far from
luxurious. Some 600 of the tenements were fully self-contained

but the rest had detached WCs and a small number of one-room flats shared WCs and sculleries. These were adequate working-class homes, nevertheless; too good to some. One correspondent to the *British Architect* expressed concern that such largesse would sap the spirit of the lower classes:

> In the evening at dinner, work over for the day, the British workman will no doubt speculate as to how long it will be before the Government not only educate him free of charge and house him for next door to the same thing, but when they really mean to allow him to pass from the partly useful to the wholly ornamental.[21]

The reality was, of course, something different. The tenements had, in the long run, to pay for themselves and their tenants had in the meanwhile to pay their rent. Fleming was far from a utopian dreamer and as a Fellow of the Royal Statistical Society (albeit a far from Gradgrindian one), he calculated in excruciating detail the 3s (15p) a room weekly rent which the alchemy of loans and sinking funds and interest rates required.

That rent was twice the sum the Old Nichol's residents had paid for their old accommodation and it barred them from enjoying the advantages of the new. The homeworkers, petty traders and labourers moved to neighbouring locales and so, in Arthur Morrison's words, 'another Jago, teeming and villainous as the one displaced, was slowly growing, in the form of a ring, round the great yellow houses'.[22] The new tenants were mostly better-paid artisans in skilled, steady employment, even some members of the middle class.

In this regard, the Boundary failed those it intended to help the most. It served – as with most early council housing – a better-off working class in stable, relatively well-paid employment but excluded those on lower or irregular incomes. Practically and morally, most housing reformers felt it wrong to 'build down' to the standards of the poorest accommodation with rents to match and they fell back on the argument that a 'filtering up' process would occur – that the slightly less slummy homes vacated by those moving to municipal housing would be taken over by the poorer working classes in the worst accommodation; everyone would climb a rung up the housing ladder.

The persistence of the slums belied such hopes, but it was a commonplace of the day. When Penshurst Parish Council in Kent built the aptly named Pioneer Cottages in 1900 (one of the very rare examples of rural council housing before 1914), Jane Escombe, the indomitable campaigner who had secured them, candidly acknowledged that their 5s (25p) weekly rent was affordable only to 'the higher class of workmen' who 'would move into our better cottages and leave theirs at a lower rent to the agricultural labourer'.[23]

When St Pancras Metropolitan Borough Council opened its own small block of tenements in 1909 on Flaxman Terrace (still there – an impressive building across the road from the British Library), a local councillor was clear that 'they would not be able to take in the submerged tenth' – the contemporary term for what would later be called the underclass: 'of course a better class of working men and women would take them' but he hoped 'the others would be able to take their places'.[24]

Liverpool was the single authority to take a different approach. Its housing conditions were among the worst in the country and a low-paid, casual workforce dominated; perhaps there simply weren't enough 'better' houses and 'better' workers to go round. At any rate, the council had determined as early as 1896 that 'the remedy' – slum clearance – 'was getting worse than the disease'. Most of those displaced either added to the overcrowding of existing slums or created new ones; some it was 'almost certain went into the workhouse'.[25] The Corporation stipulated that future council housing be reserved exclusively for those displaced by slum clearance and, crucially, at rents they could afford. At around 5s 3d (26p) for a four-bed tenement in 1903, rents were around one-third the level of those in London.

Du Cane Road, Old Oak Estate, Hammersmith

Back to London and eight miles to the west of the Boundary Estate, new municipal dreams were taking shape in what was the LCC's finest pre-war scheme, the Old Oak Estate in East Acton.

Begun in 1911, interrupted by war, the finished estate comprised 1,056 homes. This was a very different animal to the Boundary. While that was very much an *urban* village, if that, Old Oak comes close to the pastoral – a council estate idyll painted in the warm red and yellow brick of its cottage homes and floral green of its gardens and open spaces. East Acton underground station – opened in 1920, bijou and 'in keeping', as they say – lies at the heart of the estate; just to the south is the big beast of the Westway, decidedly not in keeping and a symbol of a later and failed era of planning.

The station lies on Erconwald Street, named, like a number of streets on the estate, after an early Archbishop of Canterbury to mark the LCC's purchase of its land from the Church Commissioners. The archaism seems fitting. A short walk to the east, passing under the railway bridge, brings you to the junction with Wulfstan Street and a cameo of all that its principal architect W.E. Riley (Chief Architect of the LCC and another member of the Art Workers' Guild) and his team were seeking to achieve. A short terrace of four cottages – all steeply pitched red roofs and gabling, chimney stacks and Georgian-style sash windows – lies on each corner, set diagonally and curved to provide space and vista.

Broad tree-lined streets run to the distance and along them similar but subtly varying terraces, some set back, some offset to form small, intimate closes. This was, and was intended to be, a million miles away from the densely packed and regimented grids of terraced housing that accommodated many of the working class in urban Britain. And if it reminds you of Letchworth Garden City or Hampstead Garden Suburb, that also is no accident.

Letchworth owed its existence to the singular vision and unflagging energy of one man, Ebenezer Howard. He was ostensibly an unlikely figure for such an enterprise – his day job throughout the period of his greatest labours was as a parliamentary reporter for *Hansard* – but Howard reflected and captured the spirit of the times in his rejection of an ugly and untrammelled urbanisation and, ultimately, in his demand to plan and build something better.

Rushby Mead, Letchworth – workers' housing

He first outlined his ideas in 1898 in *Tomorrow: A Peaceful Path to Real Reform* (better known in its 1902 edition as *Garden Cities of To-morrow*). He founded the Garden Cities Association (later the Town and Country Planning Association) in 1899. His company, First Garden City Ltd, formed to develop Letchworth, was established in 1903. Raymond Unwin and Barry Parker were appointed as the scheme's architects.

Howard's drawing board plans of economically self-sufficient and socially mixed new towns seemed impracticable to most people – although they were revived and to some extent implemented in the government-sponsored New Towns movement after the Second World War – and they were irrelevant to even the most ambitious of municipalities. But his guiding ideals – the reintegration of town and country, healthy homes in salubrious surrounds – had much greater resonance and wider applicability.

Brentham Gardens, for example, three miles to the west of Old Oak in Ealing, had been founded in 1901 and Unwin and Parker were appointed to plan this new 'garden suburb' five years later. This was a co-partnership scheme requiring prospective householders to invest in the company to gain tenancies and benefit from future profits, though ownership remained vested in the company and surplus income was reinvested. It was one of a number of such companies intended to harness the relative affluence and aspirations of the better-off working class.

Hampstead Garden Suburb, founded in 1906 by Henrietta Barnett, Christian socialist and co-founder with her husband Samuel of Toynbee Hall, was intended as a mixed community with smaller houses at lower rentals set aside for the working class. Several co-partnership companies were involved with its construction but overall direction was in the hands of a trust charged with maintaining its founding vision. In practice, the sheer quality of the estate and the rents it charged ensured that it would soon become the middle-class, or even upper-class enclave that we know today. Again, it was Raymond Unwin, rapidly becoming the go-to guy for schemes of this type, who was appointed the Suburb's chief planner.

Unwin was the Rotherham-born son of a Yorkshire industrialist. At Oxford, he had attended lectures by both Ruskin and Morris and, as a young man, was an active member of Morris's Socialist League. By the turn of the century, his youthful revolutionism had declined; he remained a committed Christian Socialist but his politics had taken a more practical turn. The financial model of these more or less privately developed schemes he worked on ensured they could have little relevance to the wider issues of working-class rehousing which remained his preoccupation, but he foresaw the possibilities of the new approach being pioneered by local government. 'How to provide for the Housing of the People is a problem for which our larger municipalities are now being compelled to find some solution,' he wrote; his Fabian Tract, *Cottage Plans and Common Sense*, was – with its detailed prescriptive description, illustration and plans – intended to help.[26]

His work on Hampstead Garden Suburb was of more direct relevance to the design of Old Oak Estate, however. Unwin's vision required a break with the well-meaning but unimaginative sanitary bye-laws now dictating rigid building lines and wide streets and their unintended side effect of restricting gardens and open space. A private act of parliament was secured for the Garden Suburb and this served as the prototype of the 1909 Housing and Town Planning Act that made Old Oak possible.

John Burns, no longer the socialist firebrand of his earlier years but a reforming President of the Local Government Board in Asquith's Liberal administration, guided the bill through parliament. He spoke eloquently of 'that line of beauty which Hogarth said was in a curve' and proclaimed the measure's greater object – to 'provide a domestic condition for the people in which their physical health, their morals, their character and their whole social condition can be improved'.[27]

Such heady ambition can seem far removed from the prim privet hedging and quaint Arts and Crafts vernacular of Old Oak, and its reach required the less glamorous nuts and bolts of municipalism too. A 1900 Housing Act permitted the LCC to acquire land and build beyond its restricted borders and so made these cottage suburbs possible. (Earlier estates of similar idiom but with more conventional layout had been built at Norbury in Croydon and, within London's then borders, Totterdown Fields in Tooting.) The extension of municipal transport systems and cheap workmen's fares allowed at least the better-off working class to move to them. A financial push was provided by the prohibitively high cost of land and labour in the inner city.

For all this, Old Oak represented a very English revolution: regressive to some – looking back to a past that never quite existed – and yet, in its time, progressive in the insistence that working people should live well and decently. Naturally enough in this old country, conservatism won out. Today, the estate is a Conservation Area and its design features – 'wooden mullioned window frames (both sash and casement), brick façades, pitched and gabled roofs, small dormers and panelled doors' – and landscaping details are etched in the planners' guidelines.[28]

The LCC built around 10,000 council homes before 1914. The great tenement estates – Millbank and the Bourne Estate followed on from the Boundary – and the cottage suburbs capture the eye, but many of these homes were the far less architecturally distinguished five-storey, balcony-access, walk-up flats that became ubiquitous in inner London in the years to come. Most London boroughs had neither the means nor ambition to emulate this example.

Battersea was an exception – Progressive-controlled and known as the 'Municipal Mecca', its Latchmere Estate was opened in 1903 by John Burns (the area's MP since 1892) and was the first council estate built by direct labour, the council's own workforce. A small estate of 315 homes – a terraced, two-storey mix of houses and cottage flats, it lacks the flair of the LCC's showpieces but was attractively and sturdily built. Its street names – Freedom and Reform, Odger, Matthews and Burns (local labour leaders) and even Joubert, named after a Boer general such was the council's anti-war sentiment – capture the scheme's ideals.

Elsewhere, only Liverpool, with its total of 2,747 flats and houses, had built proportionately more than London. On a smaller scale, a similar mix of tenement blocks, cottage estates and occasional terraces could be found across the country, mostly in the larger cities such as Sheffield and Manchester though with rare examples, typically driven by the zeal and energy of particular councillors, elsewhere. Overall, around 24,000 council homes had been built before 1914, housing no more than 1 per cent of the population. Nevertheless these structures offered essential precedents – in terms of both design and aspiration.

On one hand, the cottage suburbs presented a more idealistic and generous response to working-class housing needs, but pressures of space and affordability seemed to compel the tenement as a feasible solution. This contest between multi-storey living – densification in current jargon – and low-rise persisted, fought out in the competing visions of architects and planners and the conflicting priorities of politicians.

After 1914, the political class would find that the Great War created a housing crisis among a working class that it both needed and feared more strongly than ever before. This compelled a new, larger and far more generous state operation to manage housing. And so, in 1919, the first great age of council house building began.

2

'The World of the Future': The Interwar Period

The 'Homes and Property' section of the *Evening Standard* describes the Dover House Estate as 'a charming enclave on the western edge of Putney'.[1] In 1919, the local middle classes looked far less favourably on this new LCC estate. Transport links for the new residents were poor, they pointed out solicitously, and then there was another 'element for consideration': the area's 'conversion into a working-class district must enormously depreciate the rateable value of property in the vicinity'.[2] Not everyone, it seems, welcomed the 'homes for heroes' that Lloyd George had promised in the recent general election, at least not on their doorstep. Nevertheless, around 1.1 million new council homes were built in the twenty years following 1919, transforming the face of Britain and, in nearly all cases, immeasurably improving the lives of its working class.

The homes of Dover House are among the best of these and the estate was 'a show place in its day . . . visited by many from all over the world'.[3] It's worth a visit today. A turning off the surprisingly leafy section of the South Circular takes you to Dover House Road where carefully tended square-cut hedges match the square-cut red-brick, red-roofed houses. The enclave retains the prim and privetted modesty of Old Oak but here the plainer, boxier, neo-Georgian style, which came to predominate in the interwar period, prevails. Many of the houses retain their original eight-pane windows, their Crittall steel manufacture adding the 'neo-' to 'Georgian'. Short, set back, curved terraces (a device also favoured at Old Oak) and mature elms neatly frame a later mini-roundabout. A left turn takes you towards The Pleasance (the name is a merited, unpretentious archaism in the context) – the three-acre wooded open space at the heart of the estate.

At this end, the housing has a more consciously, cottagey English vernacular feel. There's an attention to detailing in porches, doors and windows and variety in a range of rooflines that could come from an architect's pattern book – gable and hipped ends, first-floor eaves, dormer windows and mansard roofs. Everything is planned to please the eye, everything contributes to a little idyll of picturesque domesticity. In later phases, further south and up the hill (the last of the estate's 1,212 homes was completed in 1927), the houses became smaller and less elaborate as economy measures kicked in. You can see both in Hawkesbury Road: at its top end, each of the short terraces completed in the earlier phases of construction is differentiated by roofline, gabling and footprint; at the lower, longer plainer terraces take over.[4]

All the estate's homes had front and back gardens, and many had side gardens too, designed to create vistas and a sense of spaciousness. Tree-lined streets, generous grass verges, mature trees retained, new ones planted and village greens too. The planners intended that every group of houses either overlooked an open space or had close access to one.[5] The nine acres of allotments provided might seem more prosaic but they spoke powerfully to housing reformers' visions of healthy self-sufficiency. Even the estate's new elementary school on Huntingfield Road was described by the LCC as 'a pavilion type [along] the lines of a sanatorium'.[6]

The Dover House Estate was begun in an almost unique period in the history of public housing when the state both insisted on the highest standards *and* provided the money to meet them. The first 600-odd houses built on the estate, some seen along Hawkesbury Road, cost £1,150 each to construct – around three times the amount of equivalent pre-war homes. This was a figure that reflected both the inflationary pressures of the post-war replacement boom and labour and materials shortages, and the willingness of central government to meet these costs in full beyond what could be raised locally by a penny on the rates.

If Dover House captures the quality of these post-war ambitions, it's the Becontree Estate in Dagenham which best captures their scale. In 1919, the government approved the LCC's plans to build 29,000 new homes to house around 145,000 residents. Of these, 24,000 were to be built on a greenfield site of 3,000 acres of market gardens, scattered cottages and country lanes beyond London's eastern borders in Essex. The first houses were completed on Chitty's Lane (there's a blue plaque to mark the occasion) in November 1921; the finished estate, by 1939, comprised 26,000 homes, housing a population of 120,000.

The cliché that it takes a war for the state to recognise the virtues of its working class – as soldiery, workforce and (though only latterly) as citizens – seems justified here. Positively, this new-found commitment to state-supported housing reflected a widespread view that those who had fought on the Western

Front deserved reward for their sacrifice. Practically, this was delivered in the 500,000 'homes for heroes' that Prime Minister Lloyd George pledged in the 1918 general election campaign. This came too late for the many who had made the ultimate sacrifice, of course, but pre-war arguments about the squalor and ill-health of slum housing – and unfitness of its population – also gained added traction as the war effort demanded healthy (albeit disposable) bodies.

Negatively, there were those who feared the potential *disloyalty* of these heroes to the established order. This was seen in the widespread fears of revolution – alarmist, exaggerated, but not completely baseless – that had been fanned by wartime militancy and the dreadful example of Russia. Trade union membership, sometimes aggressively led by a radical shop stewards' movement, had doubled to over eight million by the end of the war. The Labour Party had emerged in 1918 as the Official Opposition. In this context, the public housing programme was seen as a quite deliberate and knowing means of placating an insurgent working class.

Decent and affordable working-class housing was in short supply before 1914. It grew far scarcer, particularly in areas where arms production was concentrated, as domestic house-building and repair gave way to the military priorities of total war. The resultant crisis came to a head in an eight-month rent strike in Glasgow in 1915, involving at its peak 20,000 households, which forced the government to introduce rent controls. This unprecedented intervention into the free market reflected government fears of a working-class militancy that might threaten the war effort. Practically, it testified to the simple fact that the housing market was broken – that supply and demand were catastrophically out of kilter.

The irony, which contemporary politicians understood only too well, was that the imposition of rent controls further reduced the incentive of private builders to build for rent and for landlords to let. As the war draw to a close and the pent-up demand for new housing grew ever more pressing, it became clear that state action was unavoidable. Here, pre-war experience offered a template: a local authority housebuilding programme supported by state subsidy.

This was anticipated as early as 1917. Local Government Board Circular 86/1917 'Housing after the War' promised 'substantial financial assistance from public funds' to local councils prepared to implement approved programmes of working-class housing. If that supplied a means to new housing, the Tudor Walters Report (written in large part by Raymond Unwin) issued in 1918, suggested its form. The report stipulated – at a density of no more than twelve an acre – parlour homes (with that front room typically kept 'for best' in working-class communities) with at least two bedrooms, 'of cottage appearance', with gardens front and back, with a bathroom and a larder. All this was very largely codified in the most ambitious and generous piece of housing legislation to date, the 1919 Housing and Town Planning Act. This is often named the Addison Act after Christopher Addison, the single-minded minister appointed to oversee it. Critically, the Act required all councils to not only survey local housing needs but to implement concrete plans to tackle them.

But while all this was accepted across the political spectrum in 1917, there was a division about the scale of the operation. For most on the right wing, such projects were a necessary albeit *temporary* measure. In contrast, those on the left retained their belief, developed before the war and apparently confirmed

by it, that state provision was a positive and permanent intervention. The argument about the role and remit of council
housing would remain contested and have a powerful impact on
future debates.

An aerial view of the Becontree Estate, c1930

Returning to Becontree, it's not a pretty estate. In fact, to its
critics, it's a relentless splurge of rather anonymous municipal
suburbanism. The early estate, in particular, lacked facilities
and suffered a certain dull sameness. As one resident in those
days remembered: 'I went for a walk and when I came back, all
the houses looked alike. I was in a terrible state – in tears. The
workmen said "What's the matter, ducks?" I said, "I can't find
my house".'[7]

The LCC's architects pointed, in their defence, to the estate's
ninety-one different housing types but, in truth, it was the

overall homogeneity of those homes – front and back-gardened two-storey houses, overwhelmingly in the conventional boxy neo-Georgian style – and the flat and featureless topography within which they are set that is most striking. This, in contrast to Dover House, was a much-diminished version of the Garden City. The latter's forms were respected in the estate's scattered open spaces, curving streetscapes and plethora of cul-de-sacs and closes, but these niceties were overwhelmed by the sheer scale of Becontree and the mass and uniformity of its far plainer homes.

In contrast, the Wilson Grove Estate in Bermondsey comprised just sixty-four red-brick and white-rendered houses along three or four quiet tree-lined streets squeezed between the river and the busy Jamaica Road. In its way, though, it better captures the idealism of this brief post-war moment. A stroll down Wilson Grove to the river – you can loop round Janeway Street and Emba Street first to see the full extent of the estate and then take a right eastwards towards the Angel pub – captures a lot of the story. The pub is an early nineteenth-century hold-out, a vestige of a time when the whole area was a hub of river-trade commercialism and residents of the estate had no access to the river unless they worked on it.

Before the pub, you'll see a small group of statues – an elderly man on a bench, a rather grim-looking woman dressed in Edwardian finery, a young girl and, presumably, her pet cat. It makes for a strange ensemble without its backstory. The group (commissioned by the London Docklands Development Corporation and Southwark Council, created by Diane Gorvin) is called Dr Salter's Daydream. It depicts Alfred, a local GP, councillor and MP, his wife Ada, also a long-serving councillor, and their daughter Joyce. Alfred is shown as an old man, waving to his daughter, remembered in happier times before her early death. Alfred and Ada had met at the nearby Bermondsey Settlement, one of a number in the capital to which well-meaning Christians descended to do good works among the poor. The pair married and remained in the area: Ada continued her social work while Alfred (one of the most brilliant medical students of his generation) founded a local practice. Joyce attended a local school where she perhaps contracted the scarlet fever which killed her, aged just eight.

Alfred had long since concluded that the area was 'one huge slum' and both he and Ada had determined nothing less than a revolution in social conditions could help those in Bermondsey. In the year of Joyce's death, 1910, seven Independent Labour Party candidates contested Bermondsey's local elections. Just one – Ada Salter – was successful but the small victory was enough for Alfred to declare his dream: 'We'll pull down three-quarters of Bermondsey and build a garden city in its place.'[8]

In 1922, when local Labour secured a majority on Bermondsey Metropolitan Borough Council, the time came to attempt to put these words into practice. The party's manifesto had been clear. It rejected the LCC's inner London tenement blocks – 'No more Progressive barracks and Coalition skyscrapers!' – and demanded 'a cottage home for every family'.[9] The test came in the clearance of a notorious area of slum housing in Salisbury Street. These four acres housed some 1,300 people. Death rates from respiratory disease were three times and the infant death rate twice the London average. That the housing should be cleared was not in doubt: it had been condemned thirty years earlier. The issue was what might replace it.

The new Labour council proposed what its architect, Ewart G. Culpin, a leader of the Garden City movement, described as a small estate of 'trim structures of warm, red brick', housing only 400. The Conservative (Municipal Reform) majority on the LCC and the neighbouring boroughs baulked. Where would the unhoused 900 residents go? Their fears that many of the displaced might move to adjacent areas and add to existing problems of overcrowding were backed by the Ministry of Health, which refused loan support. But Bermondsey remained adamant that it would 'refuse to warehouse the people'. And with the support of the short-lived Labour government of 1924 and Housing Minister John Wheatley, it got its way.

The estate, built by the council's workforce, was officially opened in November 1928. The mayor spoke of a 'magnificent piece of social improvement'. He boasted too of £2,000 collected in rents and not a penny in arrears: 'people have responded magnificently to the Council's efforts on their behalf, and they are taking infinitely more pride in their homes than ever before.' It was unthinkable then that people 'sank' in council estates; rather, the estates were a key component of what local Labour had proclaimed three years earlier as a programme of 'mass upliftment'.

Alfred Salter, now the constituency MP, spoke at the same ceremony of the council's foresight in 'looking to the future and not only the present – not hurriedly throwing up dwellings which in 50 years' time will become slums and therefore a disgrace to civilisation'. That's going to seem an uncomfortably prescient critique of the 1960s council house building programme to some, but he was right about Wilson Grove. It has stood the test of time – still attractive, well cared for, a nurturing, semi-rustic haven of high-quality housing; an understated, very English 'New Jerusalem'.

But step beyond it and you'll notice that Bermondsey is not a Garden City. The council planned a second scheme on Vauban

Street along similar lines to Wilson Grove but their plans were blocked, and this time four-storey, balcony-access tenement blocks were erected instead. There's some fancy brickwork but they're otherwise conventional. What happened to Dr Salter's dream?

The short answer is that the need to rehouse inner-city popu-lations, more quickly and at greater density, and the ambition of Labour politicians to provide larger solutions, trumped the desire to build cottage suburbs and challenged their feasibility as a solution to working-class housing needs. Back in 1918, the official policy of the London-wide Labour Party had been to:

> break up London as we know it, to encourage the exodus outwards . . .
> and to plan a wide outer ring on garden city principles . . . We would
> build no more tenements . . . we would build new towns where possible,
> or garden suburbs where that was the best we could do.[10]

But a number of principally East End boroughs came under Labour control in 1919 and some of these, like Bermondsey, became socialist strongholds in the mid-1920s. Demands for slum clearance and rehousing had been central to Labour's rise; in power, the party had to combine its idealism with practicality. Take Labour in Stepney. In opposition, the borough's Labour councillors had opposed council plans to build tenements, rejecting even an innovative scheme providing lift- and deck-access and private balconies. In power, however, after 1925, one of the Labour administration's first acts was to commission Culpin to design a model six-storey maisonette scheme of their own. The lack of available building land in inner London, the necessity to house residents close to local employment, and the pressing need, above all, to build something better than the existing slums, compelled this shift for them as for others. In Stepney, where a large Jewish population needed to be 'near the market places where they can obtain Kosher meat and also to be near their Synagogues', moving out to Becontree or another of the LCC's peripheral estates was seen as even less of an option.[11]

If such local pragmatism was one factor in the retreat from the high idealism of Tudor Walters and Addison, another and more important one was a powerful shift in the national political mood. Alarmed by growing national debt and spurred by elite resentment of taxes and higher social spending, a new Conservative austerity narrative – given political clout by the by-election victories of Lord Rothermere's 'Anti-Waste League' – was in place by 1921. Lloyd George commissioned the businessman and Tory politician Sir Eric Geddes to recommend savings, and one of the major victims of the so-called 'Geddes Axe' was the post-war housing programme. Subsidies were cut with immediate effect. Addison resigned in protest; across the country, only 213,000 council houses were built under the 1919 Act he had championed.

In the 1920s, council housing policy was marked, firstly, by the reduced space standards and subsidies of the 1923 Housing Act implemented by Conservative Minister of Health and Housing, Neville Chamberlain. Its intended thrust was to boost, by means of a subsidy to building contractors, the private housing market, but where local authorities could persuade the ministry of the need for council provision, a small subsidy of £6 per house per year was offered for twenty years. The Chamberlain Act was also deliberate and explicit in reducing the design standards required for grant support. Nearly all these later homes were non-parlour and their floor area fell from an average of 900 square feet under Addison to between 750 and 850 square feet. The requirement that all homes have a fixed bath represented a small advance. A little over 75,000 new council homes were built under the Act which was, in any case, effectively superseded when the first Labour government assumed office in 1924.

In contrast, Labour's 1924 Housing Act, masterminded by John Wheatley, placed council housing centre stage. It offered local authorities a £9 per house per year subsidy for forty years and, though it maintained the reduced space standards of the Chamberlain Act, it now required that the 'fixed bath' be provided in a bathroom. In numerical terms, this was among the most effective legislation of the interwar period, producing 493,000 new council homes.

Anecdotally, one resident noted the effect of these reduced specifications on the Dover House Estate:

> As financial problems arose so each new builder made the houses smaller as they went up the hill. They were smaller and smaller so that when you got to the top ones . . . if you opened the front door you had to close all the other doors, you know, otherwise you couldn't get in.[12]

While the Wythenshawe Estate in Manchester reflected this shifting regime, it remains one of the most ambitious attempts to build at scale according to Garden City principles. The plan was formed principally in the drive and vision of three individuals – the Liberal husband and wife team, Ernest and Shena Simon (they would later, like Addison, join the Labour Party), and Labour alderman W.T. Jackson.

Alongside the vision of the Garden City, other master plans were studied by these councillors. For example, Vienna, a Social Democratic stronghold from 1919 until the fascist coup of 1934, saw the most pioneering experiments in municipal housing. The Austrian capital completed 400 housing schemes, famed for their scale and monumentalism, and 64,000 flats in the period. The most famous of them, the Karl Marx-Hof, was one kilometre (or four tram stops) long. That name signifies another aspect of these schemes – they were consciously the harbingers of a new socialist world, one that both prioritised working-class needs and fostered more communal ways of living; the housing blocks encircled large open courts that were intended to act as the focal point of the residents' social life. Additional facilities, which included laundries, bathhouses, kindergartens, healthcare services and cooperative food stores, were likewise planned to build and serve community. This collectivist endeavour and idealism excited some on the British left, but Alderman Jackson was clear: 'We are not emulating Vienna and I have not been there . . . In general we favour the cottage type of dwelling.'[13]

By 1939, there were 8,145 of these in Wythenshawe – two-storey houses, semi-detached or in short terraces (described waspishly by Pevsner as 'conventional, Quakerishly undeco-rated'),[14] set among abundant green space along tree-lined roads, each with their own front and rear gardens. At a time when 30,000 of Manchester's 80,000 inner-city homes had been officially condemned as unfit for human habitation, to the local Cooperative Women's Guild they represented nothing less than:

> the world of the future – a world where men and women workers shall be decently housed and served, where the health and safety of little children are of paramount importance, and where work and leisure may be enjoyed to the full.[15]

This new world was one where for 'every working mother' there would be 'a clean, well-planned home which will be her palace'; one, should your gender politics be bridling at this point, 'so well and wisely planned that her labour will be lightened and her strength and intelligence reserved for wider interests'.

Ernest Simon's private wealth – an industrial fortune derived from his family's engineering business – had been the seed corn of this project. He had purchased Wythenshawe Hall and its 250-acre estate south of the city in Cheshire in 1925. Donating it to Manchester, he directed only that it 'be used solely for the public good'. Jackson then persuaded the City Council to buy 2,500 acres of surrounding farmland. Government assisted through a private act of parliament in 1931 that incorporated the area to the City of Manchester proper.

Shena Simon had provided the detailed vision through her involvement in the design of the houses, school curricula and promotion of community facilities and employment. The blueprint was provided by Barry Parker, Unwin's brother-in-law and with him the co-designer of Letchworth Garden City.

Parker's plan reflected Garden City ideals of curving streetscapes and greenery. He preserved Wythenshawe Hall and Park at its centre and, though some open space has been nibbled away in later developments, thirty acres of park and woodland remain across the estate. He made two significant innovations: the parkway and neighbourhood units. The former was adapted from the more motorised America of the day, but it was not a paean to the car but rather a means of preventing ribbon development and thereby preserving green space. Parker's Princess Parkway is now the M56; perhaps not quite what he had in mind. The neighbourhood units were a planning

WITH ACKNOWLEDGMENTS TO BARRY PARKER, F.R.I.B.A., P.P.T.P.I.

Barry Parker's plan for the Wythenshawe Estate, Manchester

ideal, detailed and executed on a much larger scale after the Second World War when we will examine them again.

To the residents themselves, all this considerate masterplanning represented an enormous improvement on what they were used to. After all, 'not everyone could get a house in Wythenshawe. Before we got one an official from the Town Hall wanted to know all about us . . . We had to prove we were good tenants. We heard that some people were from the slums but we never met any of them.'[16] With rents typically set at between 13s and 15s (65p–70p) a week when average weekly wages stood at around £3, this division was not surprising. Ernest Simon calculated that rent was just affordable to the working man provided there was a 'willingness of the wage earner to be content with a very small amount of pocket money, and competent and economical management on the part of the housewife'.[17]

Some residents talked of a 'Wythenshawe ethos'. This was a commitment to making the new district 'worthy of the time and money spent on it' – a self-avowed working-class respectability which found reflection in a shift to a more privatised and domesticated focus on family and home. Gardening was the great symbol of this while less time was spent with neighbours or down the pub. Many – some residents who missed the intimacy and sociability of old haunts but also, maybe more so, middle-class observers with more or less romanticised notions of the 'community' of older slum working-class neighbourhoods – have lamented this change as a 'loss'. For now, let's just say that a great many Wythenshawe newcomers welcomed their removal from the gossip and intrusiveness of their former locales and embraced their new healthier homes and surroundings.

All this seems a far cry from 'Broken Britain' and yet Wythenshawe was where David Cameron chose, in his brief Blairite phase, to make his plea to 'hug a hoodie' in February 2007. By then, to Cameron and to others too, the estate had come to epitomise all that was wrong with such large council schemes. A *New York Times* journalist, visiting the 'endless housing project' of Wythenshawe ('pronounced WITH-en-shah', she informed us) summed it up when she wrote of 'the absent fathers, the mothers on welfare, the drugs, the arrests, the incarcerations, the wearying inevitability of it all'.[18]

It wasn't, of course, ever thus. Dover Hill again provides the acme of an alternative, prelapsarian world. In 1931 the LCC estimated that 37 per cent of its heads of household were white-collar workers while 34 per cent belonged to the skilled working class. Some families even had maids. That was exceptional but it was almost universally the case that council estates in their earlier years, and well into the post-1945 era, were the home of a (relatively) affluent and aspirational working class. Indeed, their success to a significant degree rested on just that. The true story of 'Broken Britain' is not failed council estates but an economy that failed their residents.

That early success rested, however, on a degree of exclusion – of the poorer working class still living in the slums. The persistence of slum living undercut the 'filtering up' arguments common before the war that the poorest might improve their conditions by moving into homes vacated by the better-off working class as they moved into council accommodation.

The scandal of this was recognised in the legislation of the 1930s. First, in Labour's 1930 Housing Act, which incentivised slum clearance and obliged local authorities to rehouse all those affected by it. The Act also offered a special subsidy to build flats in the inner city where the costs of acquiring and clearing land were unusually high. The pressure to build higher, which became near-irresistible from the 1950s, had been set in motion and thus by 1934 (the year they came to power on the LCC), Labour in London had so shifted from its previous blanket opposition to tenements that a party policy group concluded that 'block dwellings [were] inevitable' and that it was unwise to 'dogmatise' about their height.[19] High-rise itself, at a time when lift provision was deemed unfeasibly expensive for work-ing-class homes, was not yet an option. This would inevitably change.

There were other significant anticipations of later develop-ments. In 1933, Housing Circular 1331, passed by a 'National' (predominantly Conservative) coalition government, stipu-lated that henceforth all public housing grants be dedicated solely to slum clearance. A laudable aim but one which explic-itly demarcated a clear dividing line between those on the right who believed council housing should be reserved for the worst off and those on the left who maintained a belief that it should also serve 'general needs'.

The 1935 Housing Act added another significant criterion to definitions of unfit accommodation: that of overcrowding. All councils were required to survey overcrowding in their district and prepare construction plans to tackle it. Significantly, the Act also created a new category of 'Redevelopment Areas' replacing the more narrowly defined 'Clearance Areas' of the 1930 Act. Now, whole areas could be designated for clearance, not solely due to their insanitary character but on broader grounds of overcrowding, poor amenities and bad layout. In this context, the Second World War was, initially at least, as much an obstacle to slum clearance ambitions as a boost to them. The massive redevelopment schemes of the 1960s were sometimes seen as a delayed catch-up to these earlier aspirations.

Any housing history worth its name, therefore, should pay as much attention to the tenement blocks that predominate in inner London and feature prominently in the council housing stock of our other large cities as it does to the various schemes judged in some way 'iconic'. That said, these four-, usually five-, sometimes six- (where maisonettes formed the top two floors) storey blocks are, by definition, unremarkable. The five-storey norm was judged the maximum possible for housewives carrying shopping or managing children or their menfolk carrying coal. Most were balcony-access – that is, homes were reached along a shared balcony, usually to the rear, itself approached by a single shared, 'walk-up' staircase. In general, the desire to build cheaply at affordable rents and at scale precluded grander architectural designs.

Barville Close, Honor Oak Estate, Lewisham

The Honor Oak Estate in Lewisham can be taken as representative.[20] The estate today, subject to a plethora of improving initiatives in recent years, looks good. Its refurbished neo-Georgian-style blocks are set among well-maintained green open spaces with new children's play areas – decent housing showing little sign of its troubled origins and later turbulence.

When construction began in 1932, it was, first and foremost, a slum clearance estate, built to house 725 households displaced by slum clearance and 378 moved through overcrowding. Len White, a member of a Pacifist Service Unit drafted to the estate in 1941, characterised (not unkindly but with an outsider's middle-class perspective) the tenants, having 'lived narrow and circumscribed lives in their old environment', as 'deeply conservative and ill-fitted to adapt themselves to new conditions', conditions made more difficult by the estate's isolated location and lack of facilities.[21]

The new tenants were also predominantly low paid and often casually employed. How could council house rents be made affordable to those whom local government now had a duty to rehouse? The solution of the LCC was to reduce standards. One block of so-called 'Modified Type A' flats had baths placed in their kitchen. Four blocks of the 'Modified Type B' flats shared bathrooms. The latter were around one-fifth cheaper to build, with rents reduced to match. As such, they represented, the LCC felt, 'a successful endeavour to provide suitable hygienic accommodation for the poorer classes at a substantially lower rent than that charged for accommodation of the "normal type"'.[22]

This 'success', turning back the clock forty years, was not widely celebrated, and one of the first actions of the incoming Labour administration in 1934 (the party would retain its control of the LCC until its abolition in 1965) was to abandon such penny-pinching. Conversely, the new administration understood that, if multi-storey accommodation was a necessary response to inner-city circumstances (as its own policy group had concluded), it needed to be made more attractive and more desirable to its potential tenants.

The LCC's 'new type plan' for flats, designed by its Chief Architect, E.P. Wheeler, and unveiled in 1937, incorporated internal staircases (to overcome the overshadowing and lack of privacy which were disliked in balcony-access schemes), private balconies and a wider range of internal layouts and improved fixtures and fittings. These were trialled on the White City Estate in west London where the first of these new flats – said by the *Times* to 'almost qualify for the house-agent's description "luxury flats"' – was opened in 1939.[23]

The other occasional innovation of the later 1930s was largely cosmetic, though the sweeping white concrete balconies of the Oaklands Estate in Clapham, for example, make it a striking one. This was the LCC's attempt to emulate the late Art Deco Moderne style of the day that emphasised curving forms and long horizontal lines with an occasional deliberate echo of the grand ocean liners of the era. Oaklands wasn't exactly a land-locked *Queen Mary*, but it did represent an attractive attempt to add a previously lacking design aesthetic to the increasingly ubiquitous walk-up blocks.

Behind the façade, however, the scheme was far more conventional and a signal that London – much to the chagrin of the growing modern movement in architecture – did not wish to emulate the exciting design innovations taking place on the Continent. The Ossulston Estate (just next to the British Library in Euston) is perhaps the only scheme to make modernist hearts flutter, but even then its looks flatter to deceive. What you see are the reinforced concrete balconies, arched entranceways and white rough-cast walls – 'approximating in design to the models in Vienna which have been so greatly admired'.[24] The architect, the LCC's Chief Architect, George Topham Forrest, who had visited Vienna during the scheme's design phase, admitted this influence. What you don't see is the steel frame construction that *was* innovative, but the overall form – standard balcony-access flats – decidedly wasn't.

The Ossulston Estate, Camden

Something far more path-breaking had been envisaged in the original plans – a nine-storey development integrating privately rented shops and offices and 'flats of a character superior to the ordinary working-class dwellings' on the first three floors and council flats on the five floors above. There were no fancy ideas of social mixing here; in fact, an early form of 'poor door' was envisaged. For Topham Forrest, it was an 'essential of this idea that . . . each class of property should have its own entrance and the entrances should be as remote from one another as possible'.[25] And while for a Conservative-led LCC there were ideological attractions to such a mixed-use, public–private scheme, finance was the driver – higher-rise housing was essential to best exploit an awkward narrow site and the necessary lifts required higher private rents to pay for them. In the end, finance or its lack (government grants were not available to mixed-use schemes) also put paid to the plans.

In all, around 40 per cent of the LCC's new interwar homes were multi-storey. Elsewhere in England (Scotland was different), only Liverpool – where one in five new homes were flatted – positively embraced multi-storey housing. Most of these schemes have been demolished now, outdated and allowed to decay by the 1980s. Only St Andrew's Gardens, just east of the city centre, remains, and that is now student housing. The basic form is again conventional, but in their scale and range of facilities these blocks represented an attempt – in Owen Hatherley's words – to make 'an English city as honest about its urbanity as a Scottish or European one'.[26] The Corporation had also built multi-storey blocks along the arterial roads in the suburbs (such as Mather and Muirhead Avenues) where they were intended to create an urban massing appropriate to Liverpool's sense of self.

But above all, these were homes. It's a sign of the continuing resistance to multi-storey living that the Corporation's Director of Housing, Lancelot Keay, expressed his defence of them rhetorically, but his positive conclusion was obvious:

Is it less possible to raise an A1 community in a properly planned township of flats than in a garden city or suburb? Is there any doubt that the rising generation in the great continental cities of Europe will not be as fit physically and morally as the children of Wythenshawe and Dagenham and Norris Green?[27]

Norris Green was local – Liverpool's largest interwar cottage estate – but the reference to the European mainland reflects the familiarity of many of these foreign schemes to councillors in the UK's major cities. Keay had visited Vienna in 1926 but was critical of the small size, poor ventilation and facilities of the city's flats. He returned from a trip to the International Housing and Town Planning Congress in Berlin in 1931 more favourably impressed, particularly by Bruno Taut's grand *Hufeisensiedlung* scheme.

Similarly, Birmingham councillors undertook a grand continental tour in 1930, stopping off at Hamburg, Berlin, Prague, Vienna, Munich, Frankfurt and Cologne. Leeds councillors visited Vienna in 1932. An LCC group, led by Lewis Silkin (chair of the council's Town Planning and Housing and Public Health Committees), produced a report on 'Working-Class Housing on the Continent and the Application of Continental Ideas to the Housing Problems of the County of London' later in 1936.

The reality, however, is that despite the huffing and puffing of an emerging generation of modernist architects in this country who looked to the daring ideas being advocated on the Continent by Le Corbusier, British design and political sensibilities remained conservative. The belief persisted in the words of Charles Jenkinson, chair of Leeds City Council's Housing Committee: 'the cottage home is the best dwelling for the normal English family'.[28] The irony is that it was Jenkinson who built, in Quarry Hill, the single scheme in the UK which surpassed many of the European models touted by modernists. Clearly, there was no ideological commitment to modernism here, but rather the same pressures of slum clearance (and the consequent availability of a large inner-city site) and the need to rehouse a slum population affordably and close to their employment.

The Quarry Hill Estate housed 3,000 people in 938 flats in seven- and eight-storey blocks occupying thirty-six acres of land in inner-city Leeds. The original plans, drawn up by City Architect R.A.H. Livett, also included a community hall, seating 520, with stage and dressing rooms, twenty shops, indoor and outdoor swimming pools and wading pool, courtyards, gardens and play areas, a nursery and communal laundry, even a mortuary. There were even eighty-eight lifts, a facility lacking in the Karl Marx-Hof.

If all that gives some impression of ambition and scale, it would hardly prepare you for the appearance of the estate. The long, sweeping façades of its perimeter blocks ('somewhat forbidding though undeniably impressive' according to Pevsner), massive arched entranceways, its fortress-like strength and confidence.[29] This intimidating face to the outside world was later exacerbated by post-war planning and new roadways which created the classic 'island estate', but most residents professed to enjoying a proud and close-knit community and, contrary to all you will have read about multi-storey estates, a children's paradise: 'I lived there during the fifties and as a child it was glorious – millions of playmates and the longest roofs in the world to run around on.'[30]

If you're not local and that's whetted your appetite to visit this municipal wonder, what you'll find now is Quarry House, a central government hub, fittingly enough, home to a branch of the Department of Work and Pensions. This postmodern edifice is commonly dubbed 'The Pink Palace' or 'The Kremlin' by unimpressed natives. Around it is arrayed Leeds' Cultural Quarter. Both speak to a changed world and changed priorities.

The Quarry Hill flats came down in 1978, unlamented by many though, in fact, more flawed in their construction than their conception. The Mopin system used to build the estate (adopted from the massive Paris overspill estate in Drancy-la-Muette which Jenkinson and Livett had visited) suffered long-running structural defects and required expensive repair and maintenance. The innovative Garchey waste disposal system (also adopted from France), by which domestic refuse was flushed from the kitchen sink to a central incinerator, was smelly and prone to blockages. The swimming pools and many of the other community facilities originally planned were not built. Central government loans only covered housing; the cost savings envisaged from the Mopin system to pay for extras never materialised.

Jenkinson, like the Salters, was a Christian socialist (in fact, an Anglican vicar). Born in 1887, the son of a London docker, he left school at fourteen but secured work as a bookkeeper. He was also a chorister and Sunday school teacher at St Stephen's, Poplar, and a member of the Church Socialist League and, from 1908, the Independent Labour Party. He was a conscientious objector to the First World War but served as an orderly in the Royal Army Medical Corps while somehow studying Latin and Greek in his spare time. A law degree at Cambridge followed and then holy orders. Having requested 'the hardest parish in the country', he was appointed vicar of Holbeck in Leeds in 1927 and became a councillor in 1930.

That's a biography worth recounting in its own right, but it also serves to explain why Jenkinson approached the question of housing – and particularly the housing of the poorest – with such zeal. He was determined that 'every family will be offered the dwelling appropriate to its needs . . . at whatever rent it can afford to pay' — 'we shall not begin to talk about rent until there is sufficient money in the household to provide that family with the necessities of life'.[31]

Under his leadership, Leeds implemented the most ambitious 'rent differential scheme' in the country, uniquely setting no minimum rent payable by all. Over one-third of tenants paid no more than 5s (30p) a week under the new arrangements — an equivalent rent to the worst of Leeds' notorious back-to-backs — and around 11 per cent went rent free. But the extensive means testing was resented and some rents were increased. There lay the rub. Better-off tenants were affronted and felt their hard work and respectability were penalised: 'The average corporation tenant is a credit to the community . . . It may be that the fact that we are corporation tenants has enabled us to get good jobs.'[32]

Some feared that better-off tenants would, in effect, be driven out. 'To many in Leeds the Labour Party seemed intent on turning council housing into a Poor Law service, and the council estates into "pauper settlements".'[33] Given later shifts in the nature of and perceptions of council housing, there's a rich irony there I need hardly point out.

The landscape of Britain was transformed in the interwar period — literally by the growth of suburbia (around one-quarter of it council housing), figuratively by a politics that placed housing centre stage. The numbers are staggering. Outside London, Conservative-controlled Birmingham built the most new council homes, over 51,000. Local son, Neville Chamberlain, described the city's housebuilding record with a great deal of native pride and only a little exaggeration as 'an achievement on the part of Birmingham which has no parallel in this or any other country'.[34] Liverpool built over 40,000 and Manchester over 30,000. But council houses were built in large numbers across the country. Carlisle, with its self-defined 'anti-Socialist' council, has good claim to have built the most council houses per head of population: 4,702, meaning that 27 per cent of the town's population lived in council homes by 1939. Norwich, Labour-controlled from 1933 as slum clearance took off, rehoused fully one-quarter of its population in this period. Council housing in the countryside lagged but even here – boosted by a 1936 Act which provided 80 per cent subsidies for the construction of homes for agricultural labourers – Rural District Councils in England and Wales had built 159,000 council houses by 1939.[35]

However, it is impossible not to note that between the wars the heady idealism – or the felt political necessity – of the early Addison programme rapidly dissipated. Yet, although standards and expectations of council housing declined, the cardinal fact of the state's duty to house decently its people remained. What that meant in practice was contested. Labour retained its belief, despite its 1930 Act which prioritised slum clearance, that council housing should serve general needs. For the Conservatives, council housing was for those who could aspire to no better. For them, owner occupation and the free market would best serve the more affluent working class.

The parties were also divided on the quality of housing to be provided. Although Exchequer demands weighed heavily on both, Labour generally advocated more generous provision – higher space standards and better amenities; the Tories believed that lower standards and thereby more affordable accommodation were acceptable in providing for the poorer working class. In both cases, this was a clear prefiguring of political debates and differences that would be fought out in the post-1945 era.

As council housing reached a critical mass, especially in the large cottage suburbs, new questions arose too. Some tenants missed the neighbourliness of their former inner-city homes, more perhaps found the new estates too expensive. These voted with their feet and returned to cheaper and inferior privately rented accommodation. This alarmed an emerging profession of academic sociologists busy surveying the new estates. For Ruth Durant (better known after a second marriage as Ruth Glass), for example, the lack of local employment and the voluntary removal of around one in ten of the population back to inner London, meant that the Watling Estate in north London was 'not much more than a huge hotel without a roof'.[36]

'Community' became the Holy Grail, though a paradoxically conceptualised one – containing, as it did, both a nostalgia for the decidedly 'rough' intimacies of slum life for some and for others a distinctly 'improving' agenda of working-class respectability and rational recreation. A great deal of this came from middle-class outsiders imposing their own norms and expectations on working-class lives – maybe no more than a subtle form of the Victorian do-goodery that had helped shape the Boundary Estate, for example. Some of it came from working-class activists who were, in their way, perhaps equally unrepresentative. Whatever the case, the quest for community would preoccupy planners after the Second World War.

Planning too was an emerging expertise. Ebenezer Howard and Raymond Unwin were illustrious forebears but the idea of planning took off in the 1930s as the full impact of the catastrophic Great Depression took effect. A pusillanimous minority Labour government between 1929 and 1931 and a

Conservative 'National' government in the 1930s were not the best vehicles to implement these new ideas, but the impact of war and the machinery of state it engendered made them seem both necessary and practicable after 1945.

The war itself – and here the mobilising myth is as important as any more nuanced realities – is taken to have created a new national, social democratic, consensus: a determination to learn from the failures of the 1920s and 1930s, and this time (in the words of a famous Labour poster) to 'win the peace' for ordinary people. Good-quality housing for all would be central to this.

3
'If Only We Will': Britain
Reimagined, 1940–51

In March and April 1941, seven devastating German air raids destroyed the medieval centre of Plymouth, leaving it reportedly the most heavily damaged city in the country. Between 1941 and 1944 the city suffered fifty-nine bombing attacks in all; 1,172 of its people were killed, around 4,400 injured. And yet, in all this, there were some who saw opportunity – this 'almost complete destruction of the civic and shopping heart' provided a 'site, rarely occurring in urban existence, to replan and rebuild a Centre of really modern design'.[1]

In November 1942, Churchill cautiously proclaimed the allied victory at El Alamein as 'not the end . . . not even the beginning of the end [but] perhaps the end of the beginning'. In contrast, Plymouth's post-war planning had begun some fifteen months earlier when the City Council agreed to commission from Sir Patrick Abercrombie a comprehensive redevelopment scheme for the city. Abercrombie was, by some distance, the foremost planner of the day: a leading light of the University of Liverpool's Department of Civic Design (founded in 1909 – the first such university department in the world) from 1915 to

1935, first editor of the pioneering *Town Planning Review* and from 1935 to 1946 professor of town planning at the University of London.

He had drafted a number of planning schemes – for the cities and regions of Sheffield, Doncaster and Bristol among others – in the interwar period, but it was the unique combination of wartime destruction and post-war hopes that provided him with his greatest stage. *A Plan for Plymouth*, written by Abercrombie with City Engineer James Paton Watson, was complete by September 1943 and approved by the council the following year. The document captures all the idealism and breadth of vision of this unique moment in British history. This would be, as Viscount Astor, the Conservative mayor of Plymouth, declared, 'no half-and-half affair'.

The *Plan* aimed 'to snatch a victory for the city of the future' from the debris of the war and 'intended to cover the whole of its existence from the comfort and convenience of the smallest house and children's playground, to the magnificence of its civic centre, the spaciousness and convenience of its shopping area and the perfection of its industrial machine'.[2] This was a Britain, whose antique streetscapes and cramped lives were seen by many as tired and obsolete, not merely rebuilt but reimagined.

In the context of such vaunting ambition Plymouth today can only seem disappointing, but a visit to its centre – where the *Plan* was most fully executed – does allow at least a glimpse of these earlier ideals. The planners allowed themselves 'one great – even monumental – feature', designed to exploit the city's majestic maritime setting: 'a Garden vista – a parkway . . . with terraces, slopes, steps, pools, avenues' which ran almost one mile from the railway station down to the Hoe where once Sir

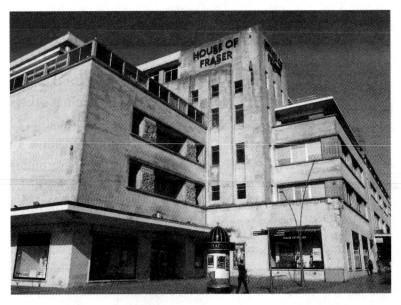

House of Fraser (formerly Dingles), Armada Way, Plymouth

Francis Drake had famously completed his game of bowls before dispatching the invading Spanish fleet. Armada Way can hardly live up to that billing. It was never fully realised and it's accumulated the clutter of contemporary consumerism since then, but look around at the grand elevations which surround it: Portland stone-faced temples of retail, finance and commerce but there's significance perhaps in the fact that the largest outlet – the only one to occupy one full block – was the Coop that once had its own domed banking hall and a cafeteria where dance bands played.

This wasn't a demotic architecture. Abercrombie's inspiration owed most to the Beaux-Arts imperialism that shaped New Delhi and Canberra in the twentieth century and Washington DC and Paris in the nineteenth. Some have criticised it all as bleak and impersonal – a contrast drawn, as ever, with the bustling hodgepodge of narrow streets it replaced. The reflex here is to condemn the planners' egotism and inhumanity but, in reality, those façades and corners were designed with real care to provide mass and symmetry and also contrast. And a closer look reveals much fine detailing. That plain Portland stone? It was envisaged as a neutral background to highly coloured shop fronts, displays and signs. Crucially, who were its clients? Not big business, nor a wealthy elite, but working-class consumers released from the constrained lives and settings that had characterised their pre-war existence. Jeremy Gould has described Plymouth as 'our first great welfare state city' and that seemingly austere centre as an 'egalitarian grid, spacious, airy, uncomplicated, accessible and gapingly open to all – the very model in stone, brick, glass and metal of the post-war welfare edifice'.[3]

Housing played its own vital role in the new and fairer society expected, but here the *Plan* was, in form at least, more conservative: there was 'no necessity to house anyone in lofty blocks of flats' and it envisaged new developments on broadly garden suburb lines. The scale of necessary reconstruction was, however, well understood. A 1935 survey had revealed around one-quarter of Plymouth's working-class population living in overcrowded conditions – a circumstance naturally exacerbated by wartime bombing. The *Plan* reported with some precision that 8,719 new houses were needed immediately to replace 6,833 lost to bomb damage, 986 to go under central redevelopment and an estimated increase of 900 new households. In the longer term – as slum clearance and 'reconstruction of decayed areas' took effect and rezoning was implemented – a further 23,986 houses would be needed to house Plymouth's people decently. The council built 10,000 by 1954.

The *Plan* was more creative in its emphasis on 'community'. Many now criticised the interwar cottage suburbs as soulless and monolithic. Abercrombie and Paton Watson suggested rather modestly in the first instance that 'a rounding off, an integration' was required; that in the new developments housing the 'decentralised population', there was 'opportunity for the latest thought in seemly community design'.

Here Abercrombie introduced his big idea and one which dominates early post-war planning, the 'neighbourhood unit' – a district of between 6,000 to 8,000 people formed around the catchment areas of infant and junior schools, bounded by distinct borders and possessing, in his words, a 'natural gravitation' towards a centre comprising a church or chapel, a library, a cinema, a restaurant, café or hotel, a public laundry and a health clinic. There was to be a 'Community Building' too, 'under the charge of a first-rate Warden, with theatre and concert halls large enough to accommodate performances by CEMA and similar organisations'. (CEMA – the Committee for the Encouragement of Music and the Arts – had been established in 1940. It metamorphosed into the Arts Council in 1946.)

We can take this latter as a simple reminder of middle-class planners' well-meant though inescapably patronising desire to 'improve' their working-class compatriots, but it speaks as powerfully to a wartime mood which, as human society plumbed its moral nadir, sought a better world. In this context, 'community' became something more than mere sociability. Abercrombie – channelling the socialist William Morris though not quite scaling his heights of eloquence – claimed it was 'community spirit . . . that inherent characteristic of all races' which had generated all that was most progressive and creative in human history:

With the return of 'community' will come the spirit of companionship
unknown to the youth of yesterday who vainly sought it in the car or the
cinema. If the individuality of the citizen is to be encouraged and
moulded into the community, then the right sort of facilities must be
found: this plan must give the craftsman, musician and painter with
undiscovered talent a chance to show himself. It must be both economical and sensible to his needs, and not cramped to the niggardly possibilities of today; a plan which allows for a higher standard of living well
within our grasp, with its call for space and beauty rather than for mere
economy.[4]

The utopian hopes betray the temper of the times as least as
much as the gendered language. Planners, who believed themselves to be unleashing such human potential and who themselves (in their own eyes, at least) personified sweet reason and
benevolent intention, can be forgiven for thinking themselves
central to the construction of this new world.

This was not entirely new. Planning had had its ideologues
and exponents since late Victorian times – Ebenezer Howard,
most obviously – but it gained a wider resonance and sought a
wider reach from the 1930s as the Great Depression hit. There
were practical elements. Building on the Special Areas Act of
1934 (which sought to boost industry in four especially hard-hit
regions), the Barlow Report in 1940 made far-reaching proposals to redistribute population and industry in order to both cut
unemployment across the country and reduce congestion in
London. Keynesianism may have been just a 'General Theory'
in 1935, but had become official government policy in the 1944
White Paper on Full Employment.

As that disdainful reference to the 'car or the cinema' suggests,
consumerism was not entirely trusted to speak to our better

natures; a 'spirit of companionship' was the higher goal. This was an ideal sometimes understood nostalgically as a revival of community feeling lost to industrialisation and urbanisation. It was a criticism too of the design failings of the interwar cottage suburbs and their alleged lack of community. And it embodied hopes that frequently invoked, perhaps exaggerated, wartime sentiments of social solidarity and shared purpose could be maintained and strengthened in the post-war world. Practically, the expectation of higher living standards, more universally enjoyed, and a belief in the fuller quality of life they enabled were strong, even heartfelt.

In short, what had once seemed radical, even utopian, became mainstream. War is the obvious pithy explanation of this but it needs unpacking. There was war, firstly, as a progressive cause: a struggle against fascism waged alongside the Soviet Union (still, for a time, the good guys) whose scientific socialism was taken by some to represent a more rational and just future world. Then, there was war as popular struggle – a democratic cause and effort in which the contribution of the working class was central. There was war as a machinery of state with government securing unprecedented powers to mobilise economy and society to the end of victory. Some of the lore of the 'People's War' can be picked apart but the mobilising myth remains as does the cardinal fact of Labour's landslide victory in 1945 and its election slogan 'And now win the peace'. There was a sense that the perceived betrayal of the promises of 1919 of a 'land fit for heroes' could not and would not be repeated.

This, then, is the 'Spirit of '45', invoked with understandable nostalgia in our contemporary neoliberal era as the moment when the working class (still around 75 per cent of the population) came of age and the British people embraced a truly progressive politics.

Revisionist accounts rightly point out how much of the Labour programme was anticipated within the wartime coalition. The Liberal William Beveridge issued his celebrated report laying the foundations of the post-war system of social security in November 1942, famously identifying the five 'Giants' – squalor, ignorance, want, idleness and disease – which had dominated the old order. (That the British public queued up to buy and bought in total 630,000 copies of this rather dry and bureaucratic tome is probably the best single illustration of the heightened consciousness and expectations of the time.) Churchill himself had heralded 'national compulsory insurance for all classes for all purposes from the cradle to the grave' in a March 1943 broadcast entitled 'After the War'.[5] 'A National Health Service' was prefigured in the White Paper of that name in March 1944.

Some argue that the programme as a whole represented little more than a reformed – kinder and therefore ultimately more efficient – capitalism. But what it represented most of all to the mass of the population was 'better' – better than what had gone before and a promise of better to come. And, if that sounds anodyne, for many in the working class this was not merely a change in degree but a change in kind. The ideological labels matter less; the dominant thrust for most working-class voters was a simple belief in 'fairness' – fair wages, proper treatment, help when needed: a more radical notion than it sounds when politically mobilised.

And for the moment, it was the Labour Party – credibility strengthened by its crucial role in the wartime coalition – whose values and aspirations clearly meshed with the country's. Though the key elements of the new Welfare State had clearly emerged before 1945, Churchill and the Tory Party he represented were not trusted to deliver them. In the general election of July 1945, Labour, capturing this progressive wave, swept to victory with 48 per cent of the vote.

It's natural and not wrong to think of all this as Britain's social democratic moment – basic ideas of fairness and class-lessness were powerful. (I think 'classlessness' better captures the mood than 'equality', which suggests something more instrumentally radical.) But maybe the unifying ideal for this moment – practical, even commonsensical and therefore with much wider purchase – was not fairness alone, but planning.

Among the bigger names within this movement was Thomas Sharp. Sharp had started his career working for the Borough Surveyor in his native Bishop Auckland and worked during the war in Lord Reith's Ministry of Works and Planning. He couldn't quite match Beveridge's sales figures, but his Penguin book *Town Planning*, published in 1940, sold 250,000 copies; the best-selling book on the subject ever written. Sharp was the most prolific of those busy designing the new world even as the bombs dropped, drawing up plans for 'Exeter Phoenix' and 'A Newer Sarum' as well as Durham, Todmorden, Oxford, Taunton, King's Lynn, Bath, Stockport, Minehead and St Andrews. In all, several hundred plans were devised for towns up and down the country, many of them unscathed by war but universally viewed as obsolescent and inadequate.[6]

Few, except in patches, were implemented but the idea of planning, presaged in the 'Redevelopment Areas' authorised by the 1935 Housing Act, had come of age. The 1946 Land Acquisition Act enhanced local councils' ability to compulso-rily purchase land but the flagship legislation – which laid the foundations of our current planning regime – was the 1947 Town and Country Planning Act. It reduced the existing mosaic of 1,400 planning authorities to 145 (formed from county and borough councils), and required each to prepare a comprehensive development plan. Local authorities were empowered not only to approve (or reject) all construction proposals but to compulsorily purchase land and carry out redevelopment plans of their own where necessary.

The Act's most radical element was the 'Development Charge', effectively a tax paid by developers amounting to the whole of the difference between the land's previous worth (its 'existing use value') and its value following redevelopment. This was intended to assure that where land increased in value as a result of a council's planning decisions that increase accrued to the community rather than to private interests. This wasn't land nationalisation as some demanded but it came close to the land value taxation which had been a favoured cause of liberal and left-wing campaigners since the late nineteenth century. The Development Charge, deemed cumbersome in operation and criticised by opponents as inhibiting enterprise, was repealed by the succeeding Conservative government.

Nevertheless, for the time being, big and bold planning ideas held sway and Abercrombie was, once more, their greatest exponent. The first edition of his *County of London Plan*, published in 1943 (co-authored with J.H. Forshaw, Chief Architect to the LCC), was a richly illustrated hardback of some 188 folio pages. (The priority given to the publication of such a lavish tome at the height of the war suggests its significance.) It sold 10,000 copies – abridged versions were also provided to schoolchildren and members of the armed forces – and 75,000, including George VI and Queen Elizabeth, attended the County Hall exhibition that previewed it. A popular Penguin edition, co-edited by the émigré architect Ernő Goldfinger, was produced in 1945.[7]

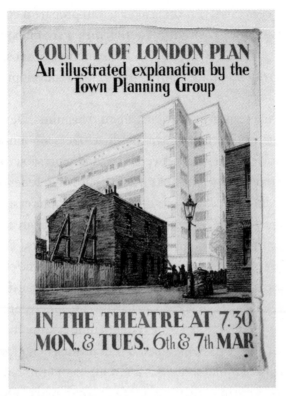

COUNTY OF LONDON PLAN
An illustrated explanation by the
Town Planning Group

IN THE THEATRE AT 7.30
MON., & TUES., 6th & 7th MAR

The Town Planning Group County of London Plan poster from Stalag Luft III

My favourite detail of the *Plan*'s astonishing reach is that a 'Town Planning Group' of British prisoners of war in Stalag Luft III (better known as the site of the 'Great Escape' in the famous 1963 film) convened a special meeting to discuss it. When these PoWs weren't planning their own great escape, they were planning Britain's escape from its benighted past. The foreword to the volume of Arthur Latham, Labour leader of the LCC, further captures the mood and rhetoric of the time: 'Just as we can move mountains when our liberties are threatened and we will have to fight for our lives, so can we when the future of our London is at stake. If only we will.' And, in a knowing echo of Beveridge, he noted that there were 'giants too in the path of city planning . . . conflicting interests, private rights, an outworn and different scale of values, and lack of vision'.[8]

While Abercrombie's language could be more measured and technocratic, his vision was all-encompassing. London, he opined, 'might be described as more planned against than planning'. An aerial image included in the volume captures the problem: 'houses close alongside railway viaducts, schools adjoining industry, tenements mixed with wharves and warehouses, an absence of private gardens and negligible public open space'. Abercrombie proposed 'conditioned yet comprehensive redevelopment' – 'conditioned' as London, despite the attentions of the *Luftwaffe*, was hardly a *tabula rasa*; 'comprehensive', such was the need and opportunity.

Chapter 1 of the *Plan* depicted this confused agglomeration of mixed districts and functions and sought – in this modern age of reason – to reconfigure them rationally, to 'zone' them in the planning jargon which would become familiar. The largest single 'zone' was the metropolitan Green Belt, first proposed by the Greater London Regional Planning Committee in 1935 but affirmed by Abercrombie and formalised in the mid-1950s – a girdle of open space and recreational land around the capital now extending up to thirty-five miles beyond London's borders, covering almost 2,000 square miles, intended to halt its further sprawl.

But community was the great mantra of this post-war age of planning. In an almost casual aside (there was no great socialist vision in the *Plan*), Abercrombie speaks to the highest hopes engendered by the 'People's War':

It is a commonplace to say that the war has done much to level incomes. There should be even less discrepancy afterwards, and this should be reflected in the Plan, which provides for a greater mingling of the different groups of London's society. It is for this new world foreshadowed in the Atlantic Charter that the Capital of the Commonwealth must prepare itself.[9]

At a micro level, the *Plan* also restates the concept, previewed in *A Plan for Plymouth*, of the neighbourhood unit, envisaged as a way of strengthening and to some degree separating existing communities through the provision of dedicated community facilities.

In other respects, those communities would be reduced in size. For example, Abercrombie envisaged that the Stepney-Poplar Reconstruction Area would see its population fall by 42 per cent. It seemed obvious at the time that London was over-crowded and overpeopled, but what to do about it? The *Plan* proposed that around 500,000 of its current population be rehoused outside the capital, both in satellites within the 'metro-politan traffic area' and outer satellites some fifty miles beyond. The first element – an extension of the LCC's programme of out-of-county estates – built upon what had been achieved before the war; the second, proposing self-sufficient new settlements, formed the basis of the post-war programme of New Towns.

One of the earliest and best known of the new generation of suburban estates was Debden, then in the Urban District of Chigwell beyond London's north-eastern borders. Its site had been identified as early as October 1942 – further evidence of the early extent of post-war planning – and land purchased in 1944. Construction began in the following year and the initial estate comprising over 4,000 homes was largely complete by the early 1950s. To a pair of early critics, these new suburban homes looked:

> row upon row . . . practically identical, each beside a concrete road, each enclosed by a fence, each with its little patch of flower garden at front and larger patch of vegetable garden at back, each with expansive front windows covered over with net curtains; all built, owned and guarded by a single responsible landlord.[10]

In their groundbreaking book, *Family and Kinship in East London*, Peter Willmott and Michael Young went on to lament what the residents, mostly from London's old East End, had lost: 'Instead of the sociable squash of people and houses, workshops and lorries, there are the drawn-out roads and spacious open ground of the usual low-density estate.'[11] To many that might seem an improvement but Willmott and Young mourned, in particular, the loss of the old matriarchal kinship networks which had, they contended, previously sustained community life. They seem blind to the bleak uniformity of the old terraces and have been criticised since for a much romanticised view of that supposedly 'sociable squash' and a selective use of evidence to support it. Still, it was an influential early sally against the legion of planners whose drawing board plans were held by critics to have decimated the working-class communities they had set out to rescue.

A slightly later study of South Oxhey, an estate of over 4,000 homes built between 1947 and 1952, just south of Watford in Hertfordshire, took a more nuanced view. It pointed out that, of the two-thirds rehoused from the LCC's waiting list, almost 55 per cent had been rehoused on health grounds (over one in ten households had a member suffering from pulmonary tuberculosis) and over one-third from previously overcrowded conditions. There were justified complaints about the early lack of facilities and poor transport links, but most praised the fresh air, open spaces and cleanliness of the new estate – the antithesis, of course, of their previous overcrowded quarters – and most were glad to have moved. This was a young population – 40 per cent were dependent children – and overwhelmingly working-class. Its children – shorter than the London average in the 1940s but by 1955 'rather taller and heavier than the London children had been in 1949' – thrived.[12] There's not much romance in that perhaps, but it certainly fulfilled the most basic goals of post-war planning.

These new schemes take us beyond the chronological confines of this chapter. In all, the LCC would build thirteen new 'out-of-county' estates in a ring around the capital beyond the interwar cottage suburbs. By 1965 (when an enlarged Greater London succeeded the LCC), 45,000 homes had been built in these estates, 39 per cent of the LCC's total post-war new build. Five were in Essex, including the largest, Harold Hill, with a population of almost 29,000. Sheerwater in Surrey and St Pauls Cray, then in Kent, were among the others.

Alan Johnson, the former Home Secretary, was raised in Notting Hill slums and then in council flats south of the river. He settled with his young family on another out-of-county estate, Britwell in Slough, in 1969. He was warned off by two police officers from whom he asked directions on his first visit – it was a trouble spot, they said, somewhere to avoid. But he came to experience it very differently – to Johnson:

It felt like a peaceful village . . . children played in the pleasant streets, men washed cars, women tended their front gardens or walked back

from the shops struggling with bags of groceries. The Britwell seemed
to me to be more Arcadian than anarchic.[13]

It was an undeniably suburban Arcadia, of course; indeed, that
was its raison d'être. As such, it has probably fulfilled the hopes
of its builders who believed simply that decent living conditions
would support lives lived decently, but it taunts those who
wanted this new world to be something more radical, something more ostensibly 'modern' and urban. As Matthew Hollow
has pointed out, Britain's early post-war planning has been criticised both for its naïve utopianism and its too timid pragmatism. The apparent contradiction can be resolved, he suggests,
if we stop treating 'utopianism and pragmatism as two mutually
exclusive concepts'.[14] There was clearly a genuine idealism and
ambition on the part of planners and politicians but it was,
unavoidably and properly, shaped by the material constraints
and cultural realities of its day. It was, in the end, a grounded
and very British utopianism.

There were criticisms too, as we'll see, of the first wave of New
Towns that emerged in the later 1940s. For the supporters of
Ebenezer Howard's Garden City movement (Howard himself
had died in 1928), these mattered little. F.J. Osborn – indefati-
gable leader of the Town and County Planning Association and
Howard's anointed successor – had been the leading advocate
of New Towns in the interwar period. But it was harsh economic
realities rather than the bucolic idealism of the Garden City
movement that played the decisive role in the creation of the
post-war programme of New Towns.

The 1940 Report of the Barlow Commission on Distribution
of Industrial Population, convened in the divided Britain of the

Great Depression, criticised the growing size and commercial dominance of London. The final report urged a 'balanced distribution of industry and the industrial population ... throughout the different areas or regions in Great Britain'. Sir Montague Barlow, a Conservative barrister and politician, concluded that 'the scheme of the Garden City is the model towards which the location of industry should work', and the report's detailed prescriptions were close to those advocated by Abercrombie and the Reith Commission on New Towns established by the incoming Labour government in 1945.[15]

Eleven New Towns were designated in the first programme of construction inaugurated by the 1946 New Towns Act. Eight of these formed a ring around London and were created to absorb the surplus population of the reduced capital Abercrombie had envisaged. Stevenage, in 1946, was the very first; Crawley, Hemel Hempstead, Harlow, Welwyn Garden City, Hatfield, Basildon and Bracknell followed by 1950. Two were in County Durham: Newton Aycliffe, established to accommodate a workforce numbering 17,000 at its peak, employed in ordnance works set up during the war, and Peterlee, intended to rehouse those living in slum conditions in local pit villages. Corby in Northamptonshire was an existing steel town expanded to take in migrants from across the country.

The New Towns embody much of the social idealism of this post-war era, particularly its hopes for greater mixing between classes. Lewis Silkin, fittingly a former member of the LCC's Town Planning and Housing and Public Health Committees and now the Minister of Town and Country Planning who introduced the new legislation, was 'most anxious that the planning should be such that different income groups living in the new towns will not be segregated'. He continued:

No doubt they may enjoy common recreational facilities, and take part in amateur theatricals or each play their part in a health centre or a community centre. But when they leave to go home I do not want the better-off people to go to the right, and the less well-off to go to the left. I want them to ask each other 'are you going my way?'[16]

It's a touching image, both as metaphor and intent.

The pit villages of east Durham might be thought by some to have contained communities of a distinct and cohesive character, but to other outside observers they 'were not so much towns as barracks: not the refuge of a civilisation but the barracks of an industry'.[17] Silkin visited Easington in 1946 and concluded that the New Town of Peterlee:

offered an outstanding opportunity for breaking with the unhappy tradition that miners and their families should be obliged to live in ugly over-crowded villages clustered around the pitheads, out of contact with people in other walks of life, and even for the most part with workers in other industries.[18]

Lord Beveridge himself, appointed chair of the Newton Aycliffe development corporation (all the New Towns were planned and built by such government-appointed quangos) in March 1948, committed himself to a surprisingly proto-feminist agenda (albeit reflecting traditional gendered roles). The New Town, he suggested, should be a 'housewife's paradise' and, to this end, he proposed that no house should be further than a ten-minute walk from local shops and nurseries be provided to look after children as their mothers did the shopping. Each group of houses – they were to be set around 'village greens' to encourage neighbourliness – would have a communal laundry and drying rooms. All this, he hoped, would enable what was possibly his most radical suggestion: a maximum forty-hour week for the female homemakers of the New Town. He told local councillors that 'we have set out to try to make a perfect town, a town in which every man, and above all, every housewife, will want to live – a town of beauty and happiness and community spirit'.[19]

There was a gulf, however, between aspiration and economic reality. The communal laundries were an early victim, axed in 1950. In 1954, housing densities were increased from eight per acre to fourteen. To the editor of the *Newtonian*, the town's monthly newsletter, all this seemed a near subversion of its founding ideals:

> The village green community is being replaced by elongated terraces in rows upon rows like barracks, with no privacy, no refinement and very little green to break them up. Altogether there seems to be no intention whatever of carrying out the original scheme.[20]

Nor were Silkin's hopes for the new Stevenage universally welcomed, at least not by many of the 6,000 residents of old Stevenage. He left a very hostile public meeting – which he had admittedly done little to mollify ('It's no good you jeering; it's going to be done') – under police escort. Those protesting this apparent central government diktat had renamed the town Silkingrad for the occasion.

And yet, resistance notwithstanding, in Stevenage a degree of social mixing emerged. By the early 1960s, 12,377 homes had been built; of these, all but 1,177 were built by and rented from the Development Corporation. There was therefore, as the journalist Gary Younge, brought up in the town in the 1970s, recalled, 'no sense of incongruity in Stevenage between being a young professional and living in social housing'.[21] In Harlow, an earlier writer had described the 'intensely idealistic section of the middle class' (she listed teachers, social workers, wardens of community centres and the clergy among them) who embraced these New Town ideals.[22]

More objective sociological analysis shows that the overall class breakdown of the New Towns was pretty similar to that of the general population, though unskilled manual workers tended to be underrepresented.[23] In Harlow, the Development Corporation ascribed this to a '"social escalator" at work whereby the unskilled rise up the ladder'.[24]

It reflected, too, the nature of more modern, light industry that the New Towns attracted. Sometimes whole factories and their workforces were transplanted and, in Harlow, 'parties of workers came down in a charabanc with their wives and spent the day looking at the town'. They did the sights in the morning and then spent the afternoon looking at possible houses: '"Everyone was always still pretty fed up by lunch-time," one girl on the Corporation staff told me, "but once we got to the houses they cheered up."'[25]

Peterlee, uniquely, was instigated as a result of the representations of local people and the advocacy of their elected representatives. 'Farewell Squalor': A Design for a New Town and Proposals for the Redevelopment of the Easington Rural District, written by the District Surveyor of Easington Rural District Council, C.W. Clarke – a follower of Howard and Osborn – was published in 1947. (Clarke also suggested the New Town's name – after Peter Lee, a much-loved miner's leader and Labour county councillor who had died in 1935.) But Peterlee, too, witnessed considerable turmoil; first in the stand-off between

Monica Felton (a former LCC Labour councillor and member of the Reith Committee appointed by Silkin to head the Development Corporation) and the local council, which resented her high-handed manner, and second, in the departure of its first architect-planner, Berthold Lubetkin, in April 1950.

Lubetkin – a Russian émigré 'artist-engineer' whose socialist ideals had been influenced by Soviet constructivism – had emerged as a major figure in British architectural modernism before the war. His Highpoint apartment complex, erected in the mid-1930s in Highgate – its first phase singled out for praise by Le Corbusier no less – provided middle-class homes but, across the capital, his political values were best showcased in the celebrated health centre designed by Lubetkin's Tecton Group for Finsbury's radical socialist council in 1938. Finsbury Health Centre was the very embodiment of Lubetkin's dictum that 'nothing is too good for the workers' and, tellingly, it featured in an Abram Games poster prepared by the Army Bureau of Current Affairs in 1943 captioned 'Your Britain: Fight For It Now'. Equally tellingly, the poster was vetoed by Churchill himself who apparently considered its depiction of a young boy with rickets, alongside the image of the new Britain represented by the health centre, a 'disgraceful libel' on working-class conditions.[26]

Silkin and Felton persuaded Lubetkin that Peterlee 'would be a sort of monument to glorify the loyalty, cohesion and courage of the mining community' and he embraced Felton's vision of Peterlee: 'neither a suburb nor a garden city, but a town that would be as truly urban in character, as compact in planning, and as distinguished in architecture as any of the great cities that belong to the great ages of town planning.'[27] Prosaically, the plans of the National Coal Board for further mining in the district precluded any such possibility and Lubetkin resigned.

Lubetkin had planned high-rise blocks in the centre of Peterlee. These had been thwarted and it was precisely the somewhat suburban and Garden City character of most of the New Towns that were condemned by modernist critics in the 1950s. Harlow in particular, perhaps unfortunate to have been selected as the venue of a 1951 site visit from their major forum – the *Congrès internationaux d'architecture moderne* (CIAM) – took the brunt of this. J.M. Richards, one of the delegates, concluded that the New Towns were 'little more than housing estates', consisting 'for the most part of scattered two-storey dwellings, separated by great spaces. Their inhabitants, instead of feeling themselves secure within an environment devoted to their convenience and pleasure, find themselves marooned in a desert of grass verges and concrete roadways.'[28] In the same edition of the *Architectural Review*, Gordon Cullen condemned what he described as the 'prairie planning' of the New Towns, lacking all characteristics of 'towniness'.[29]

This must have seemed harsh to Frederick Gibberd – Harlow's master planner and by now a preeminent figure in the British architectural and planning Establishment – and he pushed back. The use of existing topography and Harlow's 'green wedges' and expansiveness were a vital element to the New Town, he asserted, and he celebrated an English urbanism which 'prefers segregation of home and work, which enjoys open-air exercise, which has an innate love of nature'.[30]

Later, in an argument that was echoed by critics of perceived overweening architectural ambition, Gibberd was more astringent:

It has been suggested that a correct aesthetic and architectural solution would, in the end, have been the correct social one – in other words, that people should have been given what they ought to have wanted. What fun it would have been to surround the town centre with a dozen or so tower blocks like Vällingby, the new Stockholm satellite. But perhaps it is more important to encourage the development of the human personality and the English way of life.[31]

If you visit Harlow your abiding impression might well be of its suburban ordinariness, yet he had in fact commissioned a number of leading modernist architects to develop some of the New Town's housing schemes and had himself designed – and inserted against some opposition – Britain's first residential high-rise block, The Lawn, in 1951. It's a teeny ten-storey point block that actually nestles comfortably into its wooded suburban setting – a meek harbinger of the tumultuous and controversial phase that was to come.

Gibberd with his luxuriant moustache looked, appropriately for the time, like an RAF wing commander. In fact, he had spent a meritorious wartime teaching a new generation of architects and planners at the Architectural Association and designing the non-traditional BISF (British Iron and Steel Federation) steel-framed houses built in large numbers after the war. He had been a member of the Modern Architecture Research (MARS) Group – the UK's CIAM outpost – during the interwar period, a modernist who had authored (with F.R.S. Yorke) an influential book on flats. Plainly, Gibberd hadn't given up on flats. Nor had he given up on modernism, as his later tour de force, the Metropolitan Cathedral of Liverpool (know irreverently by some as 'Paddy's Wigwam'), shows. But, in overall terms, it was the moderate modernism of Gibberd's post-war designs which fitted better with contemporary sensibilities and that, to a large degree, defined the picturesque and consciously 'humanist' architecture of the 1950s.

The Lawn, Harlow

In these far more jaded times, the failure of the more utopian hopes surrounding the New Towns will seem unsurprising, although many would applaud precisely that modest humanism – an apparent contrast to the monumentalism of some now-castigated 1960s schemes – which characterised most of their planning and design. Those of the baby boomer generation who benefitted most from them look back fondly at happy childhoods: Jason Cowley remembers Harlow as 'a vibrant place, with utopian yearnings'; another recalls the town he left in 1971 as one marked by 'youthful energy, enthusiasm, and social sharing'. 'I guess the Great Dream was still alive and thriving', he concludes ruefully.[32]

For the new Conservative government that took office in 1951 the dream died early. It halted the New Town programme and sought, in its place, to expand existing smaller towns through partnerships (with Treasury support) between 'importing' and 'exporting' local authorities. In the event, progress was slow – such partnerships were never easy – and further population growth forced the creation of a second generation of New Towns in the 1960s. The current plodding progress of the latest iteration of the idea (the new so-called 'garden cities' of which Ebbsfleet is the most notable example), dependent on commercial dynamics and private finance, might make us nostalgic for an era when the state – or, as we might express it more benignly, wider society through the instrument of the state – assumed direct responsibility for housing its people decently.

4

'The Needs of the People': Council Housing, 1945–56

Not every new estate got the star treatment – in fact, as council housing grew exponentially in the post-war period, most didn't – but Derby Borough Council clearly felt that the Mackworth Estate, formally opened in 1959 but planned from 1948, was something special. In its way it was, capturing as it did so many of the dreams of the new era of public housing inaugurated by Labour's landslide victory in 1945.

The Mackworth Estate was to be developed 'as a residential neighbourhood in full accordance with contemporary town planning principles'. Its layout provided 'from the outset not only for dwellings but for schools, local shops, churches, and other buildings and, of course, recreational and ornamental open spaces'; not only meeting 'the day-to-day needs of the residents, the adults and the children [but] incidentally providing occasions for stimulating community life and feeling'.[1] This focus on 'neighbourhoods', the infrastructure that supported them and 'community' – which commentators thought lacking on the pre-war estates perceived as bland and ill-resourced – was key to the planners' vision after 1945.

Building began in 1950. Prince Charles Avenue, coming off the A52, is a mile-long spinal road that loops through the estate, separating through-traffic from residential streets. The Avenue traverses a wedge of green and wooded open space and, over a suitably sylvan roundabout and past Mornington Crescent (sounding even more incongruous now than it did in the past), you come to the main shopping centre, still anchored by a branch of the Coop. The local movement had worked closely with the Labour council in planning the new district's retail services. Carry on and you'll find most of the estate's churches and its secondary school. There were two new primary schools too, built in the eastern and western halves of the estate and envisaged as the focal points of two separate neighbourhoods.

The rest of Mackworth is an irregular streetscape of curving roads and crescents, a few cul-de-sacs and pedestrian footways,

Mayfair Crescent, Mackworth Estate, Derby

and lots and lots of houses. There is some variety here: some are pebble-dashed, white- and cream-rendered, but most are red brick, generally semi-detached or in short terraces, all in a range of the unornamented, rectangular forms favoured in this era. It's pleasant – neat and generally well cared for, over-whelmingly residential and, truth be told, with no great buzz of community despite all those good intentions.

When the estate's main shopping centre was opened, rather belatedly, in 1959, over 2,900 homes were occupied, serving a population of around 10,000. The majority of the council homes – 1,642 – were three-bed family houses but, with bungalows for the elderly and a larger number of two-bed options, there was a nod too to the newly fashionable idea of 'mixed development'. There was another, sometimes neglected, aspect to this mixed development in its broadest sense. Over 200 homes were built for private sale and nearly 300 for private leasehold. The early post-war expectation was that council estates would contain a greater *social* mix too, seen here in the provision for the better off who might choose to buy but reflected as well in council homes built for 'general needs', for a *range* of the population. Some councils also built larger council homes for middle-class rental, though Labour Derby didn't.

Mackworth was completed in the 'never had it so good' era of Macmillan, but it was begun in an era of genuine austerity when Britain somehow managed to build the Welfare State we're currently dismantling. It was an unusually ambitious project for its time, but Derby had the advantage of plentiful land (the Mackworth Estate was built on a 450-acre greenfield site on the town's north-eastern periphery) and strategic indus-tries vital to the government's export drive. It also had, in Alderman Flint, an unusually astute and energetic chair of

Housing. The Ministry of Health and Housing granted permission to proceed but could, nevertheless, only mitigate the shortages of materials and labour which hindered the government's housebuilding ambitions. Derby, like many other councils, was forced to look to alternative, non-traditional construction methods.

As a consequence, 150 'Trusteel' prefabricated homes of steel frame construction with brick cladding were erected across Derby in the immediate post-war period, and around 500 'No-Fines' houses (constructed from concrete with no fine aggregates cast in situ) were built by Wimpey's and Wates on Mackworth. There were other innovations too – not yet the central heating envisaged by the most far-seeing of the welter of reports on housing published during and after the war (Mackworth homes still had coal fires with back boilers), but there were new through lounges, generally 'felt to be a great improvement' on the stuffy parlours of the better working-class homes previously.[2] The community centre promised at the outset wasn't built, but the Townswomen's Guild (formed on the estate in 1955) suggested that the churches and church halls stepped into the breach while commenting sardonically that the four pubs – improving notions of forced temperance on council estates had declined – provided 'most men with the companionship that the majority of ladies find elsewhere'.

Later, they had far worse to complain about. The estate acquired a reputation for crime and drugs from the 1990s and the nickname 'Smackworth' (though that really owed as much to rhyme as reason). Things have quietened down since. Over half the homes on Mackworth are owner-occupied now, the first sold off under a Conservative council in 1968. But maybe the earlier words of the Townswomen's Guild are as appropriate now as they were back in 1980 as those ladies were growing old with the estate: 'There seems little likelihood of a mass exodus from this pleasant estate as residents retire.' Hardly utopian rhetoric, but it's maybe this simple decency that formed the progressive backbone of council housing hopes after the Second World War.

Housing – in new forms, in greater numbers and, crucially, state-built – was central to the post-war rebuilding. There was continuity here with the slum clearance programme prioritised in the 1930s. But the war itself added urgency and scale to the task. Around 450,000 homes had been destroyed or rendered uninhabitable by wartime bombing. In March 1945, a wartime Coalition White Paper estimated that 750,000 new homes were needed and another 500,000 to replace existing slums. In this context, a basic need for shelter trumped some of the more cele-brated aspects of the Welfare State such as the new National Health Service. It was given political clout by a squatters' movement which, after the occupation of a disused army camp in Scunthorpe in May 1946, spread like wildfire across the coun-try until by October an estimated 1,038 camps had been commandeered as emergency homes by almost 40,000 activists.

The memory of how shortages of skilled labour and building materials had hindered housebuilding efforts in the 1920s and the anticipation of similar problems to come led to early moves to investigate and promote non-traditional methods of construc-tion. This began with the Burt Committee in June 1942. The 'No-Fines' homes erected in Mackworth were among the most widely adopted but steel, timber and a range of other concrete forms were also pressed into service. Most pretty much survived their allotted sixty-year lifespan but there were structural problems in many and few cost savings at the time. As brick production stepped up, traditional methods – visually preferred in any case – were resumed.

Meanwhile, the classic prefab, which some older readers will remember, was devised as a temporary quick fix. The 1944 Housing (Temporary Accommodation) Act committed £150 million to the programme, which ended in March 1949. A total of 156,623 prefab homes were erected, allocated to local authorities according to housing need. Designed to last around ten years, there were still 67,353 in use in 1964 and in London some 10,000 were occupied into the 1970s. The 187 homes built by German and Italian prisoners of war between 1945 and 1946 on the Excalibur Estate in Catford, now (in 2017) finally being cleared against the wishes of many residents, remained a miraculous survival. Six along Persant Road have been Grade II listed by Historic England.

The Excalibur Estate, Catford

There were various forms of prefab, variations on a common theme. The largest number built were of the so-called Aluminium type. Arcon homes (steel frame with asbestos cladding), Uni-Seco (flat-roofed timber frame with asbestos wall sections) and Tarran (wooden frames with precast wooden panels) followed in rank order. Those on the Excalibur Estate were Uni-Seco with kitchen/bathroom units pre-assembled and the rest arriving in flat-pack panel units and assembled tongue-and-groove-style. The estate has (or had) a holiday village feel and, to modern eyes, the prefabs are quaint and homely, made more so through the decorative touches applied by some of the residents. They were however – with their fitted kitchens, running hot water, built-in storage and electric lighting and sockets – state-of-the-art dwellings in their time.

To Neil Kinnock, future Labour leader, brought up in a prefab, his childhood home 'was a remarkable dwelling and a piece of wonderful engineering . . . a place of wonder'.[3] Elsewhere, Eddie O'Mahoney, recently demobilised with a wife and two young children, had wanted a proper brick-built house but was reluctantly persuaded by a council housing officer to take a look at the new prefabs on Excalibur:

> We opened the door and my wife said, 'What a lovely big hall! We can get the pram in here'. There was a toilet and a bathroom. I'd been used to a toilet in the garden. The kitchen had an Electrolux refrigerator, a New World gas stove, plenty of cupboards. There was a nice garden. It was like coming into a fortune. My wife said, 'Start measuring for the lino'.[4]

Another expedient, begun under wartime emergency powers granted in 1939 but maintained through the post-war housing crisis, was requisitioning of empty properties to house those in need. A total of 71,493 properties were requisitioned during the war, and another 51,695 up to 1951.[5] Some authorities, particularly Labour ones, used the powers enthusiastically. For example, in Hackney by 1950, 3,800 homes had been taken over to house those on the waiting list. In Wandsworth, it was 3,700. A Conservative government, with greater care for the interests of property, passed legislation in 1955 ending local authorities' requisitioning powers and requiring requisitioned properties be returned or disposed of by 1960.

Permanent housing remained the goal, of course, and the incoming Labour government gave an early indication of its intentions and priorities in the 1946 Housing (Financial and Miscellaneous Provisions) Act which raised the annual Exchequer subsidy to £16.50 per home and allowed local authorities to borrow at low rates from the Public Works Loans Board. At the local level, councils were required to ensure that no more than 20 per cent of new builds were privately built; some that failed to meet this stipulation were penalised.

This testified – at a time of severe labour and materials shortages and strict rationing – to a necessary focus on state-directed programmes and the ongoing legacy of wartime state planning, but it reflected too the desire of the new Minister of Health and Housing, the left-winger Nye Bevan, to address working-class housing needs:

> Before the war the housing problems of the middle class were, roughly, solved . . . Speculative builders, supported enthusiastically, and even voraciously, by money-lending organisations, solved the problem of the higher income groups in the matter of housing. We propose to start at the other end. We propose to start to solve, first, the housing difficulties of the lower income groups.[6]

Bevan's socialist principles extended further, however. For him, the new council housing represented far more than mere bricks and mortar; in quality, design and ethos it heralded a new Britain. To this end, he was clear that mere quantity of new housing was an insufficient measure: 'While we shall be judged for a year or two by the *number* of houses we build . . . we shall be judged in ten years' time by the *type* of houses we build.'[7]

Unfortunately for Bevan and the Labour Party, the electorate's judgement came sooner and was less favourable, but in the late 1940s Bevan's idealism found support in the key official reports of the day. The Dudley Committee issued its wide-ranging report on housing design and layout in 1944, recommending firstly that post-war council homes should be larger; it suggested 900 square feet for a three-bed house over the 750–800 square feet which prevailed. In practice, Bevan chose to exceed this; by 1949, the average new three-bed council home occupied 1,055 square feet – a 37 per cent increase on the housing for the poor built during the slum clearance drive of the late 1930s. (Bevan also insisted these homes have two toilets – an unprecedented luxury in working-class homes which had more often lacked a single toilet of their own.) The report also marked a more self-consciously 'modern' approach to housing: open ranges and fires were to be replaced by gas or electric cookers and, to the pleasure of those Mackworth housewives, old-style parlours were to be traded for a single living room with the scullery now a proper working kitchen or kitchen-diner.

Dudley also criticised the pre-war cottage estates, a cause taken up more powerfully by the 1948 Committee on the Appearance of Housing Estates. This berated the look and 'feel' of the interwar estates, particularly some, in its words, 'where all individuality and homeliness have been lost in endless rows of identical semi-detached houses . . . or in severe geometrical road patterns which bear no relation to underlying landscape features'.[8] Dudley's recommendations and the changed sensibilities of the time were formalised in the 1949 *Housing Manual*.

By the end of the war, two big ideas that were to dominate post-war planning for decades had emerged: the neighbourhood unit and mixed development. A third, first mooted in the Dudley Report but highlighted in a 1953 revision to the *Housing Manual* (called matter-of-factly, *Houses 1953*) also gained considerable traction – the separation of cars and pedestrians by a system of cul-de-sacs, feeder roads and walkways along what were called Radburn lines pioneered by the town of that name in New Jersey, founded in 1929 as 'a town for the motor age'.

None of the housing and planning reports of the era embraced multi-storey construction but they did, without fanfare and with no sense that they were heralding any radical shift in the nature of public housing provision, open the door to the transition that would follow. Abercrombie and Forshaw's *County of London Plan* proposed an inner-city density of 136 persons per acre; the maths suggested that up to two-thirds of such a population would necessarily be housed in flats. The *Plan* itself, in an almost passing observation, concluded that 'a certain number of high blocks up to ten storeys might prove popular, in particular for single people and childless couples'.[9]

The Dudley Report had recommended a density of 120 persons per acre in urban areas – the same calculations applied as did the report's belief that flats remained unsuitable accommodation for families with younger children. The 1946 special

subsidy to provide lifts in housing from four storeys in height
was intended to provide working-class housewives and mothers with the same amenity enjoyed by the mansion block middle
classes but would acquire greater significance with time.

In the meantime, in the words of Salford's City Engineer, 'in
the large urban aggregations . . . flats will no doubt find a place,
but they are only the next best thing to good houses'.[10] Across
the Irwell in Manchester, which took immense pride in its interwar Wythenshawe scheme, this view was held even more
strongly. The 1945 *City of Manchester Plan* concluded:

> It would be a profound sociological mistake to force upon the British
> public, in defiance of its own widely expressed preference for separate
> houses with private gardens, a way of life that is fundamentally out of
> keeping with its traditions, instincts and opportunities.[11]

This understanding of popular sentiment appeared to be borne
out by the polling of the day: the Mass Observation survey,
People's Homes, conducted in 1943 found that only 5 per cent of
its sample 'would by choice inhabit a flat'.[12] This, however,
proved to be far from the final word on the subject.

Bevan shared these presumptions although his speech, introducing the 1949 Housing Act to the House of Commons,
demanded that the new estates – he called them, tellingly, 'town-
ships' – reflect the 'aesthetics of good modern architecture' and
contain 'the most variegated kind of housing'. Crucially, Bevan
was adamant that the new estates should not be merely housing
for the poor. If they were, they would become, in his words,
'castrated communities'. He believed 'this segregation of the
different income groups . . . a wholly evil thing'. He famously
went on to articulate this vision more fully:

It is entirely undesirable that on modern housing estates only one type of citizen should live. If we are to enable citizens to lead a full life, if they are each to be aware of the problems of their neighbours, then they should all be drawn from different sections of the community. We should try to introduce what was always the lovely feature of English and Welsh villages, where the doctor, the grocer, the butcher and the farm labourer all lived in the same street.[13]

The Act removed the stipulation that council housing be designated as working-class housing which had featured, in various forms, in every previous housing act. Bevan and Labour saw it as serving 'general needs' and a cross-section of the community.

The Festival of Britain, officially opened in May 1951, was intended as the mark and harbinger of the new Britain emerging. In the words of the official brochure, it was a 'united act of national reassessment, and [a] corporate reaffirmation of faith in the nation's future'.[14] Events were held across the country but the great showpiece of the festival was the South Bank, hitherto an area of obsolete industrial warehouses and run-down working-class housing. Here the Royal Festival Hall (designed, incidentally, by the architects of the LCC) survives as a powerful visual reminder of both the political and architectural ideals of the day. Other buildings (mostly in an International Modernist style, novel to Britain and symbolic of a new country unencumbered by the detritus of the past) were rapidly demolished by the Conservative government that took office in October 1951 for whom the Festival reeked uncomfortably of Labourist social democracy, an act of desecration in the most literal sense.

The South Bank site celebrated the land, the people and the industrial technology of the nation. Five miles down the river in the old East End, a 'Live Architecture Exhibition' was organised to showcase new housing and planning ideals. It featured a Building Research Pavilion and its counterpart 'Gremlin Grange' – a jerry-built house intended as 'a full-sized demonstration of how things may go wrong when scientific principles in building are ignored'. The themes of the Town Planning Pavilion – 'The Battle for Land', 'The Needs of the People', 'How Can These Needs Be Met?' – capture the mood and priorities of the time. But at the heart of the exhibition were the first 478 homes of the Lansbury Estate. The completed scheme comprised almost 1,200 homes: some two-storey terraced houses but the majority flats and maisonettes in a range of low-rise multi-storey blocks. It's a modest ensemble; its stock yellow brick was selected to blend in with its surroundings. And, despite the involvement of a few 'name' architects, most of its housing is unexceptional, deploying a generally conventional streetscape with a few courts and setbacks to provide variety and greenery.

Practically, the origins of the estate predated the Festival and were located first and foremost in the nature and condition of local housing. Of the estate's new residents – over half had been living in Poplar before they moved and another fifth in the neighbouring boroughs of Stepney, Bethnal Green and Shoreditch – 60 per cent had shared their previous dwellings, 63 per cent had had no access to an inside toilet and 73 per cent had had no access to a bathroom or even to a fitted bath.[15] Almost a quarter of Poplar homes had been either destroyed or seriously damaged in the Blitz. The need, embraced in *The County of London Plan*, was to rebuild and build better. The Lansbury scheme – part of the Stepney and Poplar Reconstruction Area authorised by the Ministry of Town and Country Planning in December 1947 and still in its early stages as Festival adviser Frederick Gibberd cast around for a suitable site for the proposed Live Architecture exhibition – offered potentially just the practical example of new principles and designs that was needed.

The LCC established a multi-disciplinary Reconstruction Group comprising architects, planners, surveyors and (a sign of the times) the first sociologist to be involved in such a project, Margaret Willis. Its brief was not only to build decent housing but also a community – the 'neighbourhood unit' championed by Patrick Abercrombie and endorsed in the government's 1944 *Housing Manual*. Abercrombie's object was to 'emphasise the identity of the existing communities, to increase their degree of segregation, and where necessary to reorganise them as separate and definite entities' with, to this end, each community being provided 'with its own schools, public buildings, shops, open spaces, etc.'[16] The catchment area of the local elementary school was to define the shape and population – envisaged as between 6,000 to 8,000 – of each neighbourhood.

Thus, as well as housing, the estate contained new schools and churches, pubs (one surviving as the appropriately named Festival Inn), community buildings and the country's first pedestrianised shopping precinct set around a revamped Chrisp Street Market. Here Gibberd, who became the estate's overall designer and presiding genius, also raised its single signature landmark, his 'practical folly', the Clock Tower with its fifty-five-foot-high viewing platform and separate up and down stairways.[17] (It was closed shortly afterwards for being too tempting to would-be suicides.)

In truth, this was a rare flight of fancy for the estate. Architecturally, it took its cues from the more picturesque forms of social housing pioneered in the Scandinavian welfare states – a New Humanist vision in the terms of its time. Sandy Wilson, later the architect of the British Library, then a Young Turk in the uncompromisingly modernist wing of the LCC Architect's Department inspired by Le Corbusier's more monumentalist approach, described Lansbury's 'pitched roofs, peephole windows, and "folksy" details of the current Swedish revival' as the architecture of 'cold feet'.[18] He thought it a denial of the urbanism and scale its setting demanded. J.M. Richards, editor of the *Architectural Review*, described 'the general run of the small-scale housing at Lansbury as worthy, dull and somewhat skimpy'.[19] More sympathetically he noted that 'aridity of the design' was 'undoubtedly due to so much having to be sacrificed for the sake of cheapness'.[20]

The exhibition had fallen foul of the economic crisis of the late 1940s and found its budget almost halved to £240,000. Standards (and ceilings – down to eight feet in some homes in contravention of existing bye-laws) were lowered. Even the estate's very first resident, Mrs Alice Snoddy, who moved in with her husband, two children and the family's pet tortoise on Valentine's Day, 1951, wasn't that enamoured: 'To be honest, I wasn't over-impressed when I first saw the flat in Gladstone House because I had been used to living in a house.' Still there, fifty years on, she admits that she 'must have adjusted rather well'.[21] Others were more grateful. To a lighterman's wife who had moved from a Limehouse basement it was all that she had 'hoped for': 'I've waited seven years for it. We were so desperate, we would have gone almost anywhere. I'm glad we didn't, we belong round these parts.'[22]

Beyond the architectural battles, which would run and run, those were the sentiments of most early residents. The woman who had moved from her mother's home in Millwall where her family of five had lived in two rooms said simply 'I never thought I'd see such luxury'. There were grumbles about lack of play space and nursery provision (60 per cent of the first households had children under ten), and over the rents which were high relative to those of the slums from which most had escaped. In the end, in the words of two early sociological observers, 'an environment has been created – or re-created – that is neither a pale imitation of suburban boredom, nor an apologia for city life'.[23] In that regard, the Lansbury must be accounted an overall success.

Ironically, for all the fanfare and contemporary controversy, it was, in some ways, less the first breath of a new world than the dying gasp of the old. In the mid-1950s, almost one in three of the estate's principal wage-earners worked on the docks or in ancillary trades, but the local East India Docks closed in 1965 and the last London docks, downstream in Beckton, in 1981. There were other, more current pressures too.

The construction drive of the new Conservative Minister of Housing from 1951, Harold Macmillan, required greater density and higher-rise building; by the mid-1950s new build on the estate comprised eleven-storey point blocks. Fitzgerald House, built in 1968 and towering above the Chrisp Street Market, is nineteen storeys high. That story takes us to later chapters but one major driver of this still embryonic shift to high-rise lay in the new fashion for mixed development housing.

The Lansbury made its own small contribution to this change with its inclusion of the capital's first purpose-built old people's home (since demolished), but Gibberd provided what was widely regarded as the mixed development's template in his Somerford Grove scheme for the London Borough of Hackney in 1949. This was a small estate of 150 homes but within those there was impressive variety – three-storey blocks of two- and three-bed flats, single bed and bedsitter flats, two-storey terraces of two- and three-bed houses and a terrace of bungalows for the elderly.

This was a radical break with interwar schemes dominated by two- and three-bed family housing and it reflected both a reaction to the much-criticised homogeneity of those earlier estates and a realisation that council housing must cater for a wider range of the population. Increased life expectancy and rising divorce rates in the post-war period were increasing the number of single-person and childless households; when Hackney surveyed its own 12,000-strong council housing waiting list in 1948, it found almost one-third required only a single bedroom.[24] Mixed development was intended to provide a range of housing types to cater for a range of people in different life stages.

The other great appeal of mixed development was the increased visual interest it offered housing schemes. Gibberd, speaking for a generation of post-war architects and planners, argued that 'buildings with quite different formal qualities such as blocks of flats, maisonettes and bungalows are needed to provide "contrast" and "variety" in the "composition" of an area'.[25] In Somerford Grove, Gibberd achieved this not only in the estate's range of housing forms but in its layout – a pedestrianised 'series of closes, each with its own character', embodying what he called 'precinctual theory' (a Radburn-style separation of people and traffic, in other words).

Somerford Grove, Hackney

Even surface treatments were deliberately varied: in Gibberd's description, pale pink and putty-coloured walls for the flatted houses, alternating warm brick and rendered walls on the terraced houses, dark red and blue bricks for the old people's housing.[26] It was all a hymn to Scandinavian-inspired New Humanism (and a winner of an Award for Merit from the Festival of Britain's architectural committee); according to the *Times*, at around 104 persons per acre, 'encouraging proof that even dense housing need not be inhuman'.[27] In strictly contemporary terms, part of that humanity was located in the resolutely low-rise nature of the estate. Hackney's councillors had stipulated in 1948 that no new housing scheme should exceed three storeys in height – a reminder of traditional Labour antipathy towards even the five-storey tenements which had prevailed in the 1920s and 1930s.[28]

No such proviso operated in Conservative-controlled Westminster City Council where the Churchill Gardens Estate, opened in 1951, represented an early pinnacle of mixed development ideals and implementation. The Pimlico Housing Scheme as it was originally designated was the only major project within Abercrombie's London plan to be completed. Its size – a thirty-acre site, 1,661 homes, thirty-six blocks, a population of some 5,000 – gives some indication of the scale of post-war hopes. The fact that it was designed by two recent graduates from the Architectural Association, Philip Powell and Hidalgo Moya, then aged just twenty-four and twenty-five respectively, suggests some of the youthful energy of the time.

In bare descriptive terms, the estate comprises a series of nine- to eleven-storey slab blocks interspersed by smaller blocks of three to five storeys. A seven-storey block, with ground floor shops, encloses the estate along its Lupus Street frontage. Two terraces of three-storey town houses (intended for middle-class occupation) run along the Thames-side Grosvenor Road front of the estate. That scale might alarm some, but Powell described his own 'mistrust of conscious struggling after originality . . . of the monumental approach'.[29] Churchill Gardens combines a clean-lined modernism with careful configuration of elements and unfussy landscaping that make it seem an attractive and intimate space. It's one of my favourites and, I think, a deserved winner of a Civic Trust vote in 2000 to decide the best building scheme of the preceding forty years.

Mixed development, then, was an overwhelmingly benign concept and a practical response to the reality of post-war housing needs which stretched far beyond the family homes which had been the staple of interwar development. But its incorporation of high-rise had the unanticipated consequence of licensing the multi-storey point and slab blocks which would come to dominate – in public perception at least though never numerically – the council house building of the decades to come. After the genteel precedent of The Lawn in Harlow, this began in low-key fashion. The LCC built its own first high-rise block in Southfields, Wandsworth: Oatlands Court – 'compact, not too tall (eleven storeys), with one of those plans, immediately lucid, which architects dream of, fuss over, but rarely achieve', in the words of Ian Nairn.[30] Similar blocks, this time in clusters, would be built in the early 1950s in the Fitzhugh and Ackroydon Estates nearby. This was architect-led innovation – a tribute to the LCC's Architect's Department, which was at that time, without hyperbole, the foremost architectural practice in the world – but, for the time being, few other authorities emulated this lead.

Some 804,921 council homes were built under Labour between 1945 and 1951; 190,368 in the single year 1948.[31] These are impressive figures given post-war economic dislocation and difficulties, but they fell below government targets and 1948 – a lagging indicator – represented a peak. The severe winter of 1947 and the fuel and balance of payments crises which followed forced a new focus on industrial reconstruction at the expense of social programmes. Housing completions fell. A revived Conservative Opposition made housing a prime issue in the 1951 general election, calling it in its manifesto 'the first of the social services'.[32] Macmillan was appointed, as head of the renamed Ministry of Housing and Local Government, to fulfil the Conservative pledge to build 300,000 new homes annually – a promise fulfilled with 318,000 completions in 1953.

Of that total, 229,000 were council homes, the highest annual total ever achieved. Macmillan was helped by the easing of rationing and quotas in the early 1950s but, in the first instance, his achievement rested on a pragmatic willingness to use the levers of the national and local state. Exchequer support for housebuilding increased fourfold between 1950 and 1956 and Macmillan stimulated a housebuilding drive across the country with an unashamedly corporatist machinery of regional boards comprising contractors, trades unions, civil servants and council representatives.

Another factor in Macmillan's quantitative success was a sharp reduction in council housing quality. The so-called People's Houses, which formed the bedrock of the new programme, were marked by reduced space standards. New ministry guidelines announced in 1951 made Bevan's 900 square foot minimum for a three-bed house a maximum; henceforth new council houses were again – at between 750 to 850 square feet – significantly smaller. The requirement that a five-person household be supplied with two WCs was also dropped.

This was a policy which reflected an ideological shift as much as it did any necessary practical adjustment. Such clear blue water was increasingly emphasised. The 1953 White Paper, 'Housing: The Next Step', declared 'one object of future housing policy [to] be to continue to promote, by all possible means, the building of houses for owner-occupation'.[33] In the following year, private housebuilders were freed from the obligation to secure building licences, one of the main means by which local authority housing had been prioritised in the immediate post-war years. The major change, however, was marked by the 1954 Housing Act which required that future council efforts be concentrated on redevelopment rather than general needs.

This heralded the – quite justified – attack on the slums which would dominate council housebuilding for the rest of its lifespan, but it also denoted, quite deliberately, a philosophical fissure between the two major parties. While Labour espoused – implicitly in the interwar period and explicitly from 1949 – a more egalitarian understanding of council housing which saw it serving a cross-section of society, the Conservatives saw it (and had legislated to this effect in the 1920s and 1930s) as housing for the poor. There's nothing sinister in that per se – it might even seem quite sensible – but it contains a dangerous logic which has reached its conclusion at the present time. When council housing is seen as housing of last resort – a safety net for the poorest or most vulnerable, even in present terms a *temporary* safety net – it (and its residents) are seen as second-rate.

Macmillan had moved on by 1956 but his successor, Duncan Sandys, enacted the 1956 Housing Subsidies Act which consolidated this shift. The new Act abolished completely the general needs subsidy, requiring that new council housing (unless financed by borrowing from the open market) be reserved to two designated groups – the elderly or those displaced by slum clearance. There was another change too – the new grant regime paid more the higher councils built: 'a flat in a six-storey block received 2.3 times the basic subsidy paid on a house and this ratio rose to 3.0 at fifteen storeys and 3.4 at twenty storeys'.[34]

In essence this was a simple recognition of the increased costs of multi-storey housing, as much a reflection of contemporary pressures to build high as an encouragement to them. It can be taken, however, as inaugurating the new age of council housing which will be the subject of Chapter 5.

5

'Get These People Out of the Slums': 1956–68

There are only two tower blocks in Castle Vale, a Birmingham housing estate built between 1964 and 1969 six miles to the north-east of the city centre. What you see now is a 'dignified low-rise estate' or, in the words of one gushing journalist, 'attractive new houses and mews flats, piazzas and courtyards'.[1] It wasn't ever thus.

Once the estate boasted thirty-four towers; seventeen lined up along Farnborough Road on its fringe, eight (the imaginatively named Centre 8) in the middle, others dotted around. These themselves had emerged in a fraught battle for power between the council's Public Works Department, headed by domineering City Engineer Herbert Manzoni, and its new City Architect, A.G. Sheppard Fidler. Sheppard Fidler, chief planner at Crawley New Town from 1947 to 1952, was a well-respected figure within the architectural Establishment but he found his arrival in the Midlands a baptism of fire:

The Deputy City Engineer came into my office the very first day I arrived, shoved all these plans on my desk, and said 'Carry on with these!'. He was letting contracts as fast as he could go, didn't know what he was doing . . . This rather shattered me, because we'd had very careful schemes prepared at Crawley, with very great interest on the part of the Development Corporation, whereas in Birmingham the House Building Committee could hardly care about the design as long as the numbers were kept up – I'd been used to gentle Southern people![2]

For two years, Sheppard Fidler worked under Manzoni but, even after securing his own City Architect's Department in 1954, he struggled for influence over planning decisions which Public Works felt were properly theirs. He secured a partial victory in Castle Vale when his New Town sensibilities – favouring a more Radburn-style layout and neighbourhood blocks of housing, shops and offices set around communal green spaces – were preferred against the initial, more workaday proposals of the Works Department. But Sheppard Fidler's strong support for the industrialised building methods of the French company Camus – which he felt offered architects greater flexibility and allowed a greater range of building types – was overruled in committee. He resigned shortly afterwards.

That 'Frenchness' was part of the problem, especially when set against the close relationship – to be examined later – between the council and some leading local building firms. But, in general terms, the council had little interest in the finesse which Sheppard Fidler sought to apply to planning and design. Birmingham had been the site (in Joseph Chamberlain's 'Civic Gospel') of the most extravagant expression of Victorian municipalism and it remained self-consciously Britain's second city. The council, then securely Conservative, had built more council housing than any other English authority between the

wars. Now more evenly balanced politically, the city remained
determined to build big and bold.

Sir Charles Burman (a Conservative chair of Birmingham's
Housing Committee in the 1950s), declared Sheppard Fidler:

> a very nice chap, but he was a perfectionist – he liked to get things just
> so. This meant that he did not push the housing programme along as
> quickly as he might have done, because building and planning well and
> carefully was more important to him than building a lot of houses.[3]

The unselfconscious philistinism can speak for itself but the
comment speaks to a wider culture that materialised through
the 1950s and 1960s.

Castle Vale Estate, Birmingham, 1968

The Castle Vale Estate that emerged in the mid-1960s was a
strange hybrid: a predominantly suburban low-rise estate –
terraces of two-storey housing interspersed with four-storey
flats and maisonettes – dominated by the sixteen-storey point
blocks of Centre 8 at its heart. There were around 4,800 homes

in the finished estate. Unusually 30 per cent of these – houses, of course – were owner-occupied in a nod to ideas of mixed tenure, but over half the 3,400 council homes were in the high-rise blocks. The latter appeared oddly isolated on a green island – the surrounding open space that the height of the blocks demanded – and further ringed by the estate's major service roads. The eleven-storey Farnborough Road flats at the edge of the estate, green fields to one side and suburbia to the other, looked even more isolated.

The work nevertheless fitted into the council's city-wide plans. By 1971 the Corporation owned 464 tower blocks; almost two-thirds of these lined or lay beyond the city's ring road. As a result some started to call Birmingham 'Saucer City', a reflection of its relatively low-rise centre and high-rise periphery.[4]

Why *did* Birmingham build high and why at such scale in the suburbs? The city was certainly not averse to building at scale but there had been, into the 1930s, a perceived 'prejudice against flats' and the overwhelming majority of the 51,000 new council homes completed in the interwar period were located in traditional cottage suburbs.[5] Despite that record, the council's own 1946 Housing Survey revealed more than half the city's 283,611 homes lacked a separate bathroom and some one in ten were back-to-back. Much remained to be done.

The clearance of multi-occupancy slum housing in the city centre seemed uncontroversially to demand multi-storey replacements. However beyond this, here and elsewhere, Sheppard Fidler clashed with his nemesis Herbert Manzoni. This was an era when authoritative council chief officers could exercise enormous power; nowhere more so than in Birmingham where the council's Public Works Committee – formally the decision-making body for the major schemes transforming the city in the period – was little more than a conduit for Manzoni's brusquely modernising vision. Sometimes dubbed the man who did more damage to Birmingham than the *Luftwaffe*, Manzoni, in his own words, had 'never been very certain as to the value of tangible links with the past. They are often more sentimental than valuable.'[6] And there was, indeed, little sentimentality on display when 38,000, admittedly generally poor quality, houses were cleared to make way for Birmingham's new inner ring road, completed in 1971. There was, moreover, no place for Sheppard Fidler's expertise and sensitivity in the rebuilding efforts which followed; he was deliberately excluded from the major inner-city redevelopment schemes kept firmly in the hands of the City Engineer.

It was also Manzoni who proposed building six-storey blocks on the city fringes, claiming they would 'help utilise the existing land to the fullest advantage and increase the overall density of population without destroying [its] open character'. This apparently common-sense view of housing density was, in fact, mistaken: tower blocks did not offer higher-density housing than lower-rise alternatives precisely because of the 'open character' of the space that encircled the blocks, required to avoid problems of shadowing and overlooking. In 1963 Sheppard Fidler had been instructed by the Housing Committee to aim for a density of seventy-five persons per acre in new developments. This was little more than the density of between forty-eight and sixty persons achieved by the interwar Tudor Walters standard of twelve houses per acre, but the commitment to high-rise remained.

Back in 1953, when the council found its application for a special flats subsidy in suburban Tile Cross rejected by the Ministry of Housing, it protested: 'Look, Minister, you've got to change this! We're the City of Birmingham, not some tiddly little country town – we want these rules changed!'[7] In response, a discretionary subsidy was granted, which was formalised and universalised in the 1956 subsidy regime that incentivised high-rise.

Thus Birmingham's multi-storey flats were both cause and effect of one the most crucial legislative drivers of high-rise in the period. They indicate how multi-storey blocks – once an architectural feature of choice – became, increasingly, a default for those authorities most ambitious to build at scale.

There were other forces in play too. Post-war planning – the West Midland Group's study *Conurbation* and the *West Midlands Plan* of Herbert Jackson and Sir Patrick Abercrombie, both published in 1948 – envisaged Birmingham's population stabilising and growth occurring in surrounding towns. After 1951, however, Conservative governments halted the New Town programme and Birmingham's neighbouring authorities were reluctant to embrace displaced Brummies. By 1957, just thirty-eight houses had been allocated to the city's increasing number of overspill families.

After 1960, Birmingham's own plans to build 54,000 homes on Green Belt land at Wythall in Worcestershire across the city's southern boundary, were rejected. As a result the need to build within the city borders and the logic of building at higher density came to seem unarguable – and, more positively, reflective of a new civic patriotism. As the council's Labour leader, Harry Watton, declared: 'Birmingham people are entitled to remain in Birmingham if they wish, and Birmingham industry has the right to remain in the city it has done so much to make great.'[8]

Castle Vale itself prospered in its early years. One tenant recalling that period remembered it as 'a huge improvement' on her former home in Aston. She now 'had an indoor toilet, and there was so much green space . . . it seemed like Utopia'.[9] The estate's historian Adam Mornement describes low crime rates and a small turnover of residents: 'people wanted to be there and wanted to stay there.'[10] But, despite those optimistic assessments, there were early indications of later travails. The low turnover notwithstanding, some residents felt disconnected from the wider city, and especially the central areas that had been their former home. The system-built blocks were reporting problems of water penetration through windows and faulty joints as early as 1967. Both were early indicators of troubles that would come to afflict similar estates across the country.

It was not only in Birmingham where the 1956 legislation had a direct effect on planning and construction. Labour-controlled Woolwich Metropolitan Borough had been a prodigious builder of council housing in the interwar period – 4,473 homes in all, almost 3,000 built by the council's own workforce; its direct labour department was one of the largest and most efficient in the country. As a peripheral London borough, Woolwich was unusual in the capital in having greenfield sites on which to build and, post-1945, initially resisted pressures, not least from the LCC, to build high. The need to build at density in a large central redevelopment area forced a rethink, however.

With the 1956 Act, the eleven-storey St Mary's Towers were raised to fourteen levels. For all that, the five point blocks, designed by Norman & Dawbarn, were of attractive appearance – with a butterfly-plan to maximise light and constructed of reinforced concrete frames with pinkish flint-lime brick infill panels and patterned precast concrete panels under the windows.

Hackney Metropolitan Borough Council's stipulation in 1948 of a strict three-storey maximum for all future council house construction lasted only seven years. In 1955, the council gave the go-ahead for two eleven-storey blocks in The Beckers scheme in Shacklewell, designed by Frederick Gibberd. For the time being, earlier ideals regarding the use of high-rise blocks prevailed. The Beckers, comprising one-bed flats and bedsitters, was not intended as family housing and the estate echoed Somerford Grove, Gibberd's pioneering mixed development to the south of the borough, with its low-rise block of two-bed flats, terraced three-bed houses and Scandinavian-influenced external treatments of coloured panelling and cream rendering. The two more conventional fifteen-storey blocks of the Trelawney Estate, in central Hackney, were given the go-ahead in the same year as a direct result of the impending 1956 subsidy regime.

In fact, there was a whole range of dynamics that led to the adoption of high-rise in the late 1950s. The aesthetics of mixed development were one, but the concept was boosted by the very practical realisation that a large proportion of those on the council housing waiting list did not need traditional family homes. Furthermore, in the major cities, slum clearance, higher space standards, improved community facilities on council estates, and land zoning all had the effect of reducing the area available for building. Hackney itself pleaded that the 'lack of building sites and the ever increasing cost of site purchase left the Council with no alternative but to build higher', and its shift to building high was aided by the passing of the council's old guard in the early 1950s and the emergence of a younger and more radical set of councillors.[11]

The bigger picture was provided by the Royal Institute of British Architects (RIBA) Symposium on High Flats in February 1955. Its press release reflected both the financial pressures and cultural judgements that, in its view, made an irrefutable case for taller blocks:

> the high cost of land, the encroachment of buildings on agricultural land and – too often – the featureless spread of housing estates beyond the confines of their cities are compelling a growing number of authorities to consider the contribution that the building of high flats can make to their housing and reconstruction programme.

Cynics might argue that architects had an interest in building high; in promoting eye-catching schemes that showcased their skill and daring. It's true enough that municipal suburbia gave them little scope for such display. But we shouldn't discount the genuine idealism of a generation who really believed, in the words of Ted Hollamby, that they 'had the most wonderful work to do . . . those ideas of making a better world, we thought we were actually doing it'.[12] Hollamby, later Chief Architect for Lambeth, was then a young recruit to the world's largest architectural practice, the LCC Architect's Department. In the early 1950s, the department had over 1,500 staff including 350 professional architects and trainees of whom 250 worked in the housing division. Sandy Wilson likened job adverts for the department to 'a summons to join the Forces again but in this case to win the peace by rebuilding London'.[13]

Surprisingly, the department had been sidelined in the LCC's immediate post-war reconstruction programme when responsibility for housebuilding had been placed with the council's Valuer's Department. The plan was to maximise housing output by concentrating in one department work previously split between three. Cyril Walker, who combined the roles of Chief Valuer and Director of Housing from 1945 to 1951, was responsible for acquiring land, designating its use for housing and for housing design.

The Royal Institute of Chartered Surveyors praised the scheme and, with some 18,000 permanent homes constructed in severely straitened times by 1949, it could claim success, in numerical terms at least. But RIBA had opposed the scheme from the outset for its sidelining of design and planning sensibilities; indeed, much of the new housing harked back to pre-war models. The universally critical response of the architectural press to a 1949 exhibition of the council's post-war housing achievements was sufficient to persuade the LCC to hand back responsibility for housing to its Chief Architect, Robert Matthew.[14]

The Architect's Department became, from the 1950s, the most significant *architectural* influence on the post-war design and form of council housing in the country. But the department itself was riven by disagreement – as we saw played out in criticisms of the Lansbury Estate – over what form that influence should take. A debate between the opposing sides organised by Sandy Wilson in a pub on the York Road (just opposite the department's offices) was intended to settle disagreements 'once and for all', but it lasted one day instead of the two that were planned and did little to resolve tensions.[15]

The clash would be played out on a grand scale in what an American commentator called 'probably the finest low-cost housing development in the world': the Alton Estate in Roehampton, London.[16]

The plans for Alton East, to the east of Alton Road, were first approved in October 1951 and claimed as a triumph for 'the Swedish boys'. The estate, 744 homes in all, is a mix of low-rise, red-brick, two-storey terraces and four-storey maisonettes with ten eleven-storey point blocks clad in cream-coloured brick, on its fringes, 'scattered over the bosky slope which had been covered by large Victorian gardens' in Pevsner's bucolic description.[17] The new housing was set irregularly on the footprint of the Victorian villas it replaced, preserving mature trees and giving the estate today the surprisingly verdant aspect it retains. Pevsner commended it all for its 'picturesque informality', an echo of the Scandinavian schemes that Alton East's progenitors admired.

Alton West, Wandsworth

Alton West, the second, larger phase of the scheme, was agreed in September 1953 and designed along very different lines. Here another group of LCC architects sought a more consciously monumental and uncompromisingly modernist aesthetic designed to make dramatic use of its parkland setting.

Low-rise homes feature here too, most strikingly the groups of bungalows for elderly residents in Minstead Gardens. But it is the estate's fifteen eleven-storey point blocks and the five ten-storey slab blocks which dominate; the latter ranged along the hill above Danebury Avenue providing its most iconic image. The model here was Le Corbusier's famous *Unité d'habitation* complex in Marseille, completed in 1952 and the ethos – pitted against the 'soft' New Humanism of Alton East – was a 'hard' Brutalism.

That term, Brutalism, is controversial and difficult to define. In one reading it derives from Le Corbusier's own use of exposed concrete *béton-brut* in constructing his Marseille scheme, but it owes as much to the connotations of 'toughness and primitivism' proclaimed by the style's foremost early advocate Reyner Banham. Banham was 'the towering architecture and design critic and polemicist of the post-war era', a pugnacious figure whose physical presence – 'tall, well built, a prodigious conversationalist, and, from the early 1960s onwards, patriarchally bearded' – seems almost to echo the architecture he lauded.[18]

In the early 1950s, Banham was completing his doctoral thesis on the modern movement while working for the *Architectural Review*. In a seminal 1955 article for that journal, he provided what remains probably the most precise and useful summary of Brutalism. He offered a form characterised, in his words, by '1, Memorability as an Image; 2, Clear exhibition of Structure; and 3, Valuation of Materials "as found"'.[19] There was a certain conscious monumentalism to Brutalism but, if it was statement architecture, it spoke for the moment to an architecture of social purpose and was 'widely seen as the architectural style of the Welfare State – a cheap way of building quickly, on a large scale, for housing, hospitals, comprehensive schools, and massive university expansion'.[20]

In popular terms, 'Brutalism' has now become a more encompassing descriptor – a term applied to 'any large concrete-y building from the 1960s or '70s' by some and, to its critics, something more pejoratively descriptive.[21] As such, it will take its place in the demonology of council housing. Nevertheless, Alton West and the best architect-designed estates bearing the label often provided very fine housing indeed.

Whichever side you choose, the fact is that both of the rival worldviews were attempting consciously to build a new world (though you could argue that the Brutalists were 'braver' in this respect). Both were 'modern', both envisaged a more classless architecture for a new, more classless age. In this respect, both were too late. Though mixed development remained the gold standard in Alton East and Alton West, the goal of social mix had been abandoned. This was working-class housing, as distinct in form as the cottage suburbs that had been criticised for just that reason: 'architectural style and form were still used to express and signify class position.'[22] The Barbican, built for affluent leaseholders by the City of London between 1965 and 1976, is the exception that proves the rule.

Park Hill, in Sheffield, built between 1957 and 1961 and arguably the most significant council housing scheme of the era, wears the Brutalist label with pride. The estate stands on the crest of a steep hill behind the city centre train station: a lowering symbol of the city's toughness to some (for good or ill); to others, a confident mark of an ambitious council's commitment to house its people well. Its architects, Jack Lynn and Ivor Smith, working under the guidance of Sheffield City Architect, J. Lewis Womersley, however, rejected the Brutalist label (or at

least its negative connotations): 'We didn't think we were
Brutalists. We thought we were quite nice guys.'[23]
    They were. The 996 flats replaced some of the worst slums in
the city. To one new resident, moved from a bathroomless back-
to-back where she lived with her husband, baby, parents and
brother, 'It was luxury . . . When we got here it was marvel-
lous. Three bedrooms, hot water, always warm. And the view.
It's lovely, especially at night, when it's all lit up.'
    Of course, such comments could be repeated for new council
housing schemes up and down the country, but they bear repeat-
ing as a truth so often neglected by later critics. Those that
condemn modernist estates also routinely lament the decimation of the (romanticised) 'close-knit communities' the new
housing replaced, but Lynn and Smith's design was based on an
in-depth study of working-class life and sought quite deliberately to replicate that community – old neighbours were housed
next to each other, former street names were reused, even the
cobbles of the terraced streets were used to pave the pathways
down to the station and city centre.
    Most famously, they created 'streets in the sky' – three-
metre-wide decks intended to facilitate neighbourly chat free
from the noise and danger of passing traffic save the occasional
milk float. Those decks ran the length of and joined the estate's
snaking blocks that ranged from four storeys high at the top of
Park Hill to thirteen at the lower end. The effect is powerful but
not overpowering. The thirty-two-acre site also provided four
pubs, forty-two shops, a community centre, social clubs, a
health centre, dentists and nursery and primary schools. To
Grenville Squires, a caretaker on the estate for twenty-six years,
it was 'like a medieval village; you didn't have to leave'. Park
Hill's resident sociologist (it really had one) determined the

estate an outstanding success, its 'exceptionally vigorous residents' association' sure proof against any future apathy or
alienation.[24]

In that, she was wrong. By the early 1980s, Park Hill had
become to many a very visible symbol of all that had gone
wrong with council housing. Poor maintenance had left the
estate looking shabby. The 'streets in the sky' were blamed for
rising problems of crime and antisocial behaviour. The community seemed divided and dispirited. The decimation of the local
economy – it lost 40,000 jobs from 1979 – and a reform of allocations policy which gave priority to the least well-off might
bear greater explanatory weight, however, than any inherent
design faults.

Keeling House, a tower block opened in 1959 and designed
by Denys Lasdun for Bethnal Green Metropolitan Borough
Council, offers another image of Brutalism. Its sixteen-storey
height and form – white reinforced concrete with Portland
stone finish cladding – made it stand out among the surrounding stock brick terraces and some initially thought it ugly and
intrusive. But, in my view, it's a starkly beautiful building which
seems today to sit comfortably in the local streetscape. Now it's
sold off, privately owned. In January 2017 one of its two-bed
penthouse flats went on the market at £875,000. The concierge
told me that almost half its sixty-seven flats are occupied by
architects. That's a tribute to its aesthetics and current architectural cachet but Lasdun himself, although also the designer of
the National Theatre, was designing for the working class; the
people who, in his words, 'came from little terraced houses or
something with backyards'. While he was considering the
designs he 'used to lunch with them and try and understand a
bit more about what mattered to them'.[25]

Keeling House, Bethnal Green

What mattered apparently was community and street life so, in Keeling House, Lasdun provided maisonettes as a modern version of the two-up, two-down and tried to stand those Victorian terraces on their end. His innovative 'cluster block' design (comprising a central, free-standing tower with lifts and services and separate towers containing accommodation which 'clustered' around it) offered common service areas on each floor – a place to dry clothes (before the era of tumble dryers) and meet and chat. Access balconies, each serving only two flats, faced each other but did so obliquely, in a delicate balance of neighbourliness and seclusion.

In the early years, as one long-time resident recalls, Keeling House succeeded in exactly those terms:

> It was so peaceful. Beautiful at night and you didn't have to draw your curtains. There was a very good atmosphere and we had lovely neighbours: a Jewish lady used to make us lokshen soup and latkes.[26]

Later, problems emerged. Free access to lifts and common areas left the block susceptible to vandalism and graffiti – there were no entryphone systems, let alone concierges, for council tenants in those days. A few years later some of the concrete cladding began to crumble. Years of neglect and a botched repair job in 1984 contributed to a £4 million repair bill by the early 1990s. A cash-strapped Tower Hamlets Council couldn't give it away; the Peabody Trust were offered the deeds for £1 but wouldn't take it on without guarantees of funding. In the end the council voted for demolition. It was, according to one local councillor, a 'monument to the stack-em-high principle of working-class housing'.[27]

Whatever the block's later difficulties, this was simply not true. Great thought had gone into the design of Keeling House and huge care taken to both provide good-quality homes – all a vast improvement on the squalid terraces from which their residents had come – and safeguard community. Conservative

Heritage Secretary Peter Brooke declared it rightly an 'archi-tecturally outstanding example of 1950s public housing' and became Keeling's unlikely saviour when, in 1993, he Grade II listed it, the first tower block to be so protected. In the end, Lasdun was grateful that private money saved his building, but perhaps he took equal comfort from the poignant remark of one former resident that they had 'loved living in their crumbing tower block'.

Most Brutalist buildings were multi-storey – their project and purpose demanded it. Turning to high-rise more generally, it was, at this point, part of a planned, mixed housing programme across the nation. It was normally (though this was less well observed in practice) intended for smaller households and those without young children.

In Norwich (where, to date, 70 per cent of council homes built had been three-bedroom family houses), for example, a 1957 survey of waiting list applicants showed 60 per cent were willing to live in central area flats. Norwich's plans to build a centrally located eleven-storey point block, however, were scuppered by underground chalk workings and the scheme was transplanted to the suburbs, to the Heartsease Estate on the eastern fringe of the city. There was, though, no sense of compromise in the move. Rather, in the words of Sidney Clapham, the city's mayor who performed the scheme's open-ing ceremony, the block was:

a symbol of the changing habits, thought and customs of a new genera-tion – a generation living at a fast tempo often with both husband and wife out to work all day . . . Today the tall flats are here by demand and choice. Practical in purpose and imaginative in design, they add their own character and distinction to the Heartsease Estate.[28]

Two sixteen-storey city centre blocks followed.

A tangible symbol of this sense of modernity and progress were the recommendations contained in *Homes for Today and Tomorrow* (better known as the Parker Morris Report) issued in 1961 by the Central Housing Advisory Committee. Four years earlier, Prime Minister Harold Macmillan had declared, plausibly, that 'most of our people have never had it so good'. The report echoed these sentiments, noting the changes which were 'beginning to mean an easier, more varied and more enjoyable home life . . . [the] changes in the way in which people want to live, the things which they own and use, and in their general level of prosperity'. All these made it 'timely to re-examine the kinds of homes that we ought to be building'; if the purpose of housing had been for most simply 'to provide shelter and a roof over their head', now 'an increasing proportion of the people [were] coming to expect their home to do more than fulfil the basic requirements. It must be something of which they can be proud.'[29]

In practice, and more prosaically, this meant, among other things, that all new homes should have a flushing toilet and central heating, but Parker Morris is chiefly celebrated for its insistence on increased and relatively generous space standards – between 800 and 910 square feet for standard two-storey terraced and semi-detached homes, for example.

These standards were made compulsory for new public housing in the New Towns in 1967 and across the board in 1969. While they were not enforced on private developers, Labour's Housing Minister Anthony Greenwood made it clear he saw this mandate as a significant contribution to a universal and ongoing improvement in housing quality:

I think most people would agree that the Parker Morris house is a very good house indeed; and – although we can look for even higher standards in the future, since standards are always rising – there is no doubt that the objectives which we have now set represent by far the most significant improvement in housing standards at least since the war, and probably since local authorities began building houses to rent.[30]

Despite this, home ownership was increasingly adjudged the significant metric of progress; in fact, Labour's own 1959 general election manifesto proposed a Right to Buy for sitting council tenants. Overall, the proportion of owner-occupied households rose from 32 per cent in 1953 to 43 per cent in 1961.

That trend had its own longer-term implications for the status of council housing, but the most immediate and pressing issue was the vast numbers of British people still living in slum conditions – by some estimates 4.7 million households still lived in unfit or substandard homes. The post-war surge of council housebuilding continued, but had more than halved from its 1953 peak to a low point (though the figure looks pretty impressive by current standards) of just 105,000 completions in 1961.

In the modernising Britain of the 1960s, the juxtaposition of growing affluence and the surviving slums came to seem even more jarring. A broad consensus around the Welfare State and positive role of government remained. As the two dominant parties vied for power within a highly competitive two-party system, the politics of housing came to the fore again. In 1963 a Conservative government White Paper pledged to build 350,000 new homes a year. Labour's 1964 election manifesto judged 400,000 a 'reasonable target'; two years later, it was promising a 'Government target of 500,000 houses by 1969/70'.

That same 1963 White Paper had stated that local authorities
would 'have to step up their output of houses both by rationalisation of traditional building methods and by making use of
industrial systems'.[31] In June 1963, the Ministry of Public
Building and Works became specifically responsible for promoting 'the new and rapid methods of construction [and] standard-
ising the use and production of building components'.[32]

The Conservative government expected 25 per cent of local
authority housing output to be constructed using industrialised
methods, a proportion raised by the succeeding Labour government to 40 per cent. Later, the Association of Metropolitan
Authorities (AMA) claimed that councils that 'seemed to be
co-operating were "rewarded" in terms of enhanced capital
allocations, speeding approvals, etc.' Shortages of skilled labour
– local councils were now competing fiercely with a booming
private sector – added to the pressure to use new construction
methods and materials as they had in the earlier post-war phase
of experimentation with prefabricated systems.

Here, then, was the genesis of the system-building programme
that – although most developments continued to be built by traditional methods – dominates our perceptions of the massive council housing programme of the 1960s. There was the drive to high-
rise, motivated by positive political and architectural
considerations, and compelled – many felt – by hard circumstance. There was the ambition permanently to rid the country of
the slums that still blighted the lives of so many and the requirement, therefore, to build new housing rapidly and at unprecedented scale. And then there was the lure of modernity; this was,
after all, an era when in 1963 the future prime minister, Harold
Wilson, had promised to apply the 'white heat' of the 'scientific
revolution' to outdated British traditions and practices.

By 1984, however, the AMA was keen to direct blame towards central government for what was now plainly seen as the system-building debacle. There were local dynamics too. Councillors wanted to clear the slums and some wanted to build big, to leave a visible and lasting legacy. In some of the larger authorities, there was a degree of one-upmanship and a desire to impress, or at least emulate. A Halesowen councillor who visited Hackney's Trelawney Estate (and its two towering point blocks) thought the scheme 'made his own authority, which thought it was progressive, look like a snail which had lost its way'.[33]

Local authorities had what might be seen as more self-interested motives too. Salford, for example, had initially embraced the preferred post-war solution of population dispersal. In the 1950s, the borough proposed moving almost a quarter of its population (40,000 of 178,000) to greenfield sites beyond its borders. By 1961, one Salford councillor was asserting that its very 'future as a city' depended on the Ellor Street redevelopment, a scheme that would 'add 2,800 families to our population, revitalise our trade, and give our rateable value its first boost since the war'.[34] Other Labour councillors across the country wanted, more straightforwardly, to retain working-class (and predominantly Labour-voting) families in their inner-city wards. None of this, however misguided with hindsight, was malign – but there were many who believed the results were.

One much-criticised estate in this vein was the Aylesbury in Southwark, begun in 1963 and built by Laings using their patented 12M Jespersen system. This was a so-called Large Panel System (LPS) by which concrete slabs made off-site were dropped in place by tower cranes and then bolted together.

Comprising sixteen four- to fourteen-storey slab blocks (including what was said to be the largest single housing block in Europe), eleven miles of walkway, 2,700 homes in all for a population of around 10,000 – the estate captures the ambition of the moment. To an outsider, this scale can feel overpowering; to critics, oppressive.

Even at the time, the design (by an in-house team at Southwark Council's Department of Architecture and Planning) was described as 'drab' and 'monotonous' in the architectural press. Southwark's architects, in turn, acknowledged last-minute cost-cutting which had adversely impacted the estate's public and shared spaces – 'the extensive areas of bare concrete, asphalt, and cheap obscured glass' which contributed to an 'overall feeling of low cost Local Authority housing'; 'almost an insult', they concluded, 'to the many tenants who are proud of their homes'.[35] And many were, of course: 'To get a council flat was to go up in the world . . . Oh, yes. There's no doubt about it. Coming to the new estate for most of us at that time was like Shangri-La . . . We thought we was moving into Buckingham Palace!'[36]

The new homes were, as ever, of much better quality than the slum homes vacated by the vast majority of residents. The 'streets in the sky' – though they are more properly described as walkways – were planned to promote pedestrian-friendly access and interaction. 'Route decks' were added at second-floor level for movement between blocks, which included space for shops and other community facilities and 'local decks', with play areas, within the blocks. Garaging and traffic movement took place below.

For all the good (though inadequately implemented) intentions, even as the estate was formally opened in 1970, one local

Tory councillor was describing it, unoriginally, as a 'concrete jungle'.[37] By 1976, £2.6 million had been spent on basic remedial work, rather offsetting the £1 million in earlier 'savings'.

Meanwhile, the system-building drive continued apace up and down the country. Across London, in the Metropolitan Borough of Battersea (incorporated into the new Borough of Wandsworth from 1965), the long-mooted clearance of the Winstanley Road area had begun in 1956 – a first, modest low-rise phase was followed by some higher-rise though, at this point, the taller, eighteen-storey, blocks were still conventionally built using in situ concrete. Battersea, however, facing abolition but keen to bequeath an impressive legacy, had begun investigating industrialised methods. An exploratory trip to Paris and Copenhagen by Battersea's Borough Engineer and Chief Architect in that council's final months was followed up by a similar visit from a deputation of the new Wandsworth Borough's Housing Committee.

Back on the Winstanley Estate, therefore, a final phase of lower blocks was system-built by Wates. The estate won a RIBA medal for good design in 1967, but design flaws rapidly emerged with deficient vents and doors, faulty lifts and internal condensation. That might have been a warning, but enthusiasm ran high for the scale and efficiency that system-building seemed to promise, and in June 1966 the council awarded Laings a £6.19 million contract to build the Doddington Estate using a variant of the Jespersen system. The Housing Committee declared it 'the largest industrialised building project yet undertaken in the London area'.

The finished estate comprised six long blocks, joined by pedestrian walkways at various levels, angled and shifting sharply in height from ten to fourteen storeys. Tall access towers and flue stacks combined with the unadorned grey concrete of its construction to give it, in one account at least, an 'ominous grandeur'. More ominous perhaps were early problems with vandalism and the chronic failure of the estate's ambitious district heating system. At its worst, 400 of its 970 flats lost heating and two plumbers were kept on permanent standby to deal with problems.[38]

Such grandiose ambition to build at scale often reflected the drive of individual councillors in an era when the power and status of local government could still spawn such characters and provide them with a stage. In Battersea and subsequently Wandsworth, there was Labour leader of the council, Sidney Sporle ('Mr Battersea' to some), for whom the twenty-four-storey Sporle Court on the Winstanley Estate was named. The work, however, was far beyond what could be executed by the councils' own direct labour organisations or even traditional local building firms, and was monopolised by a group of major contractors such as Laings, Taylor Woodrow, Wimpey and Wates, who competed for the multi-million-pound contracts now tendered liberally.

Negotiated and package deal contracts became the order of the day, delivering sometimes tweaked but more or less off-the-peg designs devised by the contractors' in-house teams. By 1966, at the height of the high-rise and system-built boom, 55 per cent of new public housing developments in England and Wales outside London were negotiated in package deal contracts, and some 84 per cent of industrialised construction came from non-competitive contracts.[39]

In general, this was a marriage of convenience between business and local government. As the architectural historians Miles Glendinning and Stefan Muthesius suggest, 'the contractors succeeded not because they bullied or bribed weak councils into adopting policies against their best interests, but because they gave politically strong councils what they required: high blocks, built reliably, quickly and in large numbers.'[40] But given the close relations between some councillors awarding contracts and the few firms that could deliver them, corruption did emerge. Sporle allegedly received £1,000 in connection with a drainage contract on the Doddington Estate and Laings' agent in the overall deal – a negotiated contract – was paid £19,000 for his success in winning the business. In 1971, Sporle was gaoled for four years for taking bribes. The trial also linked him with the PR company ran by T. Dan Smith, which in turn was closely associated with architect John Poulson. Poulson was a buccaneering figure whose small architectural firm, initially based in Yorkshire, had expanded hugely; firstly through his innovative practice of combining design and build services – a one-stop shop approach which speeded and accelerated the development processes and cut costs, and second, through an assiduous cultivation of links with a booming public sector.

Smith was a flamboyant character, leader of Newcastle City Council from 1959 until he resigned to build his public relations company five years later. As a politician, he had ambitions to make Newcastle the 'outstanding provincial capital in the country', even 'the Brasilia of the North'. In partnership with the powerful Chief Planning Officer Wilfred Burns, he envisaged the clearance of around a quarter of the entire city's housing stock, the decayed and outdated Victorian terraces still housing the majority of Newcastle's working class. They would be rehoused, for the most part, in the high-rise typical of the time. The five – originally ten – tower blocks of Cruddas Park to the west of the city centre, system-built by Wimpey, still stand as monument to this vision: a 'city in the sky', he called it. Smith reflected contemporary thinking, too, in his refashioning of Newcastle's city centre. The new shopping malls, office buildings and urban motorways were intended both to reflect and boost the motorised affluence of the day.

As a PR man and consultant, Smith glad-handed councillors and council officers across the country, with much of his effort dedicated to securing contracts (worth over £1 million allegedly) for Poulson. This nexus of cash and influence came crashing down when Poulson went bankrupt in 1972. As his empire unravelled, Poulson was charged with corruption and received a seven-year gaol sentence. Smith himself, it was said, had received £156,000 from Poulson for his efforts; many others were revealed to have taken their cut too. After his trail in 1973, Smith served three years in gaol. He ended his days in one of the Cruddas Park high-rises that he had built.

Goings-on in Birmingham also capture the febrile, money-charged mood of the time. The first Bison Wallframe blocks (another form of system-building) were erected in Kidderminster in 1963. Minister of Housing and Local Government, Keith Joseph, was on hand at the official opening ceremony to offer the imprimatur of central government; a deputation from Birmingham City Council enjoyed the hospitality:

> the way to the blocks was through this great marquee – which was loaded with drink and food . . . So we stayed there quite a long time and then we went out and looked at the flats. Well by this time they could have been inlaid with gold! In fact they looked pretty awful from the outside – they had this grey and white panelling. Inside they were all right.

As they left, it was decided, '"Right, we'll take five blocks."
Just as if we were buying bags of sweets.' In fact, the council
went on to place a contract for twelve standard plan eleven-
storey Bison blocks from the big local contractors Bryants. Then,
City Architect Sheppard Fidler was told to find sites for them.[41]

Between 1966 and 1968 Bryants won 66 per cent of all
Birmingham's high-rise contracts. The fact that its public relations were handled by former councillor and local Labour MP,
Dennis Howell, and that Labour alderman W.T. Bowen was
one of the firm's directors, was surely coincidental. Bryants'
2,000-strong Christmas gift list was merely a sign of the company's festive generosity, although some thought otherwise.
Private Eye tells the story of a topping-out ceremony performed
by George Brown (then a minister in the Labour government,
'tired and emotional' as he was prone to be), where Brown
'waved an all-embracing hand over the assembled dignitaries
saying "You're all in Chris Bryant's pocket" before unsteadily
despatching the last shovelful of concrete'.[42] A later City
Architect, Alan Maudsley, was found guilty of a corrupt relationship with Bryants in 1975. Subsequently, Bryants' managing director and two directors were charged with providing
gifts – bribes – to various West Midland councillors.

There's no need to sugar-coat the corruption here, although
it's fair to point out that personal gain was not always – so far
as the local government players were concerned – the dominant
driving force. William Reed, Maudsley's deputy and successor,
offers another perspective:

> It was exciting to be part of that particular period. There may have been
> things going on in the background – graft and so on – but they weren't
> the things at the top of people's minds. What was in people's thoughts

was – 'For God's sake get on and build those houses, and get these people out of the slums!'[43]

For Sidney Sporle, too, life was 'too short for regrets'. Besides, he claimed, new system-built housing was 'heaven' to its new residents: 'Now they have a separate kitchen, separate toilets. It was unheard of in the old days there. You went down the end of the garden . . . People were fighting to get in them. They were luxury flats then.'[44]

There's no record of Mrs Ivy Hodge's thoughts as she got up to make an early cup of tea on 18 May 1968 in her eighteenth-floor flat in Ronan Point in Newham, but the gas explosion she inadvertently triggered brought down the four flats above and an entire corner of the tower collapsed like a house of cards. Four people died; miraculously Mrs Hodge survived. In the short term, Ronan Point was repaired (it was eventually demolished in 1986), but its collapse and the shocking building defects it revealed are conventionally held to mark the death knell of system-built high-rise.

The official enquiry concluded that the block (built by Taylor Woodrow using an LPS system) was not strong enough to withstand high winds and fire, let alone the small explosion which occurred. Its later demolition revealed unfilled gaps between floors and walls (with some joints filled with newspaper rather than concrete), and the weight of the building resting on just two bolts per panel rather than the mortar specified.

Advocates of system-building pointed out that such systems had fared well in Scandinavia and that British problems reflected poor quality control in home-grown construction. In fact, such quality control was near non-existent. Local authorities lacked the personnel and expertise to supervise system-built construction and relied on the rather cavalier reassurances offered by the government's National Building Agency, established in 1964 specifically to promote industrialised methods of housebuilding, and the warm words of the contractors' high-pressured salesmanship. As a result – and as system-building problems multiplied in succeeding years – the high hopes placed not only in it but in modernist mass housing in general did turn, sometimes quite literally, to ashes.

It's an anti-climax but a necessary corrective to point out that much of this changed thinking had emerged before the Ronan Point disaster. A cross-disciplinary study of Deeplish in Rochdale (a 'twilight area' comprising just the type of Victorian and Edwardian terraced housing hitherto condemned as unfit), carried out for the Ministry of Housing and Local Government in 1966, concluded that individual improvement grants and a new government strategy of 'environmental improvement' could revitalise neighbourhoods previously slated for clearance.

This focus on rehabilitation rather than demolition and new build was amplified in the 1968 government White Paper, *Old Houses into New Homes*, and followed up in the 1969 Housing Act which established General Improvement Areas and Housing Action Areas to replace the 'redevelopment areas' which had previously licensed wholesale clearance. The premium payment for flats above six storeys had been abolished two years earlier. There was by now a clear and financially explicit preference for low-rise development.

All this reads like an epitaph. It was for a fevered episode in the longer story of council housing and – with its discrediting of some forms and techniques of mass housing (the phrase is properly portentous) and the exaggerated and misguided hopes

which accompanied them – it played its part in the later prevalent rejection of the broader model. In the shorter term,
however, it opened the door to what, in many ways, was a
golden age of council house building.

With lessons learnt and aspirations honed and tempered, the
decade that followed would see the construction of some of the
finest council housing ever built. Sadly, that in the end would be
its swansong.

6

'Anti-Monumental, Anti-Stylistic, and Fit for Ordinary People': 1968–79

'An absolute disaster – it shouldn't have been planned, it shouldn't have been built.'[1] That was the damning verdict of Councillor Allan Roberts, chair of Manchester City Council's Housing Committee in 1978, on the Hulme Crescents scheme, just seven years after its completion. That was a precipitous fall from grace for a development that its architects Lewis Womersley and Hugh Wilson had heralded in 1965 as 'a solution to the problems of twentieth-century living which would be the equivalent in quality of that reached for the requirements of eighteenth-century Bloomsbury and Bath'.[2] They'd even named the four six-storey, crescent-shaped blocks after Charles Barry, John Nash, Robert Adam and William Kent, the historic architects who provided their supposed inspiration.

Those ideals are best seen, as ever, in the artists' impressions included in the planning brochure. Actually, drawings of Hulme's supposed Georgian progenitors outnumber those of the new estate but there's no denying the attractiveness of the latter with the graceful sweep of the Crescents set in a thirty-eight-acre site of 'landscaped "parks" with long views, ever changing forms, grass banks and belts of trees sheltering sunken play areas'.[3]

VIEW 8

The Hulme Crescents, Manchester, as envisaged by Wilson and Womersley

The homes themselves – 989 two- and three-bed maisonettes – were designed to promote that by-now established watch-word: 'community'. Lewis Womersley, as City Architect for Sheffield, had overseen the earlier Park Hill development and he borrowed its 'streets in the sky' for the new designs. Deck-access entry to homes and walkways joining the blocks offered 'the social advantage of greater choice of friends amongst neighbours and for old people the advantage of easy contact with the passing world where they want it', he argued.[4] In an updated application of Radburn principles, given impetus by Colin Buchanan's influential 1963 report, *Traffic in Towns*, a strict separation of cars and people was embedded into the plans. Garaging was provided, with service roads to the rear

base of the blocks, while the busy Stretford Road was transformed into a 'pedestrian way'. The overall scheme, with a
library, doctors' surgeries, communal laundry and pool, several
churches and a range of pubs and clubs, was intended to offer a
new but less prescriptive version of Abercrombie's neighbourhood unit.

It goes without saying that the new flats were infinitely
superior in space and facilities to the long run-down Victorian
terraced housing they replaced. The *City of Manchester Plan
1945* – another iteration of that post-war planning and
improvement drive noted earlier – had condemned without
sentimentality 'the drab streets, the dilapidated shops, the
sordid public houses, the dingy schools, the sulphurous and
sunless atmosphere' of the inner city.[5] Twenty years later, the
city was confident in the belief that it was taking 'a unique
opportunity to create entirely new communities on the most
modern lines and to provide surroundings in step with the
20th Century'. This was to be 'a new environment' which
would create 'fuller and happier lives for the people of
Manchester'.[6]

The Hulme Crescents were completed in 1971 and for a brief
moment some of this idealism seemed to hold. One local recalls
a visit to the estate at around that time:

> They were wonderful places. Full of really new ideas and loads of hope
> for the people living in them. People talked to each other. And I can
> remember laughter with a family that lived in them. They asked me and
> my granddad in for a cup of tea. Showed us round the strange way the
> flats were designed. But the flat was so clean and nice and they were so
> proud of it. Then suddenly, about 1972 I think it was, things started to go
> wrong.[7]

The first and essential thing to 'go wrong' was the blocks' system-built construction that had initially been promoted as one of their chief advantages. The estate's design – its long, continuous blocks cut the number of lifts and link bridges required – lent itself to industrialised building (in this case, another variant of the LPS form widely used at the time). Wilson and Womersley praised not only 'greater economy and speed of erection' such methods offered but also their 'high quality of finish, both internally and externally'. It was obviously far better, they suggested, to have 'structural components, fittings and services . . . manufactured and supervised under factory conditions and not subjected to the climatic and other hazards of an open site'.[8]

Such was the theory; the practice was a modern form of jerry-building. Components were shoddily manufactured and then poorly assembled with missing reinforcing bolts and ties causing problems of water penetration. Design flaws added to the residents' woes. Inadequate insulation and ventilation caused severe condensation, and the estate's ducting allowed the rapid spread of vermin. The collapse of Ronan Point resulted in the abandonment of plans for gas-fired heating but the underfloor heating that replaced it was inefficient and, after the 1973 oil crisis, prohibitively expensive.

Leaving aside these structural issues, in truth the estate never matched those optimistic artists' impressions. Its open spaces remained formless and bleak; that pedestrian-friendly diversion of traffic enclosed and isolated it within two large dual carriageways. The street life and 'buzz' of Stretford Road were absent. Conversely, the communal routes intended to foster community – those long deck-access balconies and connecting walkways and isolated lift shafts – provided 'rat-runs' and 'escape routes' for those whose intentions were far from friendly. As problems of crime and antisocial behaviour increased on the estate, some echoed the critique emerging from across the Atlantic, which argued the form and nature of such large-scale public housing developments encouraged and facilitated criminality.

In Hulme, such structural flaws and design issues were rapidly compounded, as the council admitted, by its failure to fulfil basic tasks of maintenance and upkeep. As early as 1973, the city's Director of Works had criticised 'a general breakdown of the municipal service' on the estate and an 'atmosphere of abandonment that pervaded the whole of Hulme V'.[9] Such problems rapidly contributed to the estate becoming 'hard to let' – a contemporary euphemism that hid the reality (in another redolent phrase of the era) of a 'problem estate'. That designation became self-fulfilling as those with choices decided to live elsewhere, leaving the estate to those whose urgent needs precluded delay or options. By that same year, 44 per cent of incoming tenants to Hulme were on Supplementary Benefit, the contemporary equivalent of Income Support.

Labour's 1977 Housing (Homeless Persons) Act exacerbated this trend in Hulme and in estates across the country by placing, without additional funding, a statutory duty on local authorities to rehouse vulnerable groups with priority needs; typically pregnant women, families with dependent children and those with health issues. This was a well-meaning socialist measure, almost the embodiment of the precept 'to each according to his needs', but it had unintended consequences. Practically, it increasingly reserved council housing to the least well-off and most disadvantaged in society. Psychologically, it sent the message that council housing was for the most needy, for those incapable through their own efforts of achieving 'something better'.

Working-class owner occupation was increasing; in overall terms, the percentage of households owning their homes (or, more frequently, having a mortgage) increased from 51 per cent in 1971 to 58 per cent in 1981. At the same time, Labour – perhaps unwittingly but perhaps reflecting a deeper shift in perceptions at this time of relative affluence – had abandoned Bevan's poetry of 'the living tapestry of a mixed community' and its own prose of 'general needs' and conceded (as the Conservatives had long argued) that council housing should be, at best, a social service, reserved for the most needy, and implicitly, at worst, housing of last resort. The technical term for this shift was *residualisation*.

In addition to this, there was another dynamic running through this period. The better-known one – providing what became, in the media and popular consciousness, the general narrative – was epitomised by Hulme. It was the perception that council housing exemplified a perfect storm of social ills: 'high-rise' housing estates, badly planned, poorly built and dangerous locales whose embattled residents were swamped both by hostile circumstance and a caricatured 'underclass'. Because the image was not entirely without foundation, it was powerful but, as an image, it wrought its own damage.

This was in direct contrast with the reality that, in terms of new build, some of the best council housing ever built was erected at this time. This was often precisely because lessons were learnt from some of the overweening ambition and missteps of the preceding era of mass council housing.

Personally, I wouldn't place Robin Hood Gardens in Poplar in the former pantheon despite the affection in which it is held by the architectural great and good. Pleas for its listing have failed and it's due for demolition as part of a £500 million redevelopment scheme. At the time of writing, its two roughly parallel, concrete and glass ten- and seven-storey blocks remain; their 214 flats and maisonettes largely unoccupied. A large wooded mound (intended, it's said, to discourage the playing of noisy ball games) and scrubby grassland stand between them. It represents a lingering but forlorn tribute to the architectural vision of husband and wife team Alison and Peter Smithson who designed it. They had imagined it as 'an exemplar – a demonstration of a more enjoyable way of living . . . a model of a new mode of urban organisation which can show what life could be like'.[10]

The Smithsons were the slightly ageing *enfants terribles* of British Brutalism. Some accounts even suggest the term had something to do with Peter Smithson's nickname 'Brutus'. The couple had broken with the ultra-rationalist Modernist vision of urban living – all high blocks and spacious landscaping – in the early 1950s. Their rejected 1952 design for the City of London's Golden Lane Estate, which had pioneered streets in the sky, was a deliberate attempt to recreate working-class community and what they called 'the idea of the street' – 'effective group-spaces fulfilling the vital function of identification and enclosure'.[11] The homes themselves were large, light and airy. Brutalism as a form became much maligned and, as a descriptor, crudely applied but it must be emphasised that in its showpiece schemes the treatment of their residents was, in intent at least, very far from brutal. Ironically, in light of later criticisms, the Smithsons record one of the workmen on the Poplar scheme opining that it 'was too good for the people that were going to live in it'.[12]

But the form and appearance of Robin Hood Gardens were in part dictated by its difficult site, sandwiched between three major roads. The disposition of the fortress-like blocks was designed to create a 'stress-free central zone protected from the noise and pressures . . . a quiet green heart which all dwellings share and can look into'. The Smithsons likened this inner space – rather imaginatively – to a Georgian square.[13] The other significant feature of the scheme was the pared-down version of the 'streets in the sky' concept afforded by its wide deck-access balconies. Yet problems of crime and vandalism emerged almost as soon as the flats were opened in 1971. The walkways were placed inhospitably on the outside of the blocks – for good reason, as this located the bedrooms on their quieter inner side – and they were underused, the communal entrances forbidding. Problems of water penetration resulting from the precast concrete slab construction added to this tale of woe.

Dawson's Heights, Southwark

More successful, large-scale schemes were built, however. In London, two estates stand out as a tribute to the politics of the age. Dawson's Heights in East Dulwich, built by Southwark Borough Council and completed in 1972, was praised by those normally staid folk at English Heritage (whose request for listing was nonetheless turned down) for its 'evocative associations with ancient cities and Italian hill towns', and it's true that the estate makes superb use of its dramatic hilltop setting.[14] This was the work of Kate Macintosh, then aged twenty-six, who had studied the existing alternatives and found them wanting. The five-storey walk-up tenement blocks ubiquitous in London were, she thought, 'institutional'; the newer point and slab blocks 'unrelated to the surrounding urban grain'.[15] Post-Ronan Point, system-building was out too; here you had load-bearing cross-walls of brickwork and reinforced concrete.

Macintosh's design comprised two dramatic ziggurat-style blocks facing each other across a green expanse, so designed that two-thirds of the flats had views in both directions and each flat received sunlight, even in deepest midwinter. The scheme provided in total 296 homes – a 'Chinese puzzle of differing types to be assembled in various combinations' in Macintosh's words. 'If large blocks were to be accepted and loved, as a new way of living', she said, 'they must try to replicate the best characteristics of the terraced street; that families of different sizes and age groups should intermingle, as their needs and strengths would be diverse and complementary.'

The staggering of the blocks, their deliberately varied profiles and, perhaps above all, their warm brick outer texture created an overall scheme which, to most people, was rather beautiful and, in some intangible way, more humane than the mass housing projects of the 1960s. There were some teething troubles, unsurprising given the difficult site and complex construction, and Alice Coleman secured the later removal of two aerial walkways which had linked the blocks, but otherwise Dawson's Heights stands proud as among the best housing of its type.

The World's End Estate was built by Conservative-controlled Kensington and Chelsea Borough Council, begun in 1969 and eventually completed – its construction delayed by some of the industrial troubles of the era – in 1977, by which time its cost had risen from a tender price of £5.6 million to around £15 million. What the council got for its money was an unusually high-rise, high-density scheme for the period: 750 homes housing some 2,500 in seven high-rise tower blocks of eighteen and twenty-one storeys joined by nine four-storey walkway blocks in a figure of eight. What you see rising from this spectacular riverside setting – views were not then reserved for the more affluent – is a brown-brick, castellated vision of polygonal towers and enclosed green courts. The romantic, quasi-medieval look is deceptive – precast concrete was used in the construction and the brown brick is cladding – but it reflected the skilful overall design of architect Eric Lyons and the finesse applied by H.T. Cadbury-Brown to its fulfilment.

World's End is an attractive and popular estate now, but it didn't escape the backlash in the 1970s against such large-scale developments. By the time of its completion, chastened architectural critics were lining up to berate its apparently overbearing ambition. One commentator in the *Architectural Review* complained that 'as a "nice place to live in" it fails' – 'the internal courts have an air, not of modern domesticity, but of castle yards . . . No longer visibly a "home", the dwelling is sunk within an abstract super-image.' He hoped that it marked 'the end of this particular road'.[16] There were early reports of vandalism and another wrote that the lifts and lift areas were 'not defensible'.[17] A long-term resident, looking back, had a simpler explanation for its problems – the large number of families with teenage children then resident on the estate.[18]

Nowadays, with entryphone entrances reflecting the modern 'secured by design' wisdom (this more recent approach seeks to reduce design features held to facilitate crime and add those which enhance security) and an ageing population, the estate looks and feels good and those courts provide a true haven to the many who live in and love World's End. It did, nevertheless, as that earlier critic hoped, mark the end of one road for council housing design. Another approach and form was being trialled in the north-east.

In the early 1960s, 17,000 people lived in the Byker area of Newcastle – a densely packed district of terraced housing, backyards and alleys, outside toilets and coal sheds. Many of the homes were 'Tyneside flats' – single-storey flats upstairs and downstairs in two-storey terraces. This archetypal working-class community, however, was under existential threat. As we noted, by 1963 Newcastle's Chief Planning Officer, Wilfred Burns, working closely with city boss T. Dan Smith, planned to demolish a quarter of the city's entire housing stock in twenty years, including Byker. But, as we've seen, by the end of the decade the mood had swung and such grandiose visions were unfashionable. Byker's residents agreed they needed rehousing – they weren't that nostalgic for the close-knit terraces – but they wanted to be rehoused where they lived and with their neighbours. It was a sign of the times that Newcastle City Council agreed with them and, as a signal of its good intent, appointed Ralph Erskine to oversee the project.

Erskine was based in Sweden at the time but he had an established reputation for people-centred design, a personal philosophy rooted in his parents' Fabianism, his own Quakerism, and Scandinavian social democracy. His vision – accepted by the council in November 1968 – was for 'a complete and integrated environment for living in the widest possible sense', and this, he argued, would require considering 'the wishes of the people of all ages and many tastes' if its goal of maintaining 'as far as possible, valued traditions and characteristics of the neighbourhood itself' was to be fulfilled.[19]

These principles were executed in a pilot scheme involving forty-six households working with architects in the design of their future homes and, more significantly, by shop-front offices in the middle of the redevelopment to which residents could drop in. Practically, wider circumstances would prevent their full implementation. By 1982, when the overall scheme was completed, years of planning blight, long delays in construction, the slow pace of demolition and the sheer disruption of redevelopment had forced around 5,000 households out of the area and only about half the new homes went to locals. One critical observer concluded that 'the real power to decide what should be done, and when, lay outside the community, in the Civic Centre', perhaps inevitably given the constraints of finance and law and the politics of competing priorities.[20]

But the estate – 200 acres, 1,800 homes, a population of 9,500 – remains a marvel. Its most iconic component, the famous Byker Wall, is a 1.5-mile-long block of 620 maisonettes, rising and falling from three storeys to twelve, built to form a perimeter barrier to North Sea winds and the noise and pollution of adjacent major roads. Despite its rather forbidding exterior, there's nothing Brutalist about the Byker Wall. On the

Byker Wall, façade, Newcastle

lee side, its textured and coloured facades of brick, wood and plastic, balconies and planters, provide warmth and variety. And it shelters an extensive area of high-density, low-level housing, richly landscaped and subdivided into distinctive sections with a mix of small private gardens and larger communal spaces. Its design reflected Erskine's hopes and its quality and humanity secured it Grade II* listing in 2007, commended by English Heritage for both its 'ground-breaking design . . . influential across Europe' and the 'pioneering model of public participation' which shaped it.[21]

Did Byker live happily ever after? Some criticised Erskine's alleged tendency to over-detail his designs – in a 'Mickey Mouse way' according to the Smithsons after Disney's exaggeration of the cartoon character's eyes and ears.[22] Poor build quality has led to costly and ongoing refurbishment. But what affected the estate most powerfully was the decline of Newcastle's traditional shipbuilding economy in the 1980s. At its peak, unemployment reached 30 per cent on Byker and complaints of anti-social behaviour rose accordingly. Meanwhile, as Sarah Glynn has argued, the 'increasing residualisation of social housing as a minimally-maintained safety net for those who could not afford anything else meant that estates such as Byker became ghettos for many of those failed by society'.[23]

Norwich, to those who don't know it or think of it as only a slightly grittier Barchester, provides as good a place as any in the country to observe this history of council housing. By some measures it had the highest proportion of people living in public housing of any city in the country by the 1950s. More significantly, it was a proudly progressive and individualistic city, happy to live up to the Norfolk motto 'Do Different'. If you visit the city, you'll see a representative range of local authority housing from cottage suburbs to mixed development to deck-access and high-rise. But, to many, the most inspired and attractive of the city's council housing was built in the later 1960s and 1970s as City Architect David Percival pioneered what's been called a Vernacular Revival style.

That may sound twee to some, but given Norwich's status as an historic county town Percival was keen to respect its presiding spirit, its *genius loci*, and the result was innovative and high-quality housing. The first two phases of the Camp Grove scheme on steep slopes to the east of the city centre are a warren of landscaped blocks and courts joined by curving footpaths and unexpected entrance ways, enlivened by careful variations of texture and colour – a deliberate echo in part of the earlier street pattern and small-scale housing of the area. It is

St Leonard's Road, Norwich

Phase III, however, along Ladbrooke Place and St Leonard's Road, that is more celebrated. Designed by Tayler and Green (chiefly known for their superb council housing schemes in rural south Norfolk), it's a striking estate of eighty-seven three-storey two-bed and three-bed flats. It employs gable ends – front and back – to echo a traditional Norwich streetscape and uses, extravagantly, sixteen different types of brick and flint, cobble and colour wash, and four different pantiles to provide variation and contrast.

It's a reminder that the best council housing can be very good indeed, where scale gives way to quality, and it remains a tribute to local skills and ambitions. Norwich was unusual too in having a remarkably expert and committed City Architect's Department, employing over a dozen qualified architects at its peak during this period, when 'many council architects considered their work and capability superior to those of private architects, and certainly far above the standards of the speculative house builder'.[24]

This was also true of some of the London boroughs. Here too architects and local politicians collaborated to provide surprising variations in a form of housing too often crudely viewed as homogeneous. For instance, Southwark's local leaders continued to think big. After the completion of the Aylesbury Estate in 1970, the nearby Heygate Estate followed some four years later. Although smaller at 1,200 homes, it was subject to similar criticism and both estates suffered problems, some resulting from construction flaws, others blamed more dubiously on design issues. Controversially the Heygate has since been demolished.

The neighbouring borough of Lambeth, on the other hand, chose a very different path, largely due to influence of the borough's Chief Architect, Ted Hollamby. Hollamby, a dedicated left-winger (he finally left the Communist Party after the Soviet invasion of Czechoslovakia in 1968) had cut his architectural teeth as a member of the LCC Architect's Department through the 1950s. The nature of his appointment to Lambeth in 1962, which anticipated the enhanced role for London boroughs resulting from the 1965 reorganisation of local government, is another reminder of the idealism and energy of the day. Hollamby recalls an unusual but 'inspiring' job interview in the council chamber with half the members present. One exchange was particularly revealing. Council Leader Archie Cotton asked: 'what do you think about that chap, Le Corbusier? Do you think we ought to ask him to do something here in Lambeth?' Hollamby, in response, said he thought that Le Corbusier 'would not be bringing to Lambeth something which was essentially part of its history . . . What he would be interested in doing is imposing one of his sculptures.'

Hollamby's signature style in Lambeth became something very different, ostensibly much humbler. He had not always opposed high-rise schemes: as lead architect for the LCC's Brandon Estate, he was responsible in 1957 for what were then, at eighteen storeys, the tallest point blocks in the capital. His plans for the redevelopment of Brixton Town Centre ten years later included fourteen fifty-storey blocks. But times changed. The Brixton towers were part of an abandoned plan to build a sixty-mile London inner ring road conceived at the height of the planning mania to adapt obsolescent cities to the new motor age. When such schemes were shelved, Lambeth became an early pioneer of rehabilitation and infill housing, redeveloping areas of decay that might once have been cleared. And Hollamby became the acknowledged leader of the medium-rise, high-density council housing that came to dominate the 1970s.

In 1974, Hollamby outlined the key elements of his design philosophy: 'people', he said, 'do not desperately desire to be housed in large estates, no matter how imaginative the design and convenient the dwellings.' But this was not merely an attack on the high-rise. He continued, rhetorically, 'but do they really like the monotonous, equally vast and characterless suburb?' He concluded that they wanted 'fairly small-scale and visually comprehensible environments'. His object was an architecture that was 'anti-monumental, anti-stylistic, and fit for ordinary people'.[25]

This was implemented in a number of Lambeth schemes, most notably at Central Hill in Upper Norwood, completed in 1973, where the architect Rosemary Stjernstedt created parallel, stepped rows of three- and four-storey brick-built terraces that beautifully exploited the estate's sloping terrain and vistas. Without any now-decried monumentalism, Central Hill, in the words of Rowan Moore, 'drapes itself over its topography, creating both moments of drama and quiet enclaves in the spaces between its buildings' and provides its 374 homes with both privacy and a sense of wider belonging.[26]

Cressingham Gardens, Lambeth

Two and a half miles to the north, the site of Cressingham Gardens, completed in 1978 and adjacent to Brockwell Park, offered other opportunities. Lead architect Charles Attwood used a contour map to ensure optimum sightlines from lower-rise housing on the fringe of the estate; four-storey blocks to the rear provided a barrier to the noise of Tulse Hill Road. Without striving officiously for 'community', the estate fosters the sense of neighbourliness with Hollamby also championed by a series of small design touches – front doors facing each other; kitchen windows facing the walkways outside; and the walkways themselves as intimate, almost village-like lanes which both join and separate its elements.

Some 306 homes were built in all, including smaller units for elderly and disabled people and couples as well as family homes. Each overlooked a green open space and many benefited from another signature Hollamby innovation, the patio garden. Floor to ceiling windows, skylights and the minimisation of interior walls added to the light and airy feel of the individual flats. The Housing Committee, of which John Major (in a brief Tory interregnum) was deputy chair, congratulated the design team on a 'bold and imaginative scheme'.[27] Later, Lord Esher (Lionel Brett, past president of the RIBA), described Cressingham Gardens as 'warm and informal . . . one of the nicest small schemes in England'.[28]

That might sound like faint praise in other contexts but it's surely just the kind of encomium that Hollamby would have wished for, and it captures beautifully the shift in sensibilities that marked this latter phase of council house construction. It's a shocking sign of our changed priorities that both these fine and cherished estates are under threat from the drive towards 'densification', an ugly term for the ugly idea that council estates are 'brownfield sites' ripe for redevelopment as demand for housing in London spirals.

This was a concern shared by the newly created London Borough of Camden in this earlier period: as one of its early councillors proclaimed, 'the main aim was more housing – beginning and end'.[29] In other respects, its policies – in particular, its commitment to municipal ownership and development – were very different and, in the process, it created some of the best and most exciting council housing ever built. As a compound of the former boroughs of Hampstead, Holborn and St Pancras – respectively intellectual, wealthy and radical – the new borough was uniquely fortunate. It was the third-richest borough in the capital in terms of rateable value and it possessed a young Labour council – almost a third of the members were under forty – conscious of its role in the progressive vanguard of London politics. Finally, in Borough Architect Sydney Cook and the team he managed, it possessed some of the most gifted and innovative architects of the era.

Cook was an early opponent of the architectural fashions that held sway into the late 1960s. He rejected both system-building – 'I'll use standardised plans if you can find me a standardised site', he said – and high-rise, particularly those point blocks isolated in open terrain.[30] Neave Brown, one of Cook's team and then aged just forty, was appointed to design the Alexandra Road Estate, approved in 1969 and finally completed in 1979. Brown shared Cook's ideals: he wanted to 'build low, to fill the site, to geometrically define open space, to integrate' and he sought 'to return to housing the traditional quality of continuous background stuff, anonymous, cellular, repetitive, that has always been its virtue'.

If that sounds a bit like a return to terraced housing of yore, Alexandra Road would be a very different – and far more eye-catching – animal indeed. The estate – 520 dwellings, housing some 1,660 people – comprises two parallel pedestrianised streets and three, 300-metre-long terraces. The largest of these, seven storeys high, backs on to the West Coast mainline, and is built ziggurat-style, high at the rear, to block the noise of passing trains. Two other four-storey blocks run parallel, and between them is a four-acre park. The construction is of site-cast, board-marked, white, unpainted reinforced concrete with black-stained timber joinery. These stepped forms and materials represented what became a very distinctive Camden house-style. This was unashamed Brutalism but, if it merely sounds brutal to some, any starkness in the design was offset by the profuse greenery of its landscaping and the verdure of the residents' own balcony gardens – the 'hanging gardens of Camden' according to one critical Conservative councillor who argued the vegetation was being used to hide the architect's mistakes.[31]

There were mistakes, teething troubles, significant delays and cost escalation, of course. The initial budget ballooned from £7.15 million to £20.9 million reflecting, primarily, the troubled industrial relations climate of the period. But the scheme has been overwhelmingly acclaimed, both (most importantly) by those who live in it and by architectural commentators. To the modernist architect John Winter, it represented, 'between the system building spree of the sixties and the late seventies slide into folksiness . . . a magical moment for English housing'.[32] English Heritage listed it Grade II* in 1993 and Brown, who also designed the stunning Dunboyne Road Estate – his current home – for Camden, is the only living architect to have had all his UK work officially listed.

Elsewhere in the borough, the Branch Hill Estate, tucked away in woodland on the western fringes of Hampstead Heath, designed by Gordon Benson and Alan Forsyth (who had collaborated with Brown on the Alexandra Road scheme), is also (Grade II) listed. It provided, by some accounts, 'the most expensive council houses in England' – 'to their defenders an act of political faith, to critics socialism gone mad'.[33] That 'faith' and that 'socialism' reflected Camden Council's determination that there should be no no-go areas for council housing and that its residents were as entitled to live in leafy Hampstead as its traditionally more privileged denizens. The land alone cost £464,000 and it came with a restrictive covenant stipulating that new buildings must be semi-detached and of no more than two storeys. The architects' ingenious solution, which met the letter rather than the spirit of these onerous terms, was to create twenty-one pairs of two-storey houses in three rows, built one above the other on the site's steep slope and punctuated by a grid of walkways.

The final example of Camden's brilliant closing flourish in housing can be found at the Whittington Estate designed by Peter Tábori. At the time, Tábori was in his mid-twenties, yet his Regent Street Polytechnic diploma project had so impressed Sydney Cook that the latter commissioned him to design the first phase of the council's redevelopment of Highgate New Town. This was an area of nineteenth-century terraced housing, multi-occupied from the outset and with a troubled reputation. As 75 per cent of the homes lacked a bathroom, it was a natural target for the slum clearance drive of the 1960s.

Tábori's design – six parallel, stepped terraces, staggered and divided to make best use of their sloping site, interspersed with green open space – followed signature Camden style in form and construction. The homes, similarly, each had their own individually accessed front door and kitchens were placed to overlook walkways and allow supervision of children.

Construction began in 1972 and the estate was scheduled for completion in 1974. In the event, a not uncommon combination of construction problems and contractor failures delayed completion till 1979 and the finished estate – at £9 million – cost twice as much to build as projected. These problems were

Lulot Gardens, Whittington Estate, Camden

significant in the decision that the second phase of the redevelopment should take a very different form but perhaps of greater influence were the criticisms emerging of council estates as such.

The architect and designer Su Rogers' assessment of the Whittington Estate in 1973 was an early example of what would become conventional wisdom:

> It is difficult not to question the policy of building housing 'estates', 'areas', 'schemes' isolating one use from the more natural and spontaneous surrounding areas . . . I wonder how long it will be before the next generation will be appalled by the enormous acreage, albeit low-rise, of housing developments, self-contained within themselves with standard pedestrian decks, coloured front doors, toddler play areas, estate supermarkets and community centres which are the utopias of the local authorities.[34]

At first glance this is little more than a rehash of the charges levelled against the interwar cottage suburbs. However, in its questioning of the very post-war correctives intended to counter those earlier criticisms and directed against an imaginatively designed and relatively intimate estate such as the Whittington, there is evidence of a broader assault against not merely the *form* of council estates but the *concept*.

In part, this might be seen as a natural reaction to the enormous ambition – over-ambition to some – of the post-1945 housing drive that had seen around five million council homes built by 1981. It anticipates concerns that council estates were breeding antisocial behaviour – that genuine problem and its widespread perception began in the mid to late 1970s and became more powerful in the 1980s.

Ironically, Rogers herself had praised the Whittington's walkways for retaining 'the functions of a traditional street with much local activity, the milk float, children playing and the supervision from the dwelling units'. Less than a decade later, the local press (in an article headlined 'Haven for Hoodlums') claimed that residents lived 'in daily fear of robbery, burglary and vandalism' as a result of the estate's 'warren of lonely walkways and blind spots'.[35]

This critical turn and new thinking had emerged in the late 1960s. The official line was now gradual renewal of run-down areas through a combination of rehabilitation and selective infill. Camden itself had adopted a policy requiring all families with children to be housed on the ground floor. The next major phase of the Highgate New Town scheme, begun in 1978 and completed in 1981, reflected these ideas in its return to a more traditional streetscape. The new homes – two- and three-person flats and four- to five-person houses – were arrayed along

Dartmouth Park Hill. Camden's signature dark-stained wood remained and the scheme retained some colourful elements and flourishes in its glazed and metal-framed access stairways, white panelling and red-brick detailing, but brick-built and two or three storey, it was in essence, as Roger Stonehouse describes, 'a return to housing which is more clearly related to its surroundings'.[36] A Civic Trust commendation in 1983 made exactly this point in praising the scheme for its suggestion of the 'memories of Edwardian villas and the welcoming scale of a delightful suburbia'.[37]

Such words mark a new ethos far removed from the confident modernism that, in varying forms, had marked the first post-war decades. Most of the slum terraces cleared in that earlier phase hardly qualified as 'villas' or 'delightful suburbia' but those that remained were now – literally and metaphorically – rehabilitated. That trend, as we noted, began in the late 1960s: a reaction both to the escalating costs of high-rise and what were by now seen as its dubious benefits. It took off in the 1970s as system-building flaws became increasingly obvious and as council housing itself began to lose its aspirational sheen. The Conservative government's 1974 Housing Act established Housing Action Areas, building on the General Improvement Areas legislated by Labour five years earlier, to make renovation grants more widely available.

Meanwhile, the very notion of 'modernity' had become tainted, associated with some of the more overbearing proposals (many aborted) to adapt this old country to contemporary circumstance and raised expectations. 'Utopian', always an exaggeration of the worthy, sometimes rather homely aspirations of post-war planners, became a term of abuse. 'Conservation' became the new buzzword, celebrated in a number of books and campaigns which captured the popular imagination in the early 1970s, most notably in Adam Fergusson's polemic (an attack on the city's plans to demolish some decrepit Georgian cottages), *The Sack of Bath*, published in 1973.

Aside from the set-piece battles – the Euston Arch (demolished, though its return is threatened) and Covent Garden (preserved if somewhat transformed) – this was a war waged on the ordinary streets of the nation. And one of its heroes (assuming you favour the victors) was Nicholas Taylor, a planner and Lewisham Labour councillor, whose book, *The Village in the City*, published the same year as Fergusson's, set out its guiding principles as 'rehabilitate wherever you can rather than demolish; where you rehabilitate, do it gently so as to preserve the community'. He added the admonition that housing design shouldn't be 'an adventure playground for architects'.[38]

A neglected strand of conservation and rehabilitation politics of the 1970s is the programme of municipalisation – the purchase and council management of former privately rented homes. Municipalisation had briefly been official Labour policy in the 1950s, seen primarily as a means of rent control and property improvement. It was revived in the 1970s. The councillors of Clay Cross in Derbyshire thought of themselves 'as basic Socialists' – they regarded housing as 'a social service, not as something the private sector can profit from' – and declared in 1972 their intention to purchase every privately rented home in the district.[39] In 1974, the chair of Hackney's Housing Development Committee, Alderman J.H. Dunning JP (not a left-wing firebrand), took the view that 'the whole of the property in this Borough should come under the control of the local authority'.[40]

Practical drivers were powerful too. In general, it was clear that slum clearance and rebuilding (which tends to reduce density) did little to increase the overall housing stock. In some inner London boroughs, notably Islington and Camden, municipalisation was a pre-emptive to the gentrification threatening to price out working-class renters as the early 'knockers-through' arrived to convert the run-down terraces to middle-class *des reses*.

Islington acted early and boldly, 'buying up, at very low cost, streets at a time' until the council found itself landlord of whole swathes of Victorian and Georgian squares and terraces; an estimated 3,000 properties by March 1975.[41] Across England, some 25,600 homes were municipalised in 1974–5.[42] The expense of the policy, however, sat uncomfortably with a Labour government seeking to rein in public expenditure. The £175 million allocated to municipal acquisition in 1976 was halved in the following year; Islington, which had planned to purchase 750 homes, could only buy 300.[43]

Overall, however, the number of council-owned homes in Islington doubled – from 15,170 to 30,553 – between 1971 and 1978, and by the end of the decade amounted to around half the borough's housing. Camden's stock increased to 30,006 in the same period.[44] This represented a high-water mark for council housing in the capital where 35 per cent of homes were council-rented: in Southwark, that figure reached 65 per cent. In Tower Hamlets, an astonishing 82 per cent.[45] Across England in 1979, around 5.5 million homes – 32 per cent of all households in England – were rented from a local authority.[46] Almost 1.2 million council homes had been built since 1969.

The focus on council housing might, however, lead us to miss the bigger picture. It remained a vital and valued form of housing tenure; the numbers make that obvious, but they also conceal significant shifts in the nature of council housing and, as importantly, perceptions of its role. In the longer post-war period, around four million homes were converted, modernised and transferred from the private rented sector into owner occupation.[47] Governments might legislate to promote or constrain public housing but the stealthier operation of the free market was having, in some ways, even greater impact.

The corollary of the rise of owner occupation was, as previously noted, the residualisation of council housing. This had been prefigured in Conservative government policies – that shift in emphasis from 'general needs' to the rehousing of specific groups, principally those affected by slum clearance – in the mid-1950s and had, indeed, been anticipated in much earlier Conservative thinking. It was given major impetus by Labour's 1977 Housing Act which prioritised the rehousing of vulnerable groups.

The actuality is painted in stark form by statistics on the income and employment of council tenants. Of the 1.9 million additional households in public housing between 1962 and 1978, two-thirds had no employment earnings; the proportion of economically inactive tenants increased from just 4.8 per cent in 1961 to 28 per cent two decades later.

The social scientist Michael Harloe (in language which might today be modified) summed up the change in concluding that council housing had become 'an ambulance service concentrating its efforts on the remaining areas of housing stress and dealing with a variety of "special needs" such as the poor, the homeless, one-parent families, battered wives and blacks'.[48] Council housing allocations did indeed become a source of racial tension in this period as members of ethnic minorities, sometimes previously disqualified through lack of established residency but disproportionately living in the worst and most over-crowded of the private rented sector, were now given rehousing priority over some who had been on council waiting lists much longer.[49]

A final factor – less tangible but both cause and effect – in these shifting perceptions of council housing was the changing tone of press reports which had hailed the new housing schemes of the 1960s and now, in a crude *volte-face*, almost universally condemned them.

Thatcher and the housing revolution she engendered, despite her 1979 election victory being unexpected to some, did not then appear from clear blue water. Edward Heath's 'wet' Conservatism was far less doctrinaire in its opposition to council housing than Thatcher, but its antipathy was made clear by the 1972 Housing Finance Act and the 1974 Housing Act. The former substituted 'fair' rents for 'reasonable'. Behind the semantics was a requirement that council housing rents increase, motivated by the belief that tenants enjoyed unfairly subsidised accommodation. In Clay Cross, where rents were to increase by £1 a week from the figure, including rates, of £1.60 (admittedly the lowest in the country), the council refused to implement the legislation but – with eleven members personally surcharged and removed from office – its famous Rents Rebellion was defeated. Other councils toed the line. The legislation's introduction of a National Rent Rebate Scheme for council tenants – to replace the contemporary patchwork of local authority provision – was a palliative which did have the effect of making council housing more affordable to some of the least well-off.

The 1974 Act maintained and developed (with its creation of Housing Action Areas) the new focus on the rehabilitation of run-down and obsolete housing, but it marked a new departure too in the much increased construction subsidies (amounting to around 90 per cent of cost) paid to housing associations and the strengthened role and direct grant now given to the Housing Corporation, the quango which funded and regulated non-local authority public housing.

Housing associations had been around since the nineteenth century and the Housing Corporation itself was founded in 1964, but – in contrast to much of continental Europe – this third sector had made little impact in the UK where the national and local state had played the central role in the provision of public housing since 1890. In 1979, housing associations provided around 1.9 per cent of Britain's total housing stock; in the years since then, they have come to dominate new public housebuilding – such as it is – and the role of local government has been systematically maligned and progressively marginalised. Chapter 7 examines the revolutionary shift in the form and nature of our social housing provision that has occurred since then.

7

'Rolling Back the Frontiers of the State': 1979–91

It must have seemed that you couldn't open your daily paper in the early 1980s without seeing a picture of Margaret Thatcher handing over the keys to a suitably delighted if somewhat self-conscious family of new homeowners. These were the people who had bought their council homes under the Conservatives' flagship Right to Buy legislation. They were, in a sense, the fifth column of Mrs Thatcher's housing revolution – the former council tenants who opted, in huge numbers, to reject public ownership and embrace the property-owning democracy she so loudly proclaimed.

The year that Thatcher became prime minister, 1979, represents a watershed in British social and political history in many respects, but nowhere more so than in the field of public housing. Determined to roll back 'the frontiers of the state', during the eleven years of her premiership she oversaw the sell-off of over forty state-owned businesses, employing 600,000 workers. But by far the largest single privatisation of public goods was the sale of council homes – worth an estimated £22 billion in 1997.

Right to Buy – the purchase of council homes by sitting tenants – wasn't a new policy. It had been favoured by some Conservative-controlled authorities from the 1920s but sales initially had to be authorised by central government (which had, after all, lent the capital) and were expected to achieve the best price. Churchill's Conservative government removed those restrictions in 1952, and in 1959 Labour went even further in a manifesto commitment offering every tenant 'a chance . . . to buy from the Council the house he lives in'.[1] It also, however, pledged to take existing private, rent-controlled homes into municipal ownership. The cross-party expectation was that income from council house sales was reinvested in the programme of new council house construction that continued apace.

Thatcher's decisive 1980 Housing Act found a willing cohort of councils, especially those on the right, who had already started to sell off council housing. In Derby, briefly held by the Conservatives after 1968, homes were sold to tenants on the Mackworth Estate and across the city. Another Conservative council, Nottingham, sold off 1,635 council homes in the mid-1970s, controversially not only to sitting tenants but to anyone – including in practice to some with minimal local connection – on the waiting list.[2] In general, with house prices falling and problems of negative equity emerging, take-up was slow and only a little over 250,000 council homes had been sold across the country in the years up to 1979.[3]

The 1980 Act gave all council tenants who had rented for three years or more the right to buy their homes. It gave the Environment Secretary powers to intervene against any council held to be resisting the letter or the spirit of the new programme. (A 1982 Court of Appeal judgement against Labour-controlled

Norwich City Council, which was held to have impeded sales while pleading more important housing priorities, showed this was no idle threat.) Crucially there were generous discounts applied to the purchase price, starting at 33 per cent of market value for those with three years' tenancy and rising to a maximum of 50 per cent (to the value of £50,000) for longer-term residents. Thatcher's ideal of a property-owning democracy became tenable to many who had previously been excluded.

The intention here was to shift fundamentally the tenure make-up of Britain's housing stock; or, to put it more bluntly, to radically diminish the role of council housing. This can be seen in the fact that the vast bulk of receipts from sales went to the Treasury to pay off existing debt. There was no pretence that new council housing was to be built to replace homes lost to the market. In 1978–9, 79,160 new council homes were started in England and Wales; by 1996–7, this figure had fallen to 400.[4]

Further legislation in 1984, which extended the Right to Buy to tenants of two years' standing, and increased maximum discounts to 60 per cent, only underlined the radicalism of this assault on local government provision and ownership.[5]

Over 1.8 million council homes were sold by 1997 – around one in four of the total. Council housing, which had formed 31 per cent of total stock in England, now formed around one-fifth.

Up to this point, the case for council housing was a simple one: that society, through its agent the state, had the duty to ensure all its citizens were decently housed. State intervention might take various forms (and the British model of local government provision was, in European terms, an unusual one) but its fundamental necessity and worth were widely accepted. The case of the now ascendant New Right *against* council housing was in some respects equally simple: that it offended the efficient and beneficent operations of the free market. Conservative politicians, however, also offered an additional range of practical criticisms that resonated more broadly with popular experience and public opinion. These gave their critique credibility beyond those who might be thought to be its natural supporters.

Right-wing theorists and their supporters argued that council housing impeded choice; more negatively, they suggested it thwarted the 'natural' disciplines of the market. 'Choice' was limited by the top-down nature of council housing provision and its bureaucratic and allegedly unaccountable management. The political accountability that public housing's defenders pointed to was inadequate, vitiated by the 'vested interests' – Labour councils in cahoots with unions, direct labour organisations and subservient tenants' organisations – that governed actual service provision.

In this right-wing analysis, the public housing sector was sheltered by state funding from the financial and market disciplines which could promote more efficient and cost-effective operation. So-called 'bricks and mortar' subsidies which met housing needs by direct support for housebuilding should be replaced by greater focus on personal allowances enabling housing 'consumers' to exercise greater choice in the marketplace.

And then 'discipline' could get more personal. Low (that is below-market) rents shielded tenants from the necessary choices which economic conditions or personal ambition might otherwise have promoted. Secure tenancies and the (genuine) difficulties that tenants faced in transferring from one property to another or across geographical regions created immobility; tenants were unable or unwilling to move.

This was not an abstract point. Unemployment rose from 5.3 per cent in 1979 to a peak nationally of 12 per cent in 1984. Two years previously, the number of the unemployed had surpassed 3 million for the first time since the 1930s and remained obstinately high, particularly in working-class communities devastated by the collapse of traditional heavy industry. Norman Tebbit, Thatcher's Employment Secretary, famously recalled how his father, in that earlier depression, had 'got on his bike' to look for work.[6] The expectation, thwarted in part by the security that council housing offered, was that the contemporary jobless should do likewise.

This assault on the principles of public housing was made easier by its growing unpopularity. Even in 1966, two-thirds of the population gave owner occupation as their tenure of choice but still over one in five said they would prefer to rent from the council. By 1989, only 12 per cent gave council housing as their preferred form of tenure.[7] A survey in the mid-1980s showed that, while 74 per cent of the population thought the National Health Service was good value for money, only 42 per cent felt the same of council housing. Council housing, then, was an easy target and served as 'the perfect symbol of the failings of the public sector' for its ideological opponents. More broadly, it was 'unpopular, socially stigmatising, incompetently managed and oblivious to consumer preferences'.[8]

Critically, of course, Right to Buy was a very popular policy among council tenants. To many, it offered independence and a step up the housing ladder – though this would be chimerical to those who lost jobs and couldn't meet mortgage repayments as the economy deteriorated. To some, it was a windfall. John Holland, a security guard living on the modernist Whittington Estate in Camden, bought his five-bedroom flat – then valued

at £70,000 on the open market – for £39,000 soon after the legislation was introduced. Thirty years later, his home was worth
£600,000. 'If it weren't for Mrs Thatcher's policy, we couldn't
have afforded to buy', he says. For him, that policy was 'perfect,
absolutely perfect'.[9]

The advocates of Right to Buy also argued that the new
owner-occupiers – by definition, the most 'respectable' of
local residents and likely, it was thought, to be more emotion-
ally and financially invested in their homes and neighbourhood – would stabilise and even lift increasingly troubled
council estates. This was a dubious claim. The common-sense
anticipation that Right to Buy appealed most to the better-off
working class who in turn bought the better homes on the
better estates was borne out in practice. In the huge Norris
Green Estate – a long-established interwar estate described in
the 1970s as one of 'most stable and respectable' in Liverpool
– one-third of tenants bought their homes within five years.
The result was to highlight the deteriorating conditions of
remaining council tenants.[10] Here, and elsewhere, rather than
the beneficial 'social mix' some foresaw, the evidence was, at
best, of 'peaceful indifference' or, at worst, of tensions
between tenures.[11]

Flats, in particular, were slow to sell. This was a problem
recognised by the government when it increased the minimum
discount on flat purchases to 44 per cent and the maximum to 70
per cent in 1986. The fact that the minimum discount for flat
purchases was increased to 50 per cent when Right to Buy was
relaunched by the Conservative-Liberal Democrat coalition
government in 2012, confirms that this tinkering had little effect.
Flat sales lagged because they were less popular than traditional
two-storey homes. Second, they were more likely to be on

unpopular estates and were generally occupied by less well-off council tenants.

All this served to accelerate a process by which public housing became 'a residual or poor law service which offers undesirable second best properties to the poor'.[12] Far from stabilising communities, Right to Buy contributed to social polarisation and the concentration of poorer residents on poorer estates. That may have been an unintended consequence but it fed a powerful and damaging narrative that held, to put it crudely, that council housing was for losers.

Owner occupation increased from 55 per cent of households in 1980 to 67 per cent in 1997; nearly half that increase due to the 2.2 million council homes bought during the period of Conservative government. Mortgage Interest Relief at Source (or MIRAS), introduced in 1983, which provided tax relief to those borrowing to buy homes, provided another boost. It represented a £7.7 billion subsidy to home ownership by 1990 in a period when budgets for public housing were being slashed.

In contrast, the central government subsidy to council housing construction and maintenance fell from £2.13 billion in 1980–1 to £1.21 billion by 1990–1 – a cut of 43 per cent. In the same period, those accepted as homeless by local authorities (which therefore had a duty to rehouse them) rose from 76,342 to 178,867. This was all part of the intended shift from a 'bricks and mortar' subsidy to personal housing allowances – means-tested in the case of the poorest in receipt of Housing Benefit, but a significant perk to the middle class. At the same time, local authorities were forced to increase council housing rents – they tripled from an average £7.70 a week in 1980 to over £23 by 1990. As a result, overall local government expenditure on Housing Benefit rose from £841 million in 1980-1 to £3.35 billion by the end of the decade.[13]

For all the statistics, the bottom line is clear: this was a perfect storm of policy and law with the clear and largely accomplished aim of diminishing and marginalising council housing and, by extension, those who needed it. For those on the ideological right, for whom the 'state' was not an agent of succour and equity but the enemy of freedom and personal enterprise, council housing offered a prime and ready target for their project to limit and discredit government intervention and the communitarian values which underlay it.

Another strand to the assault on council ownership and management came in the 1988 Housing Act that introduced 'Tenants' Choice'. This gave council tenants the right to transfer their homes to another social landlord – in practice, a housing association – or set up their own Tenant Management Organisations (TMOs – first sanctioned as 'Tenant Management Cooperatives' in Labour's 1975 Housing Rents and Subsidies Act). This would, the government claimed, 'open up the closed world of the local authority housing estates to competition and to the influence of the best housing management practices of other landlords'.[14] Tenants themselves, however, preferring the security and still relatively low rents of council homes compared to those of other social providers, or perhaps just the devil they knew, were often reluctant to seize these opportunities.

TMOs, boosted by 1994 legislation giving council tenant groups with as few as twenty-five members the right to take over management functions, nevertheless remained a niche form, embracing only around 80,000 homes by the early 2000s. The far more significant process of so-called Large-Scale Voluntary Transfer also started slowly and, in fact, only 1,470 homes were transferred by demand by tenants. Instead, councils took the initiative and divested themselves of the obligation. Conservative-controlled Chiltern District Council was the first to transfer its housing stock (to the Chiltern Hundreds Housing Association), after a successful ballot of tenants in December 1988. By 1997, sixty-one local authorities had transferred some 270,000 homes to new social landlords.

These were, in this first wave, rural and suburban councils, predominantly Conservative and with an ideological predisposition to the policy. To sweeten the deal, the government provided one huge incentive to cash-strapped councils and to tenants: housing associations were allowed to borrow in order to fund repairs and improvements; councils weren't. The fiscal case made for this obvious inequity was perfunctory: that any local authority spending would have to be added to the Public Sector Borrowing Requirement that the government was committed to reducing. The low politics of such machinations are obvious.

But, the policy still faced some rearguard resistance. Large urban authorities, often Labour-controlled, were less willing to transfer their housing stock. This was bolstered by plain economics: in many metropolitan authorities in the North and Midlands the valuation of the housing stock was less than the debt it carried. This problem of 'overhanging debt' would be dealt with in later legislation, and its solution cleared the way for the flood of large-scale urban transfers that followed under New Labour.

It wasn't, however, just the organisational model of council housing that was wrong according to its opponents. On many occasions it was the new housing's actual form that came under attack. There was, by the 1980s, an established literature challenging many of the cherished ideals of modern urban planning and redevelopment. This was represented most famously in Jane Jacobs' 1961 book, *The Death and Life of Great American Cities*, which argued for dense, mixed-used neighbourhoods fostering, in her view, vibrant communities against the dead hand of those who would zone and isolate. This critique – and its defence of street life – was extended to the large public housing schemes that had appeared in some American inner cities. Their lifts, stairways and corridors were, in a sense, streets, but 'these interior streets, although completely accessible to public use, [were] closed to public view and they thus [lacked] the checks and inhibitions exerted by [the] eye-policed city street'.[15]

This was an idea taken up by American architect Oscar Newman in *Defensible Space*, published in 1972, with reference, in the first instance, to the high-rise public housing apartment blocks of New York. Such blocks, when compared to demographically similar low-rise developments, seemed prone to crime. This, Newman suggested, was a consequence of both their form and nature. Their design hindered, as Jacobs had argued previously, the 'natural surveillance' that might otherwise inhibit crime and antisocial behaviour. In addition, residents felt no sense of ownership or control, and therefore no responsibility, over these large and often labyrinthine semi-public spaces.

Newman's analysis was in many ways specific to the American 'projects' – the US term for that country's public housing schemes – but it won early support across the Atlantic as social problems increasingly emerged in their very different British equivalents. Two years after the demolition of the notoriously troubled Pruitt-Igoe complex in St Louis in 1972, Newman visited and duly condemned for the TV cameras what some saw as its British equivalent, the Aylesbury Estate in Southwark.[16]

From then on his terminology and analysis swiftly entered architectural discourse. We noted earlier how an appraisal of the newly completed showpiece World's End Estate in Chelsea in 1977 blamed vandalism on that fact that its lifts and lift areas were 'not defensible'.[17]

Newman's most vocal champion in the UK was Professor Alice Coleman of King's College London. Coleman founded the Land Use Research Unit in 1979 with a mission to examine the apparent connection between public housing design and what she termed 'social malaise'. Though lacking access to official crime figures, she contended that data on the number of children placed in care and observable measures – the extent of vandalism, graffiti, littering and even (it was a dirty job but someone had to do it) the prevalence of excrement and urine – provided quantifiable evidence of failing estates. Given that Coleman and her team studied 4,099 tower blocks containing 106,520 homes and 4,172 houses in the London boroughs of Southwark and Tower Hamlets (Oxford's low-rise Blackbird Leys Estate acted as a form of control), all this had a rigorous, even 'scientific', air.

Coleman concluded that there was a range of features common to the modern form of public housing – sixteen elements of so-called 'design disadvantagement' were identified – which promoted crime and antisocial behaviour. In a later article, she expressed these ideas even more simply:

> two or three storeys are harmless, but more are harmful. Up to four flats per corridor are harmless but more are harmful. If an entrance serves no more than six flats it is harmless but with over six it is harmful. All sixteen of these features forced families to share the same building and grounds, whereas single-family houses give households their own control.[18]

For Coleman, the ideal was the two-storey house with garden. For those not so blessed, she concluded magnanimously that 'living in a high-rise block does not force all its inhabitants to become criminals but', she continued, 'by creating anonymity, lack of surveillance and escape routes, it puts temptation in their way and makes it probable that some of the weaker brethren will succumb'.[19]

Coleman's published study, *Utopia on Trial: Vision and Reality in Planned Housing*, didn't identify individual estates, but Robin Hood Gardens in Tower Hamlets apparently scored fourteen (out of sixteen) on her 'design disadvantagement' scorecard.[20] The American architectural historian and design theorist, Charles Jencks, criticised the estate's rather narrow 'streets in the sky' as 'dark, smelly, dank passage-ways, places where, as Oscar Newman has argued . . . crime may occur more frequently than elsewhere'.[21]

An aerial view of the North Peckham and adjacent estates

The huge North Peckham Estate in Southwark was another to come under Coleman's scrutiny. Its forty-acre site contained 1,444 deck-access homes in sixty-five five-storey blocks, all linked by overhead walkways. These, in the celebratory early account of the *Southwark Civic News*, joined 'the whole scheme together, forming a network of ways containing housing, shops and other facilities'. Residents could 'walk freely along this two and half miles of deck away from the dirt, noise and danger of London traffic'.[22] Those, at least, were the good intentions, but Coleman found only danger and a 'design disadvantagement' score of 13.1 in the estate's walkways and its ninety-two vertical routes and forty-nine perimeter access points. Her criticism was echoed in more anecdotal fashion by a resident: 'you never know who's prowling around because the walkways and the stairs are open to everybody'. The editorial comment that followed again captures the extent to which the 'defensible space' critique had become the common sense of the period:

> These characteristics all contribute to a sense of anonymity due to intrusion by non-residents through each block, as well as providing escape routes for criminals. The walkways are faceless with a series of doors to upper and lower flats, and the doors frequently front directly on what is a public highway.[23]

Elsewhere and across the country, similar analysis and language was applied to a range of modern estates. Of the Castle Vale Estate in Birmingham, it was said that 'public and private domains are ill-defined, communal areas are not overlooked or supervised, and there is an intricate maze of ill-lit alleyways, making escape from the scene of crime or vandalism very easy'.[24] The Whittington Estate in Camden was a modernist low-rise estate in which a deliberate attempt had been made to create an updated streetscape, but here too council officers complained of the 'large number of potential hiding places for attackers who can then make their escape through any one of the many entrances to the area'.[25] The 'defensible space' thesis had become common currency.

All this makes depressing reading and, let's be clear from the outset, the problems which Coleman addresses of antisocial behaviour and criminality afflicting many council estates were real and distressing. Let's acknowledge too that simple design measures could improve lives – why shouldn't council flats be as secure as a middle-class mansion block? But as for the rest, Coleman's analysis is worthless – both methodologically flawed and ideologically driven.

Her method can be questioned in simple terms. There was, for example, no attempt to control for population size in her finding that large blocks of flats experience greater problems of vandalism and littering than smaller blocks. In fact, with due adjustments made, it appears that smaller blocks suffered disproportionately more from these issues. Coleman's blizzard of statistics is essentially meaningless – a 'shoddy' assemblage whose failure to control for any number of other potentially significant variables renders it invalid.[26]

The most important variable which Coleman ignores – in fact, she positively disdains it (after all, as she later stated, when her own family suffered unemployment in the 1930s they didn't turn to crime) – is, of course, poverty. That residents of council housing were likely to be poorer and more disadvantaged, that this was increasingly so at the time of her study, that tenants of the 'problem estates' on which much of her work focused were likely to be among the poorest and *most* disadvantaged was simply ignored. Socio-economic factors complicated – I would argue, invalidated – the architectural determinism on which her case rested.

Ironically, it is Oxford's Blackbird Leys Estate – which Coleman upheld as an example of the intrinsically peaceable nature of low-rise housing – that illustrates this most straightforwardly.[27] In the 1980s, unemployment on the estate peaked at 20 per cent and reached 50 per cent for those aged between sixteen and nineteen. Other measures – for example, of children under social services supervision and juvenile crime – were also much higher than the city-wide average. It was a combustible mix that came to a head in 1991 with a police crackdown on car theft and joyriding that culminated in a youth-led riot.

In ideological terms, Coleman was – quite literally – a Thatcherite who believed in the efficacy of a housing free market with, in her words, 'minimum regulation and maximum consumer choice'. This broader worldview is expressed, firstly, in her book's title in which 'Utopia' is understood as an, at best naïve, at worst quasi-totalitarian, attempt by ideologues to force society to fit some possibly well-intentioned but quite unrealistic progressive template. This, she believed, was a project that would always be found wanting. In her own introductory words:

> The first half of the century was dominated by the age old system of natural selection, which left people free to secure the best accommodation they could. The second half has embraced the Utopian ideal of housing planned by a paternalistic authority, which offered hopes of improved standards but also ran the risk of trapping people in dwellings not of their own choosing.[28]

A perspective that sees 'freedom' within the gross inequality of *laissez-faire* capitalism and oppression in the Welfare State speaks for itself. But Coleman ventured even more fantastically into an updated version of Social Darwinism with her assertion that the two-storey house and garden represented some kind of evolutionary end-game, a natural culmination of humanity's quest for shelter and territory. In this view, post-war European policy, where multi-storey urban housing was very much the norm, was clearly some disastrous wrong turning.

In 1986, Coleman was invited to Downing Street to meet Mrs Thatcher. Their mutual admiration resulted in a £50 million grant to apply her ideas in selected estates in the so-called DICE (Design Improvement Controlled Experiment) project. 'Defensible space' theory might have had good intentions and potentially beneficial results, but in the hands of the New Right, desperate to destroy both the reality of council housing and its legitimacy, it was an ideological tool. As Thatcherism waged economic war on traditional forms of working-class employment and community throughout the 1980s, this cultural assault on the form and ideals of social democracy became ever more central to ascendant Conservatism.

In an important sense, the wave of estate regeneration begun under the Conservatives (and continued more expansively under New Labour) was another front in the cultural battle *against* council housing. While, without question, regeneration addressed real problems, it was nonetheless premised on the proposition that it is the estates – and, by extension, the model of housing provision they represent – themselves that failed. And as a result the roots of poverty and disadvantage in the wider choices made by society and its political representatives are conveniently side-stepped. In this way, regeneration has served the enemies of council housing rather than its defenders. Pragmatically, of course, whatever the agenda of central government, the slew of regeneration initiatives that emerged after 1979 has been used by local politicians and housing professionals with a genuine concern to improve estates and the lives of those who live on them.

The first Conservative initiative is properly located in the concern of the preceding Labour government with the emerging problem of so-called 'difficult-to-let' estates. Labour instigated a detailed investigation of thirty such estates in 1976 resulting in a list of ranked problems. The biggest cause of their unpopularity was said to be the disproportionate number of 'problem families' they contained and the high number of children resident. Management and maintenance problems followed (including the failure to address problems of vandalism), and then their poor environment, inadequate facilities and, in some cases, the design flaws of individual homes emerged. 'The final point was the vast size; physical separateness; and labelling of the estates' – their scale and perceived anonymity, isolation and the stigmatisation they suffered in other words.[29]

In reality, the ordering of issues was almost beside the point. What had emerged was a spiral of decline in which causes interlocked and fed upon each other. From 1978, the government also asked local authorities to enumerate difficult-to-let properties in their annual Housing Investment Programme submissions to Whitehall. By 1983, these returns suggested that 6.6 per cent of council homes in England were difficult-to-let. Disproportionately it identified those in the larger and more modern estates in the larger metropolitan authorities.

In this context, the chief conclusions of the 1976 survey (not formally published until 1981) seem rather anodyne: 'At first glance what most of the case study estates needed was a thorough clean-up, not as a once and for all exercise, but *as a prelude* to continuous care and attention.' 'Maintenance should be a personal and responsive service', it continued, and it blamed, in large part, failures of housing management for 'precipitating or accelerating the downward spiral in status and acceptability of many estates'.[30] The irony of this judgement at a time of slashed housing budgets hardly needs pointing out but it contained, without doubt, a common-sense truth and was convenient to the new Conservative government whose policies were, in significant respects, contributing to the unprecedented scale of the problems emerging.

Three councils – Hackney, Bolton and Lambeth – were selected to pilot the Priority Estates Programme with the emphasis on modelling systems of local management and repair and promoting tenant participation. 'Partnership' became the new buzzword. By the end of 1980 there were twenty such initiatives across the country, including one in the benighted Honor Oak Estate in Lewisham discussed in Chapter 2. Here, as elsewhere, the scheme was accompanied by measures to improve security and the local environment.

All such schemes had some, though often short-term, beneficial effects. The potential for sustained improvement was mitigated by high levels of tenant turnover (an intrinsic feature of 'problem estates') and – as the Home Office appraisal was honest enough to admit – the 'underlying and often severe social and economic conditions' found on the estates.[31] One broader effect of the programme – as 'local authority landlords irrevocably shifted their emphasis from production to management, and from central control to service delivery' – was the impetus given to decentralisation of housing management.[32]

This had been pioneered most radically by Walsall City Council that created thirty-two neighbourhood housing offices, each covering about 1,500 homes, in 1982.

The next phase in Conservative-style regeneration opened in 1985 with the establishment of the Urban Housing Renewal Unit, renamed two years later as the Estate Action Programme. Ostensibly, it pursued a similar agenda to that of the Priority Estates Programme with its encouragement of estate-based management and range of security and environmental works. It was far more controversial, however. First, this was not additional spending but money 'top-sliced' from the Housing Investment Programme; in other words, money that would otherwise have funded council housing more generally was now being used to support a centrally administered scheme. Second, Labour authorities in particular were suspicious that its principal aim was to encourage the further privatisation of council housing stock.

Estate Action was indeed explicit in urging councils to explore options to transfer either ownership or management of estates to trusts and the sale of both tenanted estates and empty properties to private trusts or developers.[33] Of course, the encouragement to 'access private finance' – as the euphemism has it – made perfect sense to a government trying to cut public spending. The government initially targeted the sixty-nine authorities held to have the worst housing problems and, while some councils remained aloof, in the end the lure of hard cash and the needs it could meet were enough to encourage a wide take-up of the programme. By 1991, 350 Estate Action schemes were in operation, spending around £270 million and absorbing in total around one-fifth of the much-reduced total public housing budget.[34]

One of those was the North Peckham Project, awarded £40 million of Estate Action cash in 1987. To put that sum in context, Southwark had a budget of £60 million to maintain 36,000 council homes in 1979; by 1987 – with additional housing inherited from the recently abolished Greater London Council – it had £28.5 million to manage 62,000.[35] Unsurprisingly, councils took whatever money was going.

In North Peckham, some of that money was spent on renovating the largely untroubled Willowbrook Estate, a small collection of 1960s four-storey maisonettes and one twelve-storey tower block, all pleasantly located around open green courtyards. The council removed asbestos (which was necessary) and installed entryphone systems (which was sensible), but the major physical change was to add pitched roofs to the maisonette blocks. The bulk of the money, however, was spent on the North Peckham Estate itself. Here Alice Coleman had suggested a bit of top-slicing herself – the removal of all but the lower two floors of all its multi-storey blocks. That was impracticable and too costly but the radical remodelling which followed – the demolition of the estate's walkways and the creation of new ground floor entrances to flats, many of which were provided with front and rear gardens – came right out of the 'defensible space' playbook.

The Raffles Estate in Carlisle – an interwar cottage suburb of 1,500 homes – received £16 million of Estate Action funding between 1987 and 1995. Its two-storey houses abounded in 'defensible space' but the estate exemplified all the other problems which Coleman either ignored or discounted – almost one-third of residents were on Income Support, 25 per cent of its households were single adults, 13 per cent were lone parents and 28 per cent of the estate's population were under 16;

everything that made for social disadvantage or, in plain terms, poverty. The rate of burglary was said to be five times the national average – without a walkway in sight! It suffered another problem specific to a number of predominantly northern towns where there existed a crude surplus of council housing (in other words, there were more council homes than people willing to live in them) – a void rate of 30 per cent.

It was, if you choose to use the term, the very definition of a 'sink estate'. The money was spent on a number of remedial measures – traffic calming, window replacements, landscaping, for example – but all these improvements, in the rather plaintive words of the estate's would-be improvers, created 'no material change in the prosperity and stability of Raffles'.[36] Both Raffles and North Peckham would feature in later iterations of the regeneration agenda.

In all, for a total expenditure approaching £2 billion, in the precise figures provided by the Department of the Environment, 483,578 homes had been improved and the relatively small number of 32,543 transferred to the private sector.[37] In this instance pressing realities had trumped ideology. But the fixed Tory belief that council ownership and management were at the root of the problems of many estates and their resistance to public sector solutions and spending would find expression again in the policy of Housing Action Trusts (HATs) announced in 1988.

The proclaimed purpose of the HATs was to regenerate six of the 'worst' estates in the country; its not-so-secondary motive was to remove those estates from council ownership and transfer them to landlords better able, in the government's view, to manage them. Comprehensive regeneration was promised, aimed not only at repairing and modernising housing stock but 'to improve the living conditions and general environment' more widely. The HAT boards (comprising a mix of government appointees and local authority and tenants' representatives) established to oversee this process were also charged with securing a greater diversity of tenure. This reflected something fast-becoming the conventional wisdom of the day – that mono-tenure council estates were in themselves problematic. Strangely, this was an approach never applied to the vast swathes of owner-occupied middle-class suburbia; more generously, it contains an echo of post-war ideals of mixed communities. After five years, the board would hand over the estate to a new private or housing association landlord.

The government identified six potential HAT estates and promised, as a sweetener, an initial investment of £125 million. To the government's surprise, many of the council tenants it assumed would embrace the scheme found it an offer they could refuse. Protests from a radicalised tenants' movement on the Hulme Estate in Manchester, for example, forced the government to concede the principle of tenants' ballots. And when tenants in Southwark got the chance to vote on the proposal to establish a HAT in North Peckham they rejected it by a margin of 60 per cent. Many were resistant to the top-down nature of the initiative and its privatising agenda. Probably more feared – quite rightly – that rents would rise and security of tenure diminish under housing association ownership. David Trippier, the hapless government minister tasked with implementing the programme, was right to reject the accusation made by HAT opponents in a hostile public meeting in North Peckham that rents would rise fivefold, but the charge spoke to genuine concerns felt by council tenants.[38]

The government remained committed to the scheme but, somewhat chastened, it realised that it needed to find willing local government partners. With money on the table and with councils fully aware of the pressing need for estate improvements, this was not hard. John Black was someone that Trippier could do business with. Black, chair of the Housing Committee in Hull (where Labour held fifty-seven of sixty council seats), was, in his own words, not 'an idealist' – his interest, he said, was 'in seeking to achieve results, not some theory of government'.[39] The result he wanted was £50 million to £60 million to complete the refurbishment of the North Hull Estate.

22nd Avenue, the North Hull Estate

North Hull was a large, predominantly interwar cottage estate. It wasn't by any means one of the 'worst' estates in the country though – with around one in five of its working-age adults jobless – it suffered the problems common to many hit by deindustrialisation. Around half the estate had been modernised by 1989 when the money ran out, and the council found its application for Estate Action funding refused.

A two-hour car journey shared by Trippier and Black from Blackburn to Hull in July that year facilitated the beginnings of a deal that served the interests of both parties. The government needed a HAT victory and a council able and willing to deliver one. Black wanted a HAT and allied funding for the unmodernised half of the North Hull Estate. But he was in a position to demand more. Hull, uniquely, received a £5.75 million 'dowry' for its North Hull housing and was also awarded Estate Action funding for other estate projects. The government also conceded that tenants could go back to the council as landlord if they so chose when the HAT was wound up.

In April 1991, after a relentless publicity campaign by government and council, 69 per cent of tenants voting supported the creation of the North Hull HAT, the first in the country. To one resident, surely representative of many, the vote was 'a straight issue of whether you wanted your house done up in five years or twenty years'.[40]

They were duly rewarded. On top of mandatory structural repairs, tenants were allowed to choose from a 'menu' of home improvements that included such things as rear porches, French windows, wall lights and higher-quality kitchen units. An average of £31,000 was spent per home. The HAT also improved streetscapes and landscaping and – in a style that would become increasingly familiar – implemented various programmes to raise residents' health and 'self-esteem' and increase employability through training and education.

After five years, when it came to opting for a new landlord, 48 per cent elected to return to the City Council and 33 per cent to join one of the local housing associations. Owner occupation increased modestly, from 14 to 19 per cent. This might be viewed as a rare victory for local government in the period, and as something less than the housing revolution that central government desired.

Where Hull led, others, with equal pragmatism, would follow. Birmingham City Council instructed its Director of Housing, Derek Waddington, to investigate discreetly what was happening in Yorkshire. The financial case for emulating Hull became, to Waddington, unassailable:

> Eventually I had to stand in front of the Labour group and tell them the *professional* facts. And then I left the council chamber and they sorted out the political elements. In the end they accepted it. For this one simple reason . . . the Government quango gets *direct gift money* up front to plough in the infrastructure.[41]

The Castle Vale HAT was backed by 92 per cent of tenants in a 1993 ballot and the estate received £160 million in government funding. In this case, a radical and wide-ranging makeover ensued. Of the estate's original thirty-four tower blocks, just two remain. Twenty-four system-built and structurally flawed four-storey maisonette blocks have been demolished. In their place, 1,458 new homes were built and 1,381 refurbished. Some imaginatively designed new housing and pockets of self-build and 'eco-homes' showed the fuller scope of housing renewal. An incentive scheme that offered existing tenants a £10,000 grant to purchase their home helped raise owner occupation on the estate to 39 per cent by 2004.

The new HAT went further, however, than merely reconfiguring the estate's housing. It tightened tenancy regulations to facilitate the eviction of the problem households disproportionately responsible for crime on the estate. Other anti-crime initiatives followed, alongside a host of programmes designed to tackle the estate's particular problems of alcohol and drug abuse, infant mortality, domestic violence and mental illness. Latter-day consumerism and its significance was represented by the new shopping centre with a big branch of Sainsbury's as its anchor, heralded by the Progressive Conservatism Project as having a 'profound and important effect on morale and confidence' in Castle Vale, previously a 'brand desert'.[42]

The Chief Executive of Castle Vale's HAT was clear that such 'image management [was] as important as physical improvements' to the estate, and he appointed a full-time public relations officer and assistant to spread the good news.[43] We can be properly cynical about corporate PR and the prevalent triumph of style over substance, but there was a serious point here. One of the problems faced by council estates was the relentlessly negative press coverage they received and the 'postcode stigma' residents sometimes suffered.

In Birmingham, B35 was the Castle Vale Estate, and the address alone could affect your employment prospects and credit rating. Therefore positive media stories and a changed narrative did matter – to residents as well as executives. Once PR was taken seriously, the tone of coverage changed dramatically – positive press stories increased from 29 per cent in 1979 – 81 to 93 per cent in 2000 according to their PR team.

One such was quoted at the beginning of Chapter 5, in which a visiting journalist described effusively how 'these once bleak streets [were] now lined with attractive new houses and mews flats, piazzas and courtyards, travel agents and delicatessen counters'.[44]

All this made Castle Vale very much the poster child of the government's HAT programme. It is a tribute to the 'joined-up thinking' that marked these later iterations of regeneration; a realisation that the difficulties experienced by 'problem estates' stretched much further than any simple issues of design and management. But you might also conclude that it simply demonstrated the beneficial effects of properly directed public investment – £205 million from public funds in this case, with £113 million 'leveraged' from the private sector. This was investment denied to council housing as a whole.

The HAT was wound up in 2003. A ballot of the HAT's 1,327 tenants that year voted by 98 per cent to transfer housing management to the Castle Vale Community Housing Association set up in 1997. I'll confess a sneaking admiration, though, for the 18 tenants who opted to return to Birmingham City Council control – and they probably got better security of tenure and slightly lower rents to boot.

Mrs Thatcher resigned from office in November 1990 following a leadership challenge from Michael Heseltine, a powerful figure in the earlier years of her administration but latterly one of her most vehement critics. Her fall from power and John Major's succession brought about no radical shift in Conservative council housing policy but it did, under the pressure of experience and events, undergo an evolution which will be the subject of Chapter 8.

8
'Thrown-Away Places': 1991–7

The riots which devastated Meadow Well in North Shields erupted on 10 September 1991. They followed three days of rising tension after two young men from the community had been killed when the stolen car they were driving crashed into a lamppost. Their friends disbelieved police denials of a 'hot pursuit' that might have caused the crash. Protests against the police degenerated into looting and arson and emergency services attending were attacked. In all, it was said that some 400 people, overwhelmingly young men, were involved; thirty-seven were arrested. Two days later, violence spread to the Scotswood, Elswick and Benwell areas in the west end of Newcastle.

At first glance, the Meadow Well Estate might have seemed an unlikely site for such an outburst. It was a 1930s cottage suburb, designed along broadly Garden City lines though with the north-eastern peculiarity of a large number of so-called 'Tyneside flats' – two-storeyed dwellings with flats top and bottom and separate ground floor front doors. (Even after some modernisation and conversions in the 1970s, almost three-quarters of homes on the estate were flatted.) But it was very poor.

The Meadow Well Estate, North Shields, 1990

At one of the estate's primary schools, every one of the children depended on clothing grants, and three-quarters got free school meals. A quarter of young men under twenty-four were unemployed; long-term unemployment among men was the highest in the region. It was said that crime levels were the highest in the country. To Beatrix Campbell, it was 'a thrown-away place, imagined akin to Botany Bay, a place to which folks had been transported'.[1] Joe Caffrey, a local community worker, described a 'feeling of abandonment' on the estate: 'people do believe, they genuinely believe, they've been abandoned by government, by local government, by the police and by other agencies.'[2]

It was a turbulent time, one of a series of outbreaks of public disorder that marked the Thatcher years and beyond, beginning most notoriously with the disturbances in Toxteth (Liverpool), Brixton, (south London) and Handsworth

(Birmingham) in 1981. Ten years later, Blackbird Leys in Oxford initiated this latest phase, followed by the Ely Estate in Cardiff and, again, Handsworth. In all, 'riots and violent disturbances' were recorded in thirteen areas of Britain between 1991 and 1992. Twelve of the thirteen took place on council estates; all of these, bar one, were traditional estates of houses and gardens. What united them was poverty:

> All the areas where the riots happened were low-income areas with long-standing social problems and poor reputations. Most had been built to re-house slum clearance families in the 1930s, 1940s and 1950s. Unemployment levels were far above the national average and even above the average for some of the most problematic estates in the country.[3]

The City Challenge initiative, announced by John Major's Conservative government in May 1991, preceded this latest bout of urban unrest but it was, in a sense, a response to it.

In the 1980s, the government's regeneration strategy had been largely market-oriented and property-led. Where possible, it sought to bypass local government and even supersede it. The HAT experiment had shown the *practical* difficulties of this approach but – helped by Thatcher's resignation in 1990 – there was also a growing *political* understanding that local government was an essential partner in tackling what were now understood to be the deep-rooted problems of some localities.

In this respect, it was fitting that Michael Heseltine was responsible for shaping and spearheading City Challenge. Heseltine had been Minister for Housing in the first years of the Thatcher government and, having been appointed to lead the government's response to the 1981 riots in Brixton and Toxteth, he had a deeper and more empathetic understanding of inner-city woes than many of his colleagues.

The positive feature of the City Challenge programme was a formalised and strengthened commitment to economic regeneration based on the realisation that a community's physical environment was often the least of its problems. City Challenge emphasised 'partnership' – strengthened links between local councils and local businesses and close collaboration with education and training providers. Of course, all this was to fit the local community to the *new* economy; predominantly lower-paid, less regular and non-unionised service industries. This all implicitly acknowledged that there would be no return to the traditional manufacturing employment that had been the main-stay of many 'respectable' working-class communities in the past.

The process itself was also, in Conservative terms, business-like. Initially, fifteen local authorities were invited to apply for funds in a competitive public bidding process (two more partic-ipated uninvited). Eleven – whose bids most closely matched the government's criteria – were selected to receive £37.5 million each over a five-year period. A second round of compe-tition followed in the succeeding year with twenty successful bids from the fifty-seven invited to apply. In all, the programme received £1.15 billion of government funding. Again, the money was 'top-sliced' from the housing budget and denied other estates and communities in need.

Back in Meadow Well and its surrounds, the North Tyneside Metropolitan Borough Council's successful City Challenge bid in 1992 naturally emphasised employment. The limited company set up to oversee the scheme was heavily weighted towards business interests, reflecting its intention, in the disarmingly patronising turn of phrase of one commentator, to 'encourage the entrepreneurial activity of local people and their participation in community life'.[4] Probably the greatest contribution to 'community life' made by the scheme was the genuine and apparently largely successful attempt to improve police–community relations by placing sympathetic officers within the estate. (One supposes they didn't call it 'Pigsville', which had been how the local constabulary previously described the estate.)

Then, even in this two-storeyed haven, there were the requisite efforts to improve 'defensible space' by upgraded landscaping and fencing (complemented by increasingly ubiquitous CCTV). In Meadow Well, the unusual decision was taken to preserve council housing as such, but a nod towards tenure mix was made with the demolition of 750 existing homes and their replacement by 170 privately owned and 370 housing association properties.

There's little evidence of any sustained success for the project's ambition to incorporate the estate's residents into the mainstream economy. The Chirton ward, containing Meadow Well, remains among the 5 per cent most deprived wards in the country with around one in six of its adults unemployed. In today's economy, we can assume that many in work suffer irregular or precarious and low-paid employment. As one suitably judicious academic assessment concluded, 'unless the mainstream economy and politics themselves transform to incorporate an understanding of the real-life circumstances of those living in areas of concentrated disadvantage . . . the incorporation of residents of such areas into the mainstream is a chimera'.[5]

In Hulme, Manchester, a grassroots campaign had seen off the attempt to impose a HAT, but the City Council itself had in the meantime taken an 'entrepreneurial turn'.[6] A traditional ruling Labour bloc had been replaced by a modernising faction, critical of old-style paternalism and committed to decentralisation. Formerly championing a municipal socialist-style resistance to Thatcherism, by 1987 they embraced 'partnership working . . . high-profile political leadership, a strong commitment to networking with government and commerce, and the leveraging of private-sector investment'.[7] This was music to the ears of the Conservative government.

The council's successful 1992 bid for City Challenge funding was fronted by Hulme Regeneration Ltd, a joint company comprising the council's Hulme Subcommittee and construction company AMEC. The subcommittee itself included Hulme Community Homes – another three-way partnership of housing department, housing associations and tenants. The Hulme Tenant Participation Project – an autonomous body funded by City Challenge and the Housing Corporation – was formed to provide at least a semblance of the tenant input which remained, in principle, a significant element of the government's strategy. Those Byzantine structures did somehow combine to carry out one of the country's most radical regeneration transformations.

In Hulme, 'new realism' met the 'new urbanism' – the latter an attempt to 'create a new neighbourhood with the "feel" of a more traditional urban community'.[8] The Hulme Crescents went, finally demolished in 1994. What replaced them was a pretty conventional streetscape of red-brick semi-detached homes, terraces and functional low-rise flats: 'Barratt rabbit hutches' in Owen Hatherley's words.[9] Beyond this, there lay the commitment, shared by the local council and government, to mixed tenure. By 2002, 42 per cent of Hulme homes were council-rented (most would be hived off in succeeding years) and 22 per cent were managed by housing associations. Owner-occupiers made up 36 per cent of households. Crime reduction and education and training initiatives were claimed as success-ful, though there was half a suspicion that the positive data owed as much to improving national trends and the area's changed demographics.

Both Hulme and Meadow Well also benefited from the next phase of the government's evolving regeneration programme, the Single Regeneration Budget (SRB) created in 1994. Community Challenge had lasted just two years, but there was a recognition that the confusing array of government initiatives needed rationalisation and better coordination. With the SRB, twenty separate government programmes were brought within – as the name implied – a single budget. Beyond that, it strength-ened the developing emphasis on a comprehensive and inte-grated approach, one that tackled economic and social issues within estates rather than merely the narrow focus on design and management aspects that had dominated the policy of the 1980s.

An explicit language of 'social exclusion' emerged that became the *leitmotif* of New Labour policy in later years. The process of competitive bidding remained, however, and the concomitant reduction of 11 per cent in the overall regeneration budget led some to believe that the new system and its retained competitive character were intended as a smokescreen to obscure the cuts taking place.[10] A total of £1.5 billion was allo-cated to the first round of bidding; in all, six rounds took place before the programme was wound up by the new Labour government and around £5.7 billion was spent.

The North Peckham Estate and four others adjacent to it – dubbed the Five Estates though, in reality, little connected them but some loose geography – were the largest single beneficiary of the SRB, granted some £60 billion. The vehicle for the bid and its expenditure was the Peckham Partnership – a consortium comprising Southwark Council, tenant representatives, Countryside Properties plc, the Laing Group, a number of housing associations and other interested local bodies. With that emphasis on bringing in outside capital through links with private developers and housing associations, it's estimated that total spending on the Five Estates reached £290 million. Money well spent, apparently: the result, according to one journalist, was that they were 'transformed from pits of urban blight into shining examples of regeneration'.[11]

The reality, as always, was a little more complicated. Part of that lay in the disparate nature of the Five Estates themselves, which in truth offered a mixed picture of deprivation. As one local councillor recalled, 'It wasn't as if the area was all a sink estate . . . when you read the big document [the bid application], you'd imagine this area was sort of beyond repair, sinking, sinking.' But the bidding process itself created a need 'to make the area look as desperate, needy and dilapidated as possible'.[12]

Another complication was the very varied built environment of the Five Estates. The Sumner Estate was an anodyne LCC scheme of the 1930s – thirteen traditional brick-built four- to six-storey, walk-up and balcony-access tenements. Nine blocks were added in the post-war period along essentially similar lines though now with lift access and jazzed-up, white concrete-faced balconies as a nod to modernity. These were demolished. Elsewhere, the attractive Willowbrook Estate had been refurbished in an earlier phase of regeneration. Nevertheless, its innocuous and rather attractive tower block was demolished in the early 1990s. Willowbrook thus anticipated the thrust of this later phase of regeneration. The stated aim of the Peckham Partnership was to 'provide family houses and a neighbourhood environment which encourages study, work, leisure and healthy living'.

The alleged antithesis to this wholesome milieu was, of course, the North Peckham Estate and its immediate neighbour, the Camden Estate. The latter was a medium-rise, deck-access estate, of traditional brick construction, but otherwise embodying the 'design disadvantages' identified for North Peckham. Both were demolished. Given the obloquy now visited on such manifestations of 1960s design, that might seem unsurprising, but it also reflected another distortion in the nature of the programme. A strategy that emphasised private sector and housing association involvement was one that encouraged *redevelopment* – new houses built for sale and shared ownership which would reward investors – rather than *refurbishment* of existing properties. Comprehensive improvement schemes had worked elsewhere and 'selective redevelopment might have been justified by social and environmental objectives', but leveraged capital demanded its profit.[13]

The northernmost estate, facing Burgess Park, is Gloucester Grove, constructed in the mid-1960s. It is probably the most architecturally impressive of the five, with 1,210 homes in twenty-nine long, linked brick-clad three- to eight-storey blocks of heavy panel construction joined by high, semicircular, glass-tiled entrances containing stairways and lifts that provided a deliberately eye-catching 'modernist' look to the estate as a whole. Though suffering some of the same social problems as North Peckham and Camden to the south, it escaped largely unaltered, perhaps in recognition of that architectural quality, and it remains a monument to the built bravura and ambition of those earlier years.

New build on the regenerated Five Estates, North Peckham

What's replaced the rest – save for the odd hold-out – is a generic mix of terraced, two-storey housing and medium-rise blocks of flats and maisonettes in the slightly tarty style now favoured. The number of homes on the Five Estates as a whole was reduced from 4,532 to 3,694. Some 1,854 new homes were built, 70 per cent with gardens. The new work offers nothing much to dislike, yet nothing much to impress either, despite the occasional striving for effect. It is in general, as intended, modestly suburban and low-key. The makeover seems to have been popular with residents: a Southwark survey of 2002 claimed 83 per cent felt their quality of life had improved.

The other main thrust of the housing programme was to 'improve' tenure mix. This meant, naturally enough, the reduction of council tenancies. The number of council-rented homes

was reduced from 99 per cent to 60 per cent. In the new arrangements 2,154 homes were council-rented, 915 managed by housing associations and 625 owner-occupied. Steve Chance, a
director of the architectural practice appointed to oversee the
scheme, Pollard Thomas & Edwards, was clear on the goal
here: 'The intention was to have a mixed tenure neighbourhood
and make it possible for people to want to buy private property
in an area that was not popular. We are not trying to build a new
estate, we are trying to build a bit of ordinary London.'[14]

The assumptions here hardly need unpacking. Council
estates were seen in themselves as problematic and, by implica-
tion, comprising the wrong sort of people. Decent, 'ordinary
London' was something, and somewhere, else. This was a view
shared by Southwark's Labour-controlled council that had
declared itself in the ongoing redevelopment of the Aylesbury
Estate 'determined to break down the estate concept'.[15] Estates
were held to have failed *as estates*. Instead, owner-occupiers
would bring capital into the area – social capital, if you will,
which might raise educational standards and overall aspirations, and just plain capital (money, in other words) that would
improve an area's amenities and retail. The other social and
economic aspirations of the project – part of the SRB's vaunted
holistic approach – are seen in the capital allocations in the
original bid of £12.1 million to 'health, culture and sport', £10.8
million to education and some £9.7 million to 'enterprise'. The
bulk, however – some £180 million, was dedicated to housing,
still seen as the most pressing priority and, perhaps, as the most
susceptible to a quick fix.

The Conservatives' last major housing initiative before their
electoral rout in 1997 was the Estates Renewal Challenge Fund

(ERCF). This 1995 scheme returned full circle to the starting point – that much that was at fault with council estates could be laid at the door of their ownership and management. Its intention was to facilitate the transfer of run-down estates to new landlords, particularly those with 'overhanging debt', where outstanding debt and upgrading costs exceeded the notional value of a refurbished estate. It focused on smaller estates or sometimes localities in which estates were rather incongruously grouped together.

That renewed focus on stock transfer sat uncomfortably with many Labour councillors but could be attractive to tenant activists who felt their estates were being neglected. The small Lee Bank Estate in Birmingham, just south-west of the city centre, was one such example. It provides in itself a potted history of post-war council housing in the city. It had been designated (as Bath Row) one of the five major redevelopment areas after 1945. Cleared in the 1950s, the first element of the scheme was a series of six- to eight-storey blocks of traditional brick construction designed by then City Architect, A.G. Sheppard Fidler. One twelve-storey and four twenty-storey tower blocks, system-built by Wimpey, were added in the mid-1960s and more were incorporated into the estate in later years. The sharp deterioration of the estate in the 1980s – many of the flats suffered problems of damp, and antisocial behaviour was widespread – was blamed on chronic underinvestment and poor maintenance by the council.

Lee Bank was judged not quite bad enough to warrant regeneration under HAT, Estate Action or City Challenge, but by the mid-1990s it was first in the queue for the Estate Renewal Challenge. The first proposed bid for funding in 1986 found only eight backers among Birmingham Labour councillors, but a high-profile campaign by residents kept the estate's problems to the fore. A billboard erected at the entrance to the estate, for example, proclaiming 'Welcome to Lee Bank, Birmingham's Slum Quarter' grabbed press attention.

New Labour's 1997 election victory provided the council with the political cover it needed formally to support a successful ERCF bid, but Lee Bank protests to ensure its prioritisation continued. Most notably, a Town Hall demonstration coincided with Birmingham's hosting of the Eurovision Song Contest in 1998.[16] In a December ballot, 62 per cent of residents voted to transfer the estate to the Optima Community Housing Association.

Money was now found to tackle the estate's deep-rooted and long-running problems and a typical, perhaps necessary, transformation followed. In the new dispensation, the project was encouraged to find funding through private borrowing rather than public investment. The twenty-storey Charlecote and Longleat Towers were demolished in October 2000. Ironically, the contractors found them 'absolutely solid' and in good structural order, but their social problems and appalling reputation were taken to make demolition the more viable option. The other two twenty-storey blocks fell shortly after but seven others have been retained and refurbished, subject to the overcladding now held to make such buildings more attractive.

New low-rise housing and traditional street lines were added. Optima proposed that of the 1,000 new homes, only 139 would be social rented and sixty-odd shared ownership. The rest were for owner occupation. The plan was for a fifty–fifty tenure mix of social and private housing. Literacy and numeracy classes and confidence-building courses for the long-term unemployed were provided to the former council tenants who remained, but many were shifted elsewhere to make space for the new, more affluent incomers.[17]

Dawson's Heights in Southwark was, as described in Chapter 6, a very different animal – an attractive, architect-designed estate of high quality – but its tenants too were increasingly critical of the council's failure to repair and maintain its buildings. An earlier attempt in 1994, under Tenants' Choice provisions, to transfer the estate to the Samuel Lewis Housing Trust failed when the latter withdrew, having failed to secure the funding it needed.

ERCF provided a second chance: a favourable tenant ballot in September 1997 saw the estate transferred to the Trust, which received £3.35 million in public funding and leveraged in an additional £3.3 million from the private sector. The new Labour Housing Minister Hilary Armstrong called it 'a real opportunity to tackle the problems and get the estate back on its feet . . . for many years the people living on the Dawson's Heights estate have had inadequate housing'.[18] In fact, they had had very good housing but the estate had been chronically underfunded for many years. Money was found at last to deal with subsidence problems around the periphery of the estate and on providing double glazing, new roofs and improved security

Ironically, according to some residents, this was 'when it all started to go wrong'. One stated that the 'windows and roofs started leaking almost straight away . . . the security doors are always smashed . . . the estate is never cleaned and lifts are broken'.[19] The new social landlord had increased their rents too. There is no doubt (with all due allowance made for the funding problems I've highlighted) that councils have sometimes been bad landlords. The serious efforts to address these shortcomings more recently suggest that this need not be something intrinsic to the public sector, while growing complaints against housing associations indicate that the grass is not always greener on the other side of the fence.

Into the New Labour era, the new government objected to the expense rather than the politics of the ERCF. The scheme had funded some thirty-nine stock transfers involving around 43,000 homes, but the cost – some £487 million to date and rising – was judged disproportionate to the benefit and the programme was abolished in 1998.

However, many of the core assumptions that had shaped Conservative policy in the 1980s and 1990s were shared by the incoming government. Practically, New Labour seemed to agree that councils (too often at least) were poor landlords and that housing associations were better, more agile and responsive. Fiscally, it shared a desire to limit public spending – in direct terms, to keep housing costs off the Public Sector Borrowing Requirement. That renewed the necessity – one that, in any case, sat comfortably with the broad thrust of New Labour policy – to involve housing associations and private sector partners in estate regeneration. More profoundly, New Labour – after four bruising electoral defeats – had come to share Thatcher's embrace of what they both saw as an aspirational working class.

For Tony Blair, Labour leader since 1994, this was summed up in an anecdote he shared with the Labour Party conference in 1996. Four years earlier during the 1992 general election campaign, he had been canvassing 'in the Midlands on an ordinary, suburban estate' and met a man polishing his Sierra (it became a Mondeo after Ford phased out its Sierra line):

He was a self-employed electrician. His Dad always voted Labour, he said. He used to vote Labour too. But he'd bought his own house now. He'd set up his own business. He was doing quite nicely. 'So I've become a Tory,' he said. He wasn't rich. But he was doing better than he did, and as far as he was concerned, being better off meant being Tory too. In that moment, he crystallised for me the basis of our failure, the reason why a whole generation has grown up under the Tories . . . His instincts were to get on in life. And he thought our instincts were to stop him. But that was never our history or purpose.[20]

Owner occupation and Right to Buy had become the symbol of such aspiration and council housing its antithesis.

This was a sad fall from grace for a form of housing provision that had provided millions with their first decent homes – for the many for whom it had been a step up, not a step down. But in crude terms, this negative perception seemed justified by the facts. We're back to *residualisation*.

In 1980, 27 per cent of skilled manual workers (the C2s particularly targeted by New Labour) had rented their home from the council; by 1996, the proportion had fallen to 13 per cent. In 1981, 43 per cent of council housing heads of household had been in full-time employment; by 1998, that figure had plummeted to 23 per cent. (The proportion of those in part-time employment had risen from 4 to 7 per cent.) In the same period, the proportion of non-economically active heads of household (excluding the retired) expanded from 15 to 24 per cent.[21] Meanwhile, the number of those classified across Great Britain as unintentionally homeless, whom councils had a statutory duty to rehouse, increased from 60,400 to 102,410 (the number had peaked at 144,780 in 1992). The fact that just 4,700 of these were put up in temporary accommodation (bed and breakfasts, hostels and private rentals) in 1980 but over 58,000 by 1998 provides shocking evidence of the diminution of council stock.

These data are only a gloss on what many longer-term council tenants *felt* had happened to their estates in the 1980s and 1990s. In Norris Green, Liverpool, an elderly resident recalled that 'in [her] day the houses were given to steady respectable hard-working people who kept the property nice. Now though, the houses are given to anybody.' Another commented that 'terrible types [were] being given the houses nowadays'. She didn't want to talk about it further; it upset her too much.[22]

As the design and build problems of the Castle Vale Estate became ever more apparent, it became an unpopular estate spurned by those with an element of choice as to where they lived, but a convenient recourse for the council for the most disadvantaged who didn't. The estate's problems began, according to one resident, 'when people were moved here who didn't want to be here'. In the caustic words of another, it became 'a dumping ground full of single parents, alcoholics, and the mentally ill'.[23]

The shockingly misnamed 'Care in the Community' programme inaugurated in 1990 – its laudable aim was to close down institutions and provide support for people with mental health problems in their own homes – resulted in many people with severe difficulties being placed in council accommodation. In south London, it was said that a number of long-term patients of the nearby Maudsley Hospital were rehoused on the Five Estates.

Race could add an ugly element to this combustible mix. On the Brandon Estate in Southwark, one of Tony Parker's interviewees described its newcomers in stark terms: 'Every one of them are all problem families . . . and all blacks, or nearly all of them.'[24] Four miles across London, the Pepys Estate by the

Thames in Lewisham had originally been a 'white' estate. In its early years, the GLC had informally based their allocations, in the words of one housing officer of the time, on 'an assumption that black and white would rather live separately from one another'.[25] In 1981, 78 per cent of heads of households on the Pepys Estate were born in the UK or Ireland. Conversely, Milton Court, a mile to the south, was a predominantly black estate. It fell to Lewisham Borough Council (which inherited the estates from the GLC in 1979) to reverse this policy and, as it did so, the Pepys Estate's reputation for racism took off. There was, it was said, strong support for the National Front and other neo-fascist organisations and 'racist incidents', ranging from verbal harassment to physical assault and, most seriously, arson attacks on homes occupied by black and ethnic minority residents, were frequent.

The Pepys Estate, Lewisham

There's a simple reading of this phenomenon, embraced by
some in the comfortable middle class; that of white, working-
class racism. Les Back's sympathetic study of the Pepys Estate
paints a more complex picture. The estate *was* patriotic (it had
been the practice of the Tenants' Association, proud of a local
naval heritage, in its early years to formally 'adopt' a Royal
Navy frigate) and it *was* parochial. This of course, in another
context, might be understood as the 'neighbourliness' and
'community' lionised by post-war planners and politicians
before it was problematised by race. But the traditional community was being decimated by unemployment – Lewisham lost
10,000 jobs in the ten years from 1978 and unemployment
trebled. Over half those aged between sixteen and twenty-nine
were jobless by the mid-1980s. An alternative drug economy
emerged (with a particularly virulent form of cheap heroin
known as 'scag') and crime rates rose alarmingly. For some, the
new black and ethnic minority residents provided a form of
explanation or perhaps just a scapegoat for what had been lost:

> For the long-standing residents, their embitterment is essentially the
> result of what they feel is a broken promise. They were handed a resi-
> dential space, which they took as their own, and now they feel as if that
> space is being invaded by 'foreign' newcomers and a council that is
> unsympathetic to them.[26]

Back's interviews with Pepys residents capture the extent of its
decline. In its early years, one remarked, 'people were fighting
to move onto [the estate] and the lucky ones felt privileged.
They were proud to be part of a showcase.' By the early 1980s,
around a quarter of the estate's households were said to be on
the housing transfer list and its now hard-to-let properties were

increasingly allocated to those with least choice, vulnerable people housed as priority cases. These became another 'Other' – seen less as victims than culprits and sometimes with disrupted or disruptive lifestyles that may seem to have justified the antipathy that many felt towards them. Now, it was 'like [the Pepys] is the end of the road, the toilet of society and we get all the dregs. A place is only as good as the people who live there.'

Turning back to the vexed question of race, the other side of the coin was that people from the ethnic minorities had previously been the victims of what we would now understand as institutional racism when it came to the allocation of council housing. Into the 1970s, local residency criteria would often place them near to the bottom of the waiting list and many were forced into the most squalid and overcrowded housing of the private rental sector. The wholesale shift to a needs-based system marked by the 1977 Housing (Homeless Persons) Act changed things radically and it was precisely because ethnic minority citizens did live disproportionately in the worst housing that their needs were, in this particular sense, prioritised in the 1980s. This was a necessary corrective but, in the competition for an increasingly scarce resource, it in turn might be understood as unfair by white residents who saw their own children denied the council homes they might once have received when stock was more plentiful and councils typically operated local connection policies.

Institutional racism (or maybe just plain racism) lived on, however. Tower Hamlets Council, controlled by a Liberal majority between 1986 and 1994 pursuing a radical decentralisation programme that seemed to intentionally play to racial divisions, reintroduced a 'sons and daughters' policy in 1987. It was found to discriminate against the borough's Bengali population. A damning 1988 report by the Commission for Racial Equality found that 'the housing department over a period of 10 years had systemically allocated Asian applicants to poorer quality housing'.[27] An earlier and landmark Commission for Racial Equality investigation into Hackney, a left-wing Labour authority, in 1984 had found similar discriminatory practices applied to that borough's minorities. Liverpool, Oldham and Walsall were other local authorities found wanting.

Amid all this – the statistics, the tensions, the inevitable contradictions of well-intentioned (and less well-intentioned) policies – it seems to me that an essential truth about this new world of council housing is captured by a resident of the Manor Estate in Sheffield. The Manor was a classic interwar cottage suburb: an estate of 450 acres with its 3,754 homes – solid two- and three-bedroom houses with substantial gardens – set amid generous open space and greenery. Sheffield had been – no pun intended – at the cutting edge of the Industrial Revolution. Even in the interwar period, when depression had hit the city hard, a resident recalled 'everybody worked that I knew. There were very few people who didn't have a job back then.'[28]

But between 1979 and 1983, the city lost an average of 1,000 jobs a month – 21,000 jobs in the steel industry alone. Ten years later a survey of Manor found adult unemployment reaching almost 30 per cent; 50 per cent on some streets. A quarter of the unemployed had been jobless for ten years or more. It was a community which had had its heart ripped out. A working community (in every sense) had been transformed. Now, one local remarked, 'We seem to have people been brought on to the estate *with* poverty, *with* problems until the whole place is like a ghetto.'[29]

At first glance, it's a comment – in its sense of the council estate as somewhere separate and problematic – that might have been endorsed by any Conservative politician of the era. But its narrative is very different. In this personal and direct understanding of process, council estates are seen as the *victims* of wider economic dynamics in the collapse of traditional working-class employment and particular political choices in how we house our most vulnerable citizens. Estates were not the *agent* of their poverty or – as the generalised perception would have it – their dysfunction.

This might seem a trivial, even semantic, point. The reality of residualisation was powerful enough; the social problems of many council estates – not most, and where significant caused by a minority of residents – were real enough (though sometimes exaggerated by the media). But the causal chain was vital. Right-wing politicians blamed council estates – their form, their management, their population – for the problems they suffered. This was an analysis rooted in and reflecting their opposition to all forms of state intervention (except those, we might add cynically, such as MIRAS, which helped the middle class). It was also one that conveniently shifted responsibility from the structural causes of poverty and inequality – which it had been thought in the past the duty of the state or government to address – to supposedly failing neighbourhoods. Academics have a posh term for this: 'locality managerialism' – an operating assumption that 'problems of dilapidation and deprivation have predominantly spatial causes and can be tackled through area-based programmes'.[30]

All this was an approach broadly shared by New Labour. Council estates remained a problem, inherently flawed, requiring systemic reform. An explicit and strengthened 'social exclusion' agenda would focus on rescuing its marginalised communities in order to integrate them into the new, highly competitive globalised economy. The focus on environmental and managerial reforms would continue, but a lot of council housing and a great many council estates would be significantly improved. We'll look at this complex and mixed picture in Chapter 9.

9

'A Different Kind of Community': 1997–2010

On 2 June 1997, Tony Blair made his first public speech as prime minister at Southwark's Aylesbury Estate:

> I have chosen this housing estate . . . for a very simple reason. For 18 years, the poorest people in our country have been forgotten by the government. They have been left out of growing prosperity, told that they were not needed, ignored by the Government except for the purpose of blaming them. I want that to change. There will be no forgotten people in the Britain I want to build.
>
> For a generation of young men, little has come to replace the third of all manufacturing jobs that have been lost . . . Behind the statistics lie households where three generations have never had a job. There are estates where the biggest employer is the drugs industry, where all that is left of the high hopes of the post-war planners is derelict concrete.[1]

To many, including myself, a Labour foot soldier during the dark years of Thatcherism, the party's landslide general election victory in May that year was an exhilarating moment. The 'New Britain' New Labour proclaimed seemed possible; the future looked exciting. The field of housing offers an excellent prism through which to assess the ideas, policies and outcomes of that one-time future.

Returning to that speech, to begin with it was a little unfair on preceding Tory governments. As previously seen, estates such as the Aylesbury had been subject to a plethora of improving initiatives. Second, both in the telling choice of location and in its actual words, the speech in many ways reflected the assumptions of those initiatives. Blair felt he had little choice but to embrace the new globalised economy, but he also saw it as an opportunity that a younger and cooler Britannia might seize. Unemployment was a problem of people and places shut out from the new economy, unable to compete, and the two unerringly converged in the 'problem estate' and perhaps even in the form and nature of council housing more generally.

One year later, the Aylesbury Estate was awarded £56 million. It was named one of seventeen 'pathfinder partnerships' awarded cash under the government's New Deal for Communities scheme – 'a key programme in the Government's strategy to tackle multiple deprivation in the most deprived neighbourhoods in the country'.[2]

'Social exclusion' was the new buzz term, understood as 'a multi-dimensional process, in which various forms of exclusion are combined: participation in decision-making and political processes, access to employment and material resources, and integration into common cultural processes'.[3] 'Welfare', as we learnt to call the social security system, and the problem of making work pay (as it was frequently expressed) was judged to be one larger cause of this and was to be tackled by the new minimum wage and benefits reforms. Nevertheless, the focus on specific localities and their particular problems remained strong. In this analysis, Britain's 'socially excluded neighbourhoods were populated by individuals without the skills required by the contemporary workplace' and were areas 'where long-term economic inactivity had produced cultures and behaviours that collectively challenged the employability of residents'.[4]

The new government's Social Exclusion Unit was established in December 1997 with a remit to reduce social exclusion by producing 'joined-up solutions to joined-up problems'. One of its earliest and most important projects was the New Deal for Communities (NDC) programme launched the following year; its 'vision that, within 10 to 20 years, no-one should be seriously disadvantaged by where they live'.[5] Over the course of the scheme, thirty-nine of the country's 'most deprived neighbourhoods' were selected: seventeen in the first tranche in 1998, and twenty-two in 1999. It's estimated that the overall programme had cost something over £1.7 billion by 2008 with a further £730 million 'leveraged in' – as was intended – from other public, private and voluntary sector sources.

Aylesbury offers a case study of the approach and some salutary lessons. For all the hype around the new holistic approach to tackling 'multiple deprivation', much of the Aylesbury NDC's money and effort was committed to housing regeneration. In this instance, that bland term concealed a £243 million scheme to demolish the existing 2,700-home estate and transfer existing council tenancies in new 'social rented' properties to the newly formed Faraday Housing Association. To fill the funding gap, sixty acres of the estate were to be sold to private developers and some 1,000–1,500 private homes built for sale. Overall housing densities would increase significantly. The 'starchitect' Will Alsop (who had worked on the Five Estates project in nearby North Peckham) was brought in to produce the master plan.

There's much to unpick here. There was an operating assumption (or perhaps it was just a useful pretext for demolition, one endorsed by Blair himself in his reference to 'derelict concrete') that the estate's system-built housing was irredeemably, structurally, flawed. There had certainly been significant teething troubles in the original construction, but these were largely rectified. Individual homes, built to Parker Morris plus standards, were well-liked. The tenants themselves believed that the estate's problems were to be blamed not on the fabric but on years of neglect and poor upkeep.

'Defensible space' arguments persisted to bolster media portrayals of the Aylesbury as a crime hot-spot. These, too, were challenged by those who actually lived on the estate:

> Our lived experience of crime on the Estate does not match the myth – and this is borne out by the statistics. We need to counter these pernicious negative stereotypes . . . We are not going to be bullied into giving up good sound insulation, light, views and space because of exterior neglect and delays in re-housing growing families due to current housing scarcity.[6]

A potent symbol of the stigmatisation of the Aylesbury Estate (though here it merely stood as a cipher for all such modernist, multi-storey estates) was the Channel Four ident, first deployed in 2004, which presented a truly dystopian vision of its 'streets in the sky', recreated here with every imaginable trope of urban decay as litter-strewn, graffiti-laden, dank and threatening. The residents later produced their own more positive portrayal of the estate's decks and community in rebuttal.[7]

Of course, it wasn't Shangri-La. How could it be, given all that had happened to council housing since 1979? It was officially rated as one of the poorest inner-city areas of the capital and, while around one-third of residents had lived on the estate for over twenty years (an important reminder of the settled and 'respectable' community which persisted on demonised council estates), it had increasingly come to house a disadvantaged population, disproportionately from the black and ethnic minorities. The estate was also used as a reception area for refugees and asylum seekers.[8]

It was, then, less a 'problem estate' than an estate with problems, but the label was important in justifying the social engineering – the belief in 'mixed communities' – that lay at the heart of this New Labour project. The government wanted a tenure mix – a range of housing tenures but one which, critically, included private ownership. It believed the insertion of better-off middle-class owner-occupiers (as well as more affluent private renters) would 'lift' the area and benefit the community as a whole.

This belief in the beneficial effects of so-called 'mixed communities' was one increasingly shared by councils which were, in any case (as central government support diminished), anxious to increase local tax revenues. All this is neatly summarised in a later Southwark Council report on the Aylesbury: 'mixed communities', it asserted, 'help to overcome the problems associated with areas of deprivation such as reduced local business activity, limited local jobs and employment ambitions, downward pressures on school quality, high levels of crime and disorder, and health inequalities.'[9]

And yet the residents rejected this version of their future. In December 2001, on a turnout of 76 per cent, 73 per cent of them voted against stock transfer. Some tenants may have feared a middle-class takeover; others were concerned that they might lose gardens or access to open space and parking places. They were worried that their new flats would become smaller and that their rights would diminish while their rents rose under a new social landlord.[10] The whole scheme was blown out of the water.

Southwark was sent back to the drawing board. The council considered the refurbishment option but concluded that the alleged £350 million price tag was prohibitive. The figure was contested but in the wider context it probably was the case that regeneration without the private capital that redevelopment brought in was a non-starter in the current terms of the financial game. In 2005, the council, then under Liberal Democrat leadership, voted again for demolition. Further master plans followed until in January 2007 what was apparently the sixth iteration was agreed in partnership with the London & Quadrant Housing Group. L&Q, which now owns and manages around 70,000 homes in London and the South-East, claims to be the largest landlord in the capital. It is also one of the most aggressively entrepreneurial of the new breed of housing associations.

This twenty-year scheme lumbers on. The withdrawal of projected Private Finance Initiative (PFI) funding of £181 million in 2010 added further delay. Nevertheless, Phase 1a of a nine-phase project has been completed: one council block has been demolished, replaced by six new buildings in which 48 per cent of homes are private, 39 per cent designated 'affordable' and 13 per cent 'intermediate' (generally shared equity). Overall, the new scheme plans to replace the estate's 2,250 council-rented and 500 privately owned homes (some 17 per cent of the flats have been purchased under Right to Buy) with 4,200 new homes. Of these, around half are classified as 'affordable'; that is, they will be let at up to 80 per cent of prevailing market rates for the area. Three-quarters of these will be social rented and one-quarter 'intermediate' (for those not qualifying for social rented property).

The detail is important for it exposes the realities of current regeneration practices and the so-called 'mixed communities' on the ground. First, council housing is abolished and is only partially replaced with fewer, more expensive and less secure housing association homes. Second, 'affordable' homes are unaffordable precisely to those who need them most. In 2015, it was calculated that a household income of over £52,000 was required to pay the average £303 weekly rent of a so-called 'affordable' two-bed home in Aylesbury's SE5 postcode area. Currently, over one in five of the borough's workers earn less than the London Living Wage (roughly £19,000 a year).[11] The benefit cap, reduced by the Conservative government to £23,000 for a couple with or without children in London in November 2016, rules out those on social security.

For the time being, the Aylesbury survives and its residents battle on. Its leaseholders were unexpectedly buoyed by Communities Secretary Sajid Javid's decision in September 2016 to quash Southwark's request for a compulsory purchase order on their homes. Leaseholders had been offered an average £187,000 in compensation when comparable properties in the neighbourhood were on the market at over £450,000. A planning inspector concluded that many would be forced to leave the area and he suggested that Southwark's request and paltry financial offer represented a clear breach of the leaseholders' human rights.[12]

The Heygate Estate, about a mile to the north, has been less fortunate. Its 1,200 council homes have been razed and their former residents scattered to the winds. Of the estate's 1,034 households formerly renting from the council, now just 216 remain in the local SE17 postcode.[13] Of 2,535 homes in Elephant Park, the new Lend Lease development which replaces it, just seventy-nine will be social rented.

In inner London, where property prices are high and councils desperate to generate income, it's not hard to see this process as social cleansing. Let's concede the good intentions of some of the actors involved, those who wish to improve decayed estates and help troubled communities. Let's acknowledge how, in the current framing of housing and local government finances, the necessity to redevelop in partnership with private sector interests and cash may have seemed inevitable. Southwark Council has promised to build 11,000 new council homes through these mechanisms by 2043. But, in practice, the conclusion that poor people have been deliberately displaced to make way for more affluent newcomers and that truly affordable housing has been sacrificed for commercial profit seems inescapable. The charge of state-led gentrification here – and elsewhere – is a persuasive one.

The irony, not unusual to the process, is that the Aylesbury has been blighted by regeneration or, at least, by the drawn-out and disruptive saga which commonly accompanies it. The added irony – though some might claim this as a success for the *social* regeneration heralded as an integral element of the NDC programme – is that the estate has improved by some measures even as its physical environment deteriorated. In 2007, *The People* reported – in tabloid-style but in sharp contrast to earlier media 'exposés' – that crime on the Aylesbury was down by a third, fear of crime had halved, drug use had fallen by a quarter and education results had improved by 300 per cent.[14]

This is a reminder that the 'destigmatisation' of changing, more positive storylines might be as potent a tool in the revival of estates as the physical alterations deemed to be central. One year later, 47 per cent of residents reported that the activities of the NDC had improved the area as a place to live.[15] Around £20 million was spent under NDC on various community initiatives to improve residents' well-being and resources. The charity Creation Trust has continued the work since the NDC was wound up in 2009. These efforts are most obviously seen in Southwark Council's new eye-catching Will Alsop-designed Faraday Community School, opened in September 2010 at a cost of £12 million. Of course, none of this area-based regeneration has done much to challenge overarching and intractable economic realities. In 2012, the estate's unemployment rate stood at 16.3 per cent compared to the borough rate of 10.8.[16]

Around a third of national NDC spend since 2002 went on housing and the physical environment, the rest on measures tackling ill-health, crime and worklessness and improving local education and 'community'. These were the metrics by which the success or failure of the programme was to be measured. The official final assessment was positive: 'Between 2002 and 2008 NDC areas saw an improvement in 32 of 36 core indicators.'[17] Significantly however, 'worklessness' was not one of these and, in general, the report conceded it was easier to achieve 'positive place-related change' than improvements in 'people-related outcomes'. It's true, as the report argued, that changing the tenure mix helped the latter: increasing owner occupation tended to 'dilute the scale of problems more likely to be apparent in households living in rented accommodation' while displacing many existing council tenants.[18]

I don't like the term 'social cleansing'. It's crude and emotive; it ascribes malignancy to what were undoubtedly intended as beneficial reforms, implemented – for the most part – by progressive actors. And benefits did accrue, as they do when you invest positively in people and communities. To muddy the waters further, there *is* a strong case to be made for mixed communities. It was, after all, Nye Bevan himself who urged that council estates should never be 'colonies of low-income people' well before homelessness legislation, Right to Buy, the cessation of new build and mass unemployment contrived increasingly to create that reality. That was a form of largely unrecognised social engineering. Council estates had been mixed communities and, though now housing disproportionately many of our poorest citizens, they remained so, far removed from the 'ghetto' caricature embraced by the media and some politicians.

An attempt to reverse engineer mixed communities isn't inherently objectionable therefore, but its actual form and practice has been deeply flawed. This is particularly so in London – uncoincidentally the location of ten of the thirty-nine NDC schemes – where the combination of soaring house prices and rising demand made investment in building for sale particularly attractive.[19] Actual regeneration has reduced council housing stock and forced many council tenants to move, often to peripheral areas far from their original homes. Inner London has become increasingly the preserve of an affluent middle class. The fault lies not necessarily, or not always, in intent but rather in a public investment strategy tied to the demands and interests of private capital and in a poverty reduction programme which in practice is as focused on removing the poor as it is in reducing their poverty, and in an approach premised on the belief that council estates themselves are part of the problem rather than an essential element of any genuinely inclusive solution.

Here the New Labour government, for all its genuinely progressive politics and more radical policy ambition, shared in essence the presumptions of its Conservative predecessors.

Nowhere was this seen more clearly than in the continuing and expanded programme of Large-Scale Voluntary Transfer. The rate of transfer from council to housing association ownership averaged 50,000 properties annually under the Conservatives but reached 100,000 a year between 2000 and 2002. Of 1.4 million homes transferred between 1988 and 2008, around 80 per cent occurred under New Labour.

There was resistance to what some opponents saw as back-door privatisation as we saw at the Aylesbury. The group Defend Council Housing brought an activist political agenda to the fight but found a sympathetic audience among many council tenants with a well-founded concern that their rights might diminish under the new regime. For all the storm and stress, however, of 133 tenant ballots between 1999 and 2004, only sixteen rejected transfer. By 2010, when Labour departed office, housing associations had overtaken councils as the country's main social hous-ing providers, managing 2.2 million homes in England compared to the 1.8 million remaining in council hands.[20]

This, then, is a story which can be told multiple times, but we'll return to the Norris Green Estate in Liverpool as an exemplar of the bigger picture. The estate was ageing and its so-called 'Boot homes' in particular – 3,000 houses built of precast concrete as a means of circumventing shortages of tradi-tional materials and skilled labour in the 1930s – had reached the end of their useful life. They had been flawed from the outset; the cheap sulphur clinker used in the manufacture of the concrete had led to cracking and shrinkage within two years of their construction and they continued to be plagued by prob-lems of damp and rust, though not formally declared defective and unmortgageable until 1985. The estate as a whole was granted £27 million of Estate Action funding in 1993: 1,700 homes were upgraded but the demolition of the remaining 1,500 Boot homes didn't begin until 2000.

In that year, the Labour government unveiled its vision for housing in its Green Paper, *Quality and Choice: A Decent Home for All*. A central objective was to transfer 200,000 council homes a year to new social landlords. This new world of social housing finance and management reached Liverpool in March 2002 when two-thirds of the city's council tenants agreed to the transfer of their homes to Cobalt Housing, a housing association formed for the purpose.

Cobalt continued with the redevelopment of what had become known colloquially but pervasively as the 'Boot Estate', but it worked hand-in-hand with the property development company New City Vision. In Phase 1 of the Ellergreen scheme (as the Boot Estate was rebranded) in 2006, ninety houses were built for social rent but 104 for sale: 'two and three-bedroom mews and semis, three and four-bed detached houses and a four-bedroomed, three-storey mews property' in the developer-speak employed. Five years later, Inpartnership (a 'Manchester-based niche regeneration specialist') and their 'development partner' Countryside Properties began the first stage of a six-phase, £200 million scheme to redevelop another sixty-three-acre area of Norris Green, initially providing sixty homes – fifteen properties for sale on the open market, twenty-five social rented and twenty shared ownership 'intermediate units'.

In all of this and elsewhere, the role of Liverpool City Council was transformed. In 2008, the last of its housing stock – comprising at its peak in the 1980s some 60,000 homes – was transferred to new social landlords. The Corporation now saw itself as a 'strategic partner' in the provision of social and affordable housing – an enabler not a provider in the jargon of the Third Way championed by Blair.

Local government had once been very much a housing provider. Nowhere more so than in Tower Hamlets in London's East End where, in 1981, an astonishing 82 per cent of the borough's households lived in council homes.[21] The proportion had fallen to 61 per cent ten years later, mostly due to stock transfer to housing associations. At the same time, owner occupation had risen from 14 per cent to 39 per cent in the same period, partly through new build around the new financial hub of Canary Wharf. Right to Buy saw one-quarter of council homes sold to former tenants.[22]

Fast forward twenty years and the largest single form of housing tenure in Tower Hamlets was private rental, accounting for some 39 per cent of households. This was helped by the fact that a similar proportion of the borough's former council homes sold under Right to Buy were now owned by private landlords. Only around 36 per cent of households lived in social rented properties.[23] Some fifty-six registered providers of social housing – housing associations, large and small – were operating in the borough.

This tenure revolution was hard-fought and remains a controversial process. Poplar Harca (Harca is an acronym for Housing and Regeneration Community Association) had been set up by the council to receive some 4,500 homes transferred from council ownership in 1998. In 2001, the council balloted all eighty of its remaining estates on an 'in principle' look at stock transfer and secured agreement in each. George Galloway, who would become the process's arch-enemy, described the 'mismatch of resources' – the 'leaflets and little paper posters' of opponents ranged against the council's 'DVDs and glossy magazines' – which helped secure this result. Eight ballots followed which agreed to actual transfer, but by 2005 a complex communal politics, heightened by local opposition to the Iraq War, had found a charismatic champion in Galloway, who was elected Respect MP for the constituency of Bethnal Green and Bow that year. Of seven ballots in 2005, vigorously contested by Galloway and Defend Council Housing, two voted no; that on the Cranbrook Estate in Bethnal Green opposed transfer to the Swan Housing Association by 72 per cent.[24]

Elsewhere in Tower Hamlets, the process continued – for the time being at least – without controversy. Further successful ballots and transfers followed, including that on the Brownfield Estate in Poplar in 2006. Tenants were promised new kitchens, new bathrooms, a whole range of repairs and improvements, basically the kind of necessary upgrade that local councils were financially unable to offer.

At Poplar's Balfron Tower – Ernő Goldfinger's lowering masterpiece (Grade II listed in 1996) – residents were offered new homes on the estate if they moved out to allow some flats in the tower block to be sold off to the private sector. In 2010, the rules of the game changed and it was determined that *all* of the block's flats would have to be decanted. It became swiftly clear that the tower as a whole was to be sold into private ownership. In the meantime property guardians and artists in residence were moved in. Various more or less well-meaning arts events and happenings were organised in the now vacated homes of East End residents. Critics accused Poplar Harca of 'artwashing', a public relations strategy in which corporations use arts activities to distract from their essentially commercial agenda. The reality that could not be disguised was that homes built for working-class Londoners were being marketed to hip and affluent incomers at a time when Tower Hamlets had 23,500 households on its

Balfron Tower, Poplar

social housing waiting list and some 1,500 households, officially homeless, living in temporary accommodation.

Poplar Harca reckoned it would cost £137,000 to refurbish each of Balfron's flats, an expensive job made more expensive by the block's listed status. It could point too to a positive record in carrying out improvements elsewhere, in building new homes and developing other community resources. Regarded, with some reason, as one of the 'good guy' housing associations, its reputation has been tarnished by the sell-off of Balfron. The building has become iconic for all the wrong reasons: an example of council housing seemingly judged too good for the poorer local citizens for whom it was originally built. To many, the loss of Balfron is a symbol of the malignancy of our current social housing actors and providers. At the very least, it is an indictment of a contemporary system of housing finance which minimises public investment and betrays the shared social vision and purpose which formerly inspired it.

As for the Cranbrook Estate, it was transferred to Tower Hamlets Homes, an 'Arms-Length Management Organisation' (ALMO) set up by the council in 2008 that now oversees the 12,000 social rented homes in the borough remaining in council ownership. The council had estimated it needed £400 million to upgrade its existing housing stock, an amount it couldn't begin to finance from its own resources and which it was legally debarred from borrowing. ALMOs were an option first mooted by Labour in the 2000 Green Paper – wholly owned local authority non-profit companies set up by the council to manage and improve all or part of its stock, controlled by a board of directors made up of tenants, independent members and council nominees. Councils retained ownership and strategic oversight while the ALMOs took care of day-to-day management. They appealed, deliberately, to those councils reluctant to lose their housing stock.

That was the carrot; the stick was the threat that capital for housing investment would only be made to those councils which set up ALMOs. From 2002 to 2006, some £2.1 billion was provided through this route. In latter years, in another indication of New Labour's performance-driven ethos, money was only distributed to those organisations rated 3★ ('Excellent') or 2★ ('Good') by the Audit Commission's newly established Housing Inspectorate.[25] By 2010, ALMOs managed over half of all council housing – more than one million homes across sixty-five local authorities. Nottingham City Homes, set up in 2005 and managing 28,000 properties, and Hackney Homes, set up one year later and managing almost 34,000, were among the largest.

Changes in funding rules made by the new coalition government from 2010 gave councils greater flexibility in housing investment, alongside the suggestion – or perhaps veiled threat – that ALMOs should be transformed into fully functioning and separate housing associations. This was sufficient cause to encourage some councils to bring their operations back in-house. Labour-controlled Islington and Sheffield were notable early examples. In Rotherham, where its perhaps significantly named ALMO, Rotherham 2010, had accessed £218 million in government funding for housing upgrades, nine out of ten tenants voted to return to council management in 2011.[26] Hackney followed suit in 2016. Positive arguments for this reversion to council control centred on the savings made possible by cutting a layer of bureaucracy and, challenging the by-now conventional critique of local authority inflexibility and paternalism, the case for direct democratic accountability.

Other councils, including Labour-controlled authorities, continue to value the work of their ALMOs and have extended their contracts. As of March 2017, thirty-five ALMOs remain in existence managing around 500,000 homes. Other ALMOs – such as Gloucester's in 2015 – have been transformed into independent housing associations. And at the ideological extremes lie Labour Rochdale, fittingly self-styled the 'Home of Cooperation', and Conservative Barnet, known to its critics as the 'easy Council' for its 'no-frills' outsourced model of service provision. In 2011, Rochdale's ALMO, Rochdale Boroughwide Housing, managing 13,700 homes, became the country's first tenant- and employee-owned Mutual Housing Society. In 2012, Barnet Homes and its stock of 15,000 homes became part of the Barnet Group, a local authority trading company incorporating Your Choice Barnet which provides adult care.[27]

This is where the attack on local authority housing provision and management has got us. At worst, we see a crude commercialisation of public services and a shocking assault on the ethos which sustained them. At best, the current market-facing hybrid has replaced a model which could be, as many tenants would testify, monolithic and inefficient with something genuinely more customer-oriented and responsive.

New Labour also promoted the TMOs that its predecessor had first mooted in 1975 and that succeeding Conservative governments had since actively encouraged. With little effect by either party, it seems: by 2010 there were reported to be no more than 200 TMOs in operation, managing around 80,000 homes.[28] It's a reminder to both left and right that most people's housing activism probably extends to a little DIY around the home.

The system of 'choice-based lettings', by which tenants or prospective tenants of social housing could bid for properties advertised online, introduced in 2001, was a more popular and practical means of introducing some customer focus into a system that had thus far been heavily top-down. To Labour Housing Minister, Nick Raynsford, it was proof that we had 'left behind the 20th century framework where . . . the ethos was based on assumptions that the state would provide and people should be grateful for being allocated the benefit of a home'.[29] It had been taken up by a third of councils within five years and was compulsory by 2010. It didn't supersede the priority criteria of needs-based allocations, nor could it overcome the overall shortage of council housing, but it was a modestly successful attempt to deal with the problem of low-demand estates and introduce some of the market rigours of supply and demand now believed essential. An attempt to launch a National Mobility Scheme in 2004 with the aim of enabling tenants to exchange homes across local authority boundaries failed to get off the ground.

That faith in market solutions to housing problems was seen most dramatically in the Housing Market Renewal Initiative, better known as the Pathfinder programme, inaugurated in 2002. This, for once, wasn't targeted specifically at 'problem' council estates, though several were caught up in its web. Pathfinder identified a real problem: urban neighbourhoods hard hit by the collapse of traditional employment, blighted by poverty – those we now call 'left behind'. In housing terms, they were marked by high vacancy rates and – a typically British concern – falling house prices.

As a result, increased demand and rising prices were to be a major measure of the initiative's success. In the words of the House of Commons Public Accounts Committee, 'In such neighbourhoods, the high concentrations of difficult-to-let or -sell properties, the loss of population and the inability to attract new households had created neighbourhood decline and deprivation'.[30] It's a telling formulation which seems to reverse any proper understanding of the causal chain involved, but the assumptions it contained allowed another typical response – a focus on property-based solutions and an assumption that the market knew best.

Nine areas in the North and the Midlands were selected as the test bed of this approach, a larger-scale initiative than those that had preceded it, encompassing some 800,000 properties in total. Regeneration here focused on housing markets and was to be achieved by a programme of selective demolition of older properties (some derelict and poorly equipped but many still decent homes), refurbishment and new build. The irony that many similar properties were in high demand in London and the South-East and commanding inflated prices might suggest that the housing itself was not the problem.

Low Hill in Wolverhampton, an interwar cottage suburb of over 4,000 homes, was one such troubled council estate that Pathfinder addressed. As early as 1971 (when, by the way, the local unemployment rate stood at 4 per cent), parts of Low Hill had become hard to let and, to one observer, the estate 'already found itself locked in a spiral whereby few people other than those in desperate need of accommodation will choose to live there'. He continued that because such people tended 'to come from those sectors of the community which are looked down upon by "respectable" people, their presence serves to further lower the reputation of the estate'.[31] By 2001, as the major companies on the nearby industrial estate shut up shop, unemployment stood at 15 per cent and the estate's problems had worsened.

The Bushbury Hill Estate Management Board, a TMO set up to manage some 840 homes on the estate in 1998 (the rest remained with the ALMO Wolverhampton Homes), was one response. Pathfinder's contribution to a solution was to demolish around 500 homes, replaced – in this instance – largely by open terrain and some small-scale new developments such as the fifty new 'eco-friendly' homes built in Showell Park. These were built for private sale and shared ownership; a few were offered for social rent. Improvements in management and better community provision have raised the estate since then. It would be hard to measure the impact of Pathfinder but not difficult to conclude that it was probably minimal.

In 1995, after a local school had been destroyed in an arson attack, the MP Roy Hattersley (a chair of Sheffield's Housing Committee in the 1960s) dubbed the city's Manor Estate 'the worst estate in Britain'. That was unfair to its community and there were plenty of others vying for the dubious tabloid accolade. It is true, however, that Sheffield had lost 21,000 jobs in the steel industry alone in preceding decades and around one in three of the Manor's adult population were workless. Sixteen hundred homes – many suffering genuine structural deficiencies – had been demolished in the Urban Programme scheme of the 1980s. Only 500 new homes were built to replace them. Alongside other, more constructive initiatives, Pathfinder arrived in 2005 with the mission to 'build and support sustainable communities and successful neighbourhoods' by adding to the 'quality and choice of housing'.[32] This was accomplished by further demolition and selective new build, naturally with the tenure mix now deemed requisite.

Of the decayed or not so decayed pre-1914 terraces that provided the thrust of the Pathfinder programme, the most famous example was the Welsh Streets in Liverpool – 'tinned up' for years, their early decommissioning adding its own element to the neighbourhood's urban blight. Liverpool suffered an almost Detroit-style decline in the second half of the twentieth century (its population fell from a peak of

846,000 in 1931 to around 470,000 today), but has faced it with a Liverpool-style resilience. Such a fall from grace left a lot of empty homes. Nevertheless, an active campaign by residents and housing and heritage activists, helped by the fact that 9 Madryn Street was the birthplace of Ringo Starr, has led clearance plans to stall. Alternative proposals are being formulated.

Fifty miles to the east, the remaining Edwardian terraces of Pendleton in Salford were another Pathfinder target. The refurbishment scheme by arch-gentrifiers Urban Splash (of Park Hill notoriety) in Chimney Pot Park offers a cameo of the programme's hopes. The so-called 'upside-down houses' (with bedrooms and bathrooms on the ground floor and kitchen and living rooms above) are nice enough; in fact, they are 'achingly fashionable', designed, as they were, for 'a new community of urban pioneers' and 'aspirational young couples'.[33] But, at an initial sale price of £120,000 (judged three times what might count as 'affordable' in local terms at the time), they had little relevance to the lives of those who once lived there or those who live in the social housing nearby.

Here we are confronted directly with the class politics implied more or less directly within the Pathfinder initiative. In overall terms and in contrast to its dominant visual imagery, the programme appears to have built more houses than it demolished. Some 21,190 houses were cleared, 29,126 built and over 85,000 homes refurbished. The fullest study to date concludes it 'achieved some positive impacts', although the authors counsel that these 'took place within the context of a uniquely favourable phase of economic and urban development'.[34] In other words, relative prosperity raised those communities just as its earlier opposite had damaged them. Other criticisms remain from those who argue that 'sustainability' (one of Pathfinder's proclaimed ends) is better safeguarded by not demolishing structurally sound homes. Meanwhile, others make the more difficult accusation that it was a 'programme of class cleansing'.[35] That might seem overstated but it's sad to see, in practice, how often the ostensible goal of 'mixed communities' seems to require the removal of the poor and the importation of the more affluent.

Staying in Salford, we can examine how the final of New Labour's vehicles to finance and manage regeneration worked in practice. The PFI, inaugurated by John Major in 1992, was another scheme inherited from the Conservatives that took off after 1997. For a government desperate to advertise its fiscal prudence and committed to meeting previously announced Conservative public spending targets, it must have seemed a good wheeze. Under PFI, private consortia were commissioned to finance, design and often manage major capital projects – typically schools and hospitals but, in some fifty cases, council estate regeneration, covering around 28,000 homes. For their efforts, the consortia received annual payments, usually over a contract period of around thirty years, from the authorities concerned – local councils in the case of housing – paying for services rendered and effectively leasing back privately owned public assets. It kept large-scale capital expenditure off the books, replacing those bigger sums with far smaller annual payments, though the latter would in the end cost far more than any direct upfront payment. If there lay the financial logic of the scheme, such as it was, critics on the left also saw 'a neoliberal agenda designed to open up the provision and management of public services to the private sector'.[36]

Broadwalk, Pendleton Estate, Salford

In 2008, 93 per cent of Pendleton's housing stock was still council-owned. The 'target position' – outlined in the 'Benefits Realisation Plan' behind 'Creating a New Pendleton' one year later – was to fashion 'a mixed tenure residential area'. Four years later, the PFI charged with implementing this plan was finally established. The objects of the thirty-year contract were: to refurbish 1,253 council properties, demolish 960 (including four multi-storey blocks of flats) and 'deliver a minimum of 460 homes for affordable rent, around 950 for market sale and a minimum of 25 for shared ownership'.[37]

The consortium in charge, Pendleton Together, comprised, among others, the housing association Together Housing Group, 'building and regeneration specialist' Keepmoat, architects and planners Lathams, and Salford City Council. Its vision was outlined in a glossy brochure called 'An Ideal for Living'.[38] The immediate beneficiaries of this vision were financiers:

> Investec Bank arranged the bond issue on behalf of joint venture FHW Dalmore, with £71.7 million of Class A senior secured notes at 5.414% and £10.9 million of Class B junior secured notes at 8.35%. The two-tranche approach sees subordinated B loan notes offering protection to A note investors, with the debt on-lent to the borrower as a single loan at a blended margin, and a standard project finance covenant package.[39]

It's worth quoting that financial mechanism (and perhaps you understand it better than me) as an insight to the mystificatory process involved that, behind all the smoke and mirrors, rewards capital at the expense of social need. Things were much simpler and surely much more cost-effective when council housing was financed by the Public Works Loans Board.

Given the long delays, the results are at best a work in progress. Pendleton is another area – though parts of it have undoubtedly been changed for the better through the various improvement initiatives of recent years – currently blighted by regeneration, with large swathes of cleared land and so far relatively little rede-velopment. All this, for PFI, is very much par for the course. The programme has been marked by escalating expense (the first seven PFI schemes cost 88 per cent above initial estimates), delayed implementation (an average of thirty-six months in the first thirteen contracts agreed) and poor oversight.[40] Even the measured language of the National Audit Office acknowledges cost overruns, long delays and inadequate auditing and supervi-sion.[41] In overall terms, it's reckoned that the overall programme has created a £210 billion debt (of which £4.3 billion relates to housing) to be paid back over thirty years.[42] The programme remains one of the more inglorious legacies of the New Labour governments.

In contrast, the Decent Homes Programme is something in which Labour can take justifiable pride – a scheme whose modest title but practical objectives improved the lives of millions. In many ways, it is the most transformative of all the initiatives described in this chapter and, without doubt, the most directly beneficial. I've come to it late for one simple reason – that its implementation was bound inescapably to the central tenet of New Labour's housing policy: that councils were poor landlords and that council housing as such should be reduced. There was a clear recognition that decades of cuts and underinvestment had left social housing in a parlous state and with, in straightforward terms, a £19 billion backlog of needed repairs and refurbishments. But if a council were unable to fund these improvements from its own resources (which, of course, none could), they had the three options explained so far: Large-Scale Voluntary Transfer, ALMO or PFI. The entirely laudable aims of the Decent Homes Programme were thus intimately connected to the government's broader housing agenda.

The Decent Homes Standard, instigated in 2000, required all homes to be in a reasonable state of repair and to enjoy reasonably modern facilities and services. A home lacking three or more of the following was deemed to fail the standard: a kitchen, of adequate size and layout, which was less than twenty years old; an appropriately located bathroom and toilet less than thirty years old; adequate noise and thermal insulation; and, in the case of blocks of flats, adequate size and layout of common areas. The requirements don't seem unduly demanding and it's an indication of the years of neglect suffered by much of our social housing stock (and don't forget that most was, by definition, unaffected by all those locality-based initiatives discussed earlier) that an estimated 1.6 million social rented homes were non-decent in 2001 – 1.2 million in properties managed by local authorities and 400,000 by housing associations.

Together they equated to 39 per cent of all social housing (43 per cent of households in the private sector also suffered non-decent accommodation).[43] Landlords were given ten years to put the deficiencies right. By November 2009, the Department for Communities and Local Government reckoned 1.4 million local authority homes had been improved under the programme at a cost of some £22 billion. It estimated that 92 per cent of such homes would meet the Decent Homes Standard by the end of 2010, leaving just 305,000 homes with works underway or in the pipeline.[44] This, by any standards, was a major achievement and one insufficiently recognised. Paying for it and managing it all was another question.

In Woodberry Down, Hackney, the council's 2002 'Structural Evaluation Report' on the estate concluded that thirty-one out of its fifty-seven multi-storey blocks, mostly built in the late 1940s and early 1950s, were 'beyond economic repair' with wide-ranging problems including subsidence, damp, faulty drainage, poor insulation, asbestos and lack of disabled access and lifts. This led the regeneration strategy – perhaps conveniently – to shift from upgrade to redevelopment: the 1,980 council or former council homes on the estate would be demolished and 4,644 new homes constructed. The 1,458 socially rented homes would be 're-provided' while an additional 2,700 homes were to be built by private developers for sale. The tenure mix of the estate would shift from 67 per cent socially rented to 34 per cent socially rented, 65 per cent privately owned. The latter made the scheme self-financing and gave the developers, Berkeley Homes, a contractually guaranteed 21 per cent profit.

Hackney Council, for its part, takes pride in the fact that the actual size of the social housing stock (now managed by the Genesis Housing Association) will not be diminished and that, at 41 per cent, the overall proportion of 'affordable housing' on the new estate is relatively high. To the tenants who don't get the new prestige flats with water views, to some forced out during the lengthy rebuilding process, to the inadequately compensated leaseholders, the process remains controversial. To its critics, this is nothing less than 'state-sponsored gentrification'.[45]

Other examples are less controversial but equally indicative. In Salford, the PFI has raised 1,253 former council homes to the Decent Homes Standard. Other stock was improved by Salix Homes, launched as an ALMO in 2007 and an independent housing association since 2015. Sheffield's Manor Estate was transferred to Pennine Housing 2000. Around £15 million of Decent Homes improvements followed. A lot else had happened on the estate too, and a revised narrative for the 'worse estate in Britain' emerged: 'While many people perceive Sheffield's biggest council estate to be a hotbed of unemployment, teenage mothers and anti-social behaviour, to those who live and work there it's a homely haven.'[46]

The Raffles Estate in Carlisle had already been subject to Estate Action and SRB initiatives. In 2002, it got £3 million to bring its social housing (transferred that year to the Carlisle Housing Association by a narrow 52 per cent majority) up to the Decent Homes Standard. The 'Raffles Vision', built on an earlier 1999 Area Report, set out 'a four-year programme of decanting, demolition and redevelopment', which planned to reduce the number of council homes – 624, almost half, were to be demolished. In consequence, it would 'create opportunities for tenure diversification'.[47]

The immediate impact of the overall programme is best seen in the changing tenor of local press headlines. The *News and Star* headed a 2003 article on the regeneration of Raffles, '£100,000 for a New Home as Rundown Estate Goes Posh'. By 2006, it was proclaiming Raffles 'The Trendy New Place to Live'. In 2013, the *Cumberland News* stated that the £30 million investment had left 'Carlisle Estate's Bad Old Days in Past'.[48] By 2014, 500 council houses had been demolished and some 262 new properties built. Of these, just forty-nine were for afford-able rent with fifty-eight more planned.

The actual changes were a classic mix of all the by-now standard elements of the regeneration playbook: the clearance of unpopular council homes, the introduction of mixed tenure with a range of owner-occupied, social rented and 'affordable' homes, and a diversity of housing type. But they seem to have had an effect. Kath Queen, a Raffles resident for nearly forty years and a leading light in the estate's Living Well Trust, believed it 'has got better – by a long way . . . It's created a different kind of community.' Ken Swales, resident for forty-five years, concurred: 'It's nice now. At one time you couldn't leave your house, but it hasn't half quietened down.' The anec-dotal testimony was seemingly backed up by hard evidence: overall crime down by 13 per cent, criminal damage almost halved and car theft reduced by 70 per cent.[49]

Estates have needed regeneration and much good has been done. But, Carlisle City Council, having overseen the demoli-tion of good council housing, soon came to identify a net annual shortfall of 708 affordable homes over the next five years.[50] I doubt that Carlisle – far away from the overheated housing markets and relative affluence of the South-East – has suffered an excess of gentrification, but the Alice in Wonderland logic of tackling a housing crisis by destroying solid, genuinely afford-able and much-needed council homes seems plain.

Despite that criticism, it's nevertheless important to make one simple observation. I've probably seen more council estates (many of them no longer 'council', of course) than most people in recent years and the vast majority of them look good: well-maintained, attractively landscaped, overwhelmingly – unless my experience is very unrepresentative or Panglossian – quiet and respectable. In a word, decent. That might seem partisan, given the whole purpose and overall tenor of this book, or partial – the latter must, of course, be to some extent true – but I would pit these impressions against the demonising caricature that has afflicted council homes and their communities since the late 1970s. In that sense, the now more positive media headlines are important and I hope they've contributed in part to a new 'common sense' around social housing: that it provides good and desperately needed affordable homes at a time when, once again, the free market is failing ordinary people.

There was, however, no revival of council house building under New Labour. Between 1997 and 2010, of 2.61 million new homes constructed, just 0.3 per cent were local authority – a grand total of 7,870 new council homes built under the Blair and Brown governments. Housing associations fared better, with some 350,000 new homes completed in the same timescale.[51] In part, this reflected the fiscal (and electoral) 'prudence' that was so central to New Labour's strategy to power. Not only did the new Blair government stick, as promised, to announced Tory spending plans, in its first term of office spending on social housing overall fell significantly below that of the preceding Major government.

Only after a third election victory – and as a national short-age of affordable housing became clearer – did ambitions rise.

An annual target of 200,000 new homes annually was announced in 2005, increased to 240,000 in 2007 when Gordon Brown became prime minister. That year saw 224,680 homes built across the UK in all sectors – the highest figure since 1981 and the first time in two decades that the number of new social rented homes surpassed those lost through Right to Buy.[52]

The 2004 *Review of Housing Supply* commissioned by the government from Bank of England economist Kate Barker had largely focused on interventionist planning reforms and modest fiscal measures as a means of boosting house construction, but even she recommended that what she termed misleadingly 'subsidised housing' numbers be increased – to 23,000 completions a year if both current demographic trends and a mounting backlog of needs were to be addressed.[53] In the event, *Homes for All* – the government's big policy statement which followed – committed to just 10,000. Its thrust was market renewal (including the Pathfinder scheme) and a range of gimmicks to promote owner occupation – a First Time Buyer Initiative for key workers and a HomeBuy scheme for social housing tenants, both for shared ownership.[54] In practice, home ownership in Britain fell from 69 per cent of households in 2005 to a little over 65 per cent by the time Labour left office.

Government priorities were further amplified in the independent report commissioned from the LSE academic John Hills and published in 2007. His brief was to 'stand back and ask what role social housing can play in 21st Century housing policy'; the key questions tackled:

- What can social housing do in helping create genuinely mixed communities?

- Can the way we run it encourage social mobility and opportunities, including in the labour market, for people to get on in their lives?
- Can social housing and other support be more responsive to changing needs and enable greater geographical mobility?[55]

Ends and Means: The Future Roles of Social Housing in England was in many ways an estimable undertaking – over 200 pages of closely packed analysis and data, invaluable to anyone with an interest in the past, present and future of social housing. It would be curmudgeonly even to bridle at the issues and objectives it addressed. And yet it encapsulates so much of the present thinking around council housing – for it is *council* housing rather than social housing managed by housing associations that is problematised. Should council estates house mixed communities? Yes, and they once did. Should they encourage social mobility? Yes, and they were once its key location as working-class job security and living standards rose. Should social housing more generally be flexible and responsive? Yes, and at its best – as design and forms evolved – and, belatedly, as its management improved, it has been. Should it facilitate geographical mobility? Yes, and this historically has been a significant deficiency, ironically one which has been exacerbated by the housing policies pursued by governments of all stripes since 1979.

The obvious riposte to my lament is to point to a changing world, a globalised economy which has edged out past assumptions of full employment and greater social equality with increased public investment as a means to both. But our unalloyed obeisance to the market seems to have created as many problems as it has solved. And those problems have been disproportionately visited upon the poorest of our people, those housed disproportionately on our council estates.

In this reading, council estates are not a cause of our economic and social woes but their victim. With this understanding, we should view them not as a problem but as a solution – offering secure and affordable housing – to the low pay and insecure employment which affects so many. That reluctance to invest in public housing looked all the more suspect as the global economic crisis hit in 2008. New completions plummeted and the £1.5 billion boost to housing investment announced that year was largely dedicated to the rescue of a private market in crisis.

Readers should come to their own judgement about New Labour's record in office but housing policy and achievement does offer an excellent yardstick. Even as it pursued its generally progressive social ends, New Labour undoubtedly pursued a broadly neoliberal agenda, one that gave economic primacy to the market and its disciplines, one which privileged private finance and the profit motive over public investment. Its social housing policies which rested in essence in a diffuse but pervasive belief in competitiveness – personal and institutional – afford one of the clearest illustrations of this overarching belief-system and, to many, will suggest its limitations. In terms of council housing – I mean social housing now, of course – New Labour and its chosen agents improved both its fabric and management, but in a way which perpetuated the prejudices against it and undermined the values which sustained it.

That failure – in fact, the unwillingness – to challenge existing assumptions about the nature and role of council housing left it open to the even greater threats it faced in the politics which followed.

10

'People Need Homes; These Homes Need People': 2010 to the Present

In different ways to different people, the burnt hulk of Grenfell Tower will stand as some dystopic cipher for all that has 'gone wrong' with social housing. In the early hours of Wednesday 14 June 2017, a small electrical fire broke out in a fourth-floor flat of this recently refurbished twenty-four-storey west London tower block. It spread rapidly until flames engulfed the building's upper floors. The official death toll, announced in November 2017 after painstaking investigation, was seventy-one. The pain and anger of victims is almost unimaginable but the event sparked a much wider and agonised public debate about how such a needless tragedy could occur in twenty-first-century Britain.

To some, 'the lesson from Grenfell [was] simple: stop building residential towers'; they were 'antisocial, high-maintenance, disempowering, unnecessary, mostly ugly, and they [could] never be truly safe'.[1] Each of those adjectives is questionable. The more nuanced truth is that tower blocks, while not perfect (which housing form is for every type of household?), have provided good homes for many thousands. In fact, tower blocks are back in fashion as the displacement of social housing tenants from ex-council blocks in the right postcodes by affluent middle-class incomers reminds us. But, more importantly, we need to challenge the stereotype of tower block living which misrepresents it as some kind of hellish anomie. In the worst circumstances imaginable, Grenfell showed us community, strong and diverse; families, friends and neighbours together. And all, of course, joined with and connected to others in our wider community. As a reminder of our common humanity, perhaps Grenfell will act as a corrective to the demonising caricature of social housing tenants prevalent in recent years.

Many of the questions raised were, at first glance at least, more narrowly technical. The recent £10 million renovation of the block had added the new shiny thermal cladding, now *de rigueur* in such work. The flammability of that cladding seems to have been a major cause of the fire's rapid spread. The failure of 'compartmentalisation' – the means by which any outbreak of fire is contained – appears equally culpable. Most residential blocks in the UK employ what is called 'passive' fire protection, using means that prevent the spread of fire rather than sprinkler systems which actively extinguish it. The fire safety advice issued to residents of Grenfell (as is the case in similar blocks) was to remain in their flats until what should have been a limited outbreak was dealt with by the emergency services. It's a sound model *if it works*. At Grenfell, it failed disastrously. There are now widespread calls for 'active' systems to be installed in all comparably vulnerable buildings. What now appears to be the widespread use of combustible cladding in tower block renewals stands condemned.

The management of the block has also been sharply criticised. Grenfell Tower was owned by the Borough of Kensington and Chelsea but managed by the TMO which, unusually, has run the borough's entire social housing stock of around 9,700 homes since 1996. Residents' concerns about fire dangers resulting from a botched renovation had been powerfully voiced by the unofficial Grenfell Action Group. In a tragically prescient blog post in November 2016 entitled 'Playing with Fire', the group feared it would take 'a catastrophic event . . . an incident that results in serious loss of life' to truly expose the incompetence of the Kensington and Chelsea TMOs and its mismanagement of recent works.[2] Many others have extended this criticism of weakened democratic controls and blurred lines of accountability to the entire system of devolved social housing management which has come to dominate the sector since the 1980s. It would be wrong to condemn all registered social landlords and naïve to assume council management automatically provided more responsive management. But the case for strengthened democratic controls and oversight and stronger accountability to residents – the experts on the ground when it comes to their own housing – is clear.

Grenfell Tower also shines a disturbing light on the near-universal contemporary model of regeneration dependent on opaque public–private partnerships and private capital and driven by commercial interests. At Grenfell, it is claimed that managers and contractors cut costs by using cheaper and less fire-resistant cladding. Such decisions are integral to a system which privileges private profit while it limits – and decries – public investment.

But ruthless cost-cutting extends much further. It appears that expert recommendations to strengthen fire safety regulations, particularly those made after a fire at Lakanal House in Southwark which killed six people in July 2009, have been consistently delayed and sidelined by government.[3] Meanwhile the local authority building control departments whose job it is to enforce fire safety regulations have been 'eviscerated'.[4] Some of their functions have been privatised while the oversight role of independent fire officers has been replaced by a form of self-certification. No-one is likely to use the phrase a 'bonfire of red tape' again – its echoes have become too chilling – but here is the value, the absolute necessity, of the health and safety measures so widely derided in recent years. And if 'austerity' can sometimes seem a piece of empty political rhetoric, this is its reality. For almost four decades, we have been taught the neoliberal mantra 'private good, public bad' and encouraged to see public spending as an evil; ruthless economising as a virtue. We have come to know the price of everything and the value of nothing and have ended with the funeral pyre of Grenfell Tower.

As I write, in late 2017, it is too soon to predict what will be Grenfell's longer-term impact on the social housing sector. It will, alongside the unexpected result of the general election which occurred just one week earlier, disturb the existing policy narrative, but how far and in which direction is hard to know. In general, housing policy has been shifting terrain since 2010 with a pattern of radical statements followed by apparently pragmatic retreat. Defenders of social housing's role and ethos have been left grateful – more grateful than they should be perhaps – for the concessions wrested from the maximalist positions originally taken by government. Because of those shifts and current uncertainties, this chapter examines this detail in the context of the bigger themes and issues around social housing, allowing us to revisit questions of its

past and present purpose and perhaps to assess the form and
nature of its future.

Looking back at council housing's history, we saw how in its
early years it housed a relatively affluent working class, those in
steady employment who could be reliably expected to pay its
comparatively high rents. In this sense, councils were like any
other landlord: they wanted 'respectable' tenants for their housing and a guarantee that its capital costs would be paid off and
running expenses met. This should remind us that council housing is not, in any meaningful sense, 'subsidised'. Construction
loans are repaid and, in most cases, the homes themselves
become an asset, not only to those who live in them but a financial – and income-generating – asset to the local authority. To
those to whom council housing did not cater – the 'submerged
tenth', the 'residuum', the casually employed, low-waged or
unemployed slum working class, a 'filtering up' theory was
applied. They, it was hoped, would move into the slightly less
slummy housing vacated by their immediate superiors.

This changed, but changed slowly. Slum clearance in the
1930s combined with the impact of the Great Depression
brought a poorer working class into council housing for the first
time, and with it some of the perceived problems and demonising stereotypes applied to council tenants more generally in
recent years. The policy shift reflected a political division
between Conservative politicians who believed council housing
should properly be reserved for the neediest (the market would
provide for the rest) and those on the left who saw it as serving
'general needs'. Full employment and rising living standards
after the Second World War reinvigorated the sense that council housing catered predominantly for a relatively prosperous
and aspirational working class. But, from the 1970s, politics and

economics combined to lower its status and that of its community.

The National Rent Rebate Scheme implemented in 1973 (it became Housing Benefit in 1982), increasing access to council housing for the less well-off, was a significant factor in the shift. The 1977 Housing (Homeless Persons) Act, prioritising council housing for the most vulnerable and cementing a system of needs-based allocations, was central to it. Right to Buy and the near cessation of new build in the 1980s was determinant. The concomitant collapse – or destruction – of the traditional manufacturing economy and loss of jobs that went with it was, in this context, just a bonus. All that made for, in one word, residualisation: the increasing confinement of council housing (and by this time social housing) to the poorest of our citizens and, disproportionately, those classified as 'vulnerable' in some way. (That estates continued, in fact, to house a cross-section, albeit a narrower one, of our community goes without saying.)

In the 1980s, residualisation may have been a partly unintended consequence of housing policies pursued with varying ideological intent. Since 2010, and more so since the return of single-party Conservative government in 2015, we've seen something further: welfarisation – 'a conception of social housing as a very small, highly residualised sector catering only for the very poorest, and those with additional social "vulnerabilities", on a short-term "ambulance" basis'.[5] To some extent, this replicates the agenda of Conservatives in the 1930s and, with Harold Macmillan's abolition of the 'General Needs' subsidy in 1954, it represents in its present form something deeper and more dangerous. In the years after 1945, we talked first of 'social security' – a universalist provision protecting all sections of the populace. Now we use the language of 'welfare' adopted from the US and with it all the freighted notions of the scrounging underclass popularised by TV exposés of those on benefits. From this perspective, those who need social security – I would say 'depend' on it but for the political use of the term 'dependency' to signify some failure of will and character – are placed on society's margins and stigmatised. 'Council estates' – the preferred term for the negative connotations it carries despite the huge changes in the social housing sector – take their place in this dystopic pantheon.

The practice of welfarisation has taken a number of forms in recent years, but perhaps the most powerful has been the attempt to end lifetime security of tenure for those living in social housing, made first by the Conservative-Liberal Democrat coalition government in office from 2010 to 2015 and latterly by the Conservatives alone. Technically, lifetime security only came into place in 1980 – a by-product of Right to Buy. The understanding was always that tenants who paid their rent and otherwise behaved responsibly enjoyed a home for life though they have, of course, always been subject to eviction for breaches of their conditions of tenancy. This in itself, to ideologues of the Right, was a form of dependency, inhibiting the ambition and social and geographical mobility appropriate to citizens of a free market. To others, and I remember the late social scientist and geographer Doreen Massey, raised on the Wythenshawe Estate, making this point eloquently at a housing conference, it has offered precisely the security which has enabled their lives to flourish.

In presenting the 2011 Localism Act which empowered social landlords to offer 'flexible', fixed-term tenancies of two to five years in duration, however, ministers offered apparently more pragmatic arguments. (Housing associations already had the right to offer assured short-term shorthold tenancies but this was hedged by the requirement that they also 'offer and issue the most secure form of tenancy compatible with the purpose of the housing and the sustainability of the community'.)[6] It was, the then Housing Minister Grant Shapps suggested, 'no longer right to require that every social tenancy should be for life – regardless of the household's particular circumstances'.[7] Critics pointed to the irony that the threat of losing a council tenancy through an advantageous change of circumstance (new-found employment or a better-paid job, for example) might be a disincentive to precisely the enterprise the legislation was supposed to encourage.

Shapps claimed too that the bill gave councils and housing associations more freedom in managing their housing stock and would allow them, in particular, to address the problem of underoccupancy – the fact that some tenants had more bedrooms than their needs apparently warranted. The latter was not something viewed as a problem in owner-occupied homes, but in the case of social housing the stated aim, as Shapps argued, was to 'create a more flexible system so that scarce public resources can be focused on those who need it most'. The thinly veiled implications of this – that the homes of social housing tenants were regarded as a gift to be granted or withdrawn according to higher interests and that the sector as a whole be reserved to the neediest – hardly need highlighting.

Some of the more aggressively proactive housing associations welcomed the scheme, those labelled by the housing academics Suzanne Fitzpatrick and Beth Watts as either 'interventionists' (keen to 'improve' their tenants and move them on and up) or as 'utility maximisers' (wanting to manage their stock as efficiently and as commercially as possible). More traditional housing associations and Labour-controlled local authorities were generally hostile, while flagship Tory councils such as Wandsworth and Barnet embraced the legislation and its underlying ethos.[8] Overall, however, by 2015 only some 15 per cent of new general needs tenancies were being offered on a fixed-term basis.

This was clearly the wrong sort of 'localism' and, after the 2015 general election, a newly unfettered single-party Conservative government proposed in its 2015 Housing and Planning Bill to *compel* the use of fixed-term, two- to five-year tenancies for nearly all new council house lettings. Powerful opposition in the Lords forced concessions. For certain groups such as older and disabled people, the maximum tenancy period was raised to ten years and it was also accepted that secure tenancies should cover the full period of a child's schooling to the age of nineteen. These were concessions which, although confined to those judged 'vulnerable', confirmed practically the arguments made by those who opposed short-term tenancies more broadly: that it was precisely the security and stability of so-called tenancies for life which enabled individuals and communities to grow.

Another component in the Conservatives' welfarisation agenda came with 'Pay to Stay'. Again, it came with a 'common-sense' proposition – that it was 'simply not fair that hard-working people [were] subsidising the lifestyles of those on higher than average incomes'.[9] Even better, it came with a suitably (in government terms) ugly face – the late Bob Crow who, as the 'union boss' of RMT, was making life difficult for commuters while earning a six-figure, executive salary *and* living in a council house. The *Telegraph* reckoned there were 5,000 others earning over £100,000 similarly placed – an impressive example of council homes promoting social mobility, you might think, though in truth the figures are dubious.[10] The initial plan, announced by Chancellor of the Exchequer George Osborne in the July 2015 Budget, was straightforward: social housing households earning over £40,000 in London and over £31,000 elsewhere in the country would be required to pay the equivalent of local private sector rents.

The Tory-controlled Local Government Association – alongside most working in the housing field – provided the obvious retort: first, that such incomes (particularly where there was more than one breadwinner or a number of dependent children) couldn't properly be considered high-earning; and second, that the proposed rules disincentivised 'hard-working people' and those aspiring to earn more. A study commissioned by the association concluded that the policy would hit 214,000 households across England and that up to 70,000 – unable to afford the new rent levels – would be forced to leave the homes and areas in which they lived.[11] By October, the new Housing Minister Gavin Barwell was suggesting that a tapered system (in which rents rose more gradually in line with incomes) might operate to offset the undeniably drastic effects of the original ill-conceived proposal. One year later, the scheme was scrapped; councils and housing associations were to be given discretion. The government had listened, Barwell claimed. In reality, practicalities had, for once, outweighed ideology.

The ideology remained, however, manifested in the basic assumption that social rented housing was for the poorest, for those who could do no better. Back in 1980, Right to Buy had been the clearest expression of this idea and, in Conservative quarters, it was still viewed – with some justification – as an electoral masterstroke. The coalition had extended its provisions in 2012 – reducing the eligibility period to three years from five and increasing discounts – and had been rewarded by a significant boost in sales from around 2,500 a year to 11,000. By this time it was reckoned that 1.88 million council homes had been lost through Right to Buy since 1980 – around 37 per cent of the total – with just 345,000 new council homes built to replace them in the period.[12] Scotland's devolved government has halted Right to Buy in that country; similar proposals were promulgated in Wales in March 2017.

As council housing households declined, the numbers renting from housing associations rose – to about 2.5 million in total. Going into the 2015 general election, the Conservatives promised Right to Buy 2; legislation which would give housing association tenants the same right to purchase their property as council tenants. Conservative strategists hoped to tap into the same reservoir of 'aspirational' voters which had supposedly backed Thatcher so strongly. For the rest of us, the sweetener was that there would be a one-for-one replacement of homes sold; in London, the new government even promised two 'affordable' homes would replace every one sold. The issue remained how to finance this policy: housing associations would need compensating for the loss of their assets; the new homes promised would need to be paid for. Fortunately, the Conservatives had a cunning plan – the entire scheme was to be paid for by the forced sell-off of 'high-value' council homes which, in turn, would finance their own replacement by lesser value 'affordable' housing (which, incidentally, might include low-cost homes for private sale or shared ownership). That money was doing a lot of work.

The headline deficiency of the scheme – the further loss of genuinely affordable council-rented homes at a time of housing crisis – was obvious, but detailed number-crunching brought it into sharp relief. Shelter estimated that 113,000 council homes across the country would have to be forcibly sold off but, given the exigencies of the housing market, some local authorities would be catastrophically affected. Unsurprisingly, of the twenty councils hardest hit, half were in inner London. In Grenfell's Kensington and Chelsea, fully 97 per cent of council homes breached the 'high-value' threshold; in Westminster 76 per cent. Almost half of Camden's 22,000 council homes would be liable to sell-off. Outside London, Cambridge, York, Leeds and Warwick were among other badly affected authorities.[13] Furthermore, such sell-offs inhibited the possibility of new council housing – why would councils build if they faced the immediate loss of these new homes; why would financial institutions lend as council assets were progressively diminished?

Councils almost universally opposed the proposals; housing associations were surprisingly equivocal, divided between the realpolitik of, typically, the larger and more entrepreneurial associations who wished to curry favour with their political masters and those who remembered their charitable foundations and social purpose. Their trade body, the National Housing Federation, cut a deal and, after a poll of members whose representativeness was queried by some, endorsed a government concession making the Right to Buy element voluntary.[14] In a small-scale pilot of the scheme, would-be purchasers are required to have been resident for ten years rather than the three originally proposed and, to date, only 5 per cent of those eligible have pursued the option.[15] In the meantime, Brexit brought new priorities and new challenges for the government and the more radical politics of housing reform was put on the back-burner.

Those basic Conservative instincts, represented in the long-running commitment to a gold standard of owner occupation, were obvious in the 2015 election when David Cameron pledged to deliver 200,000 so-called Starter Homes – available to first-time buyers under forty at 20 per cent below local market rates – by 2020. Shelter's invaluable research team again exposed the limitations, the essential dishonesty, of the proposals. Families on the National Living Wage could afford a Starter Home in only one in fifty local authorities; Starter Homes would be unaffordable to households on average wages in almost 60 per cent of local authorities.[16] The difficulties of enforcing the strict planning stipulations which the scheme required and the resistance of the private building sector led, once more, to a flagship, ideologically driven policy being diluted, and in this case, to all intents and purposes, abandoned. The January 2017 Housing White Paper announced that 200,000 new homeowners would instead be created through a broader range of measures including loan guarantee schemes and shared ownership.

The determination of Conservative governments to restrict the supply of the one genuine form of affordable housing – social housing – as waiting lists lengthened was perhaps impressive testimony to their core beliefs and principles. Some critics saw lower political motives. Nick Clegg, Liberal Democrat deputy prime minister in the coalition, recalls a leadership meeting at which he proposed building more social housing:

One of them [David Cameron or George Osborne] – I honestly can't remember whom – looked genuinely nonplussed and said, 'I don't understand why you keep going on about the need for more social housing – it just creates Labour voters.' They genuinely saw housing as a Petri dish for voters. It was unbelievable.[17]

But for all the desperate but ineffectual measures to promote home ownership and a Conservative-inclined property-owning democracy, owner occupation is in decline. The *English Housing Survey* of 2015 – 16 showed 63 per cent of households as owner-occupiers (29 per cent of households were, in fact, mortgagors) – a fall of 8 per cent since numbers peaked in 2003 and the lowest level of home ownership for almost thirty years. The number of private renters had exceeded those in social housing four years earlier for the first time since such records began in 1980. In 1980, a little over 31 per cent of households were social renters (then, of course, they rented overwhelmingly from the council) and just 11.9 from the private sector. In 2015 – 26, the 4.5 million households renting privately accounted for one in five of all households; 3.9 million households – 17 per cent – rented from social landlords.[18]

Currently, the government pays around £9.3 billion a year in Housing Benefit to private landlords supporting some 1.5 million households, almost half of whom are in work. If all these people were renting socially, we'd be saving £1.5 billion on benefits payments at a time when the country is investing just £1.2 billion annually on building new 'affordable' housing.[19] If you factor in the calculation that every new social home built generates an additional £108,000 for the economy and creates 2.3 jobs, it's merely understated to argue, in the words of one social housing pressure group, that 'making a long-term switch of public spending from Housing Benefit into bricks and mortar would make social and financial sense'.[20]

Of course, there have been efforts to cut spending on social security. The coalition's 2012 Welfare Reform Act introduced the bedroom tax; in this case, the government's preferred euphemism, the 'removal of the spare room subsidy', never caught on. Social housing tenants with one bedroom deemed surplus faced a 14 per cent hike in rents; tenants with two or more, 25 per cent. Two children of the same gender under sixteen were expected to share a room, likewise two children under ten regardless of gender. The ostensible rationale was to free up larger homes for those in overcrowded or otherwise inadequate accommodation as those who occupied them 'unnecessarily' were encouraged to move. The question as to where – with our public housing stock so grossly diminished – these smaller homes might be found was largely left unanswered.

From April 2013, an estimated 600,000 households – around one-third of all social housing tenants on Housing Benefit – faced an average cut of between £14 and £25 in their weekly benefit. To pay the rent, to maintain their tenancies, this shortfall had to be made up from their own pockets. To disabled people who needed a 'spare' room to store equipment or simply to provide a quieter haven for non-disabled partners, to families who couldn't reasonably expect their younger children to share a room, to those who quite simply needed a space for visiting children, relatives and friends, to all those with a right to expect this small token of a civilised and decent society, the policy was potentially disastrous. And to all its victims, typically among the poorest of our community already, it was financially punitive.

These obvious judgements hardly need proof but the scheme's operation has amply justified its many critics. A National Housing Federation survey found over half of those affected had 'often' run out of money, one in four had gone without meals, one in five had cut back on heating.[21] Another, academic, study revealed the human stories behind the bare statistics:

The money that we get, the bills comes out of that and we don't have a lot for food. So we both go on sort of, like, days . . . weeks where we don't get enough food in for ourselves . . . We've lived on, and that's the honest truth, at Christmas, we've lived on just tins of soup.

I got pneumonia twice. I was in hospital for ten days once . . . I was really ill . . . because I hadn't put my heating on . . . and obviously if you haven't got much money and the bills are high anyway you tend to not put the heating on . . . I find I do spend a lot of time in bed . . . if you're asleep, one, you're not using the water, two, you're not using the electricity, you're not using the gas, and then I'm not eating the food that is there.[22]

The legislation's impact on health and well-being was obvious and predictable. Conversely, the requirement announced in 2015 that all registered providers of social housing reduce rents by 1 per cent annually over four years might, in another context, have been portrayed as some kind of gift to social renters. The reality, as Chancellor of the Exchequer George Osborne had the grace to admit, was that it was another effort to cut spending on Housing Benefit. It had, however, the collateral impact of further reducing the capital available for reinvesting in social housing. Genesis – admittedly one of the new breed of more commercially minded housing associations which probably didn't need too much incentive to recalibrate its priorities – announced it would cut the amount of social rent homes it was building in order to concentrate on shared ownership and homes for market rent and sale.[23]

Meanwhile, market rents became unaffordable to many more on Housing Benefit as a result of the 2016 Welfare Reform and Work Act which reduced the benefits cap to £23,000 in London households and £20,000 for those outside the capital. This 'incentive to find work' as the Department of Work and Pensions described it, was predicted to affect 116,000 families (and some 320,000 children) across the UK and make, in swathes of the country, private rented housing unaffordable to those in receipt of social security.[24] Increased pressure on local councils to rehouse those declared statutorily homeless and, in practice, increased use of temporary, bed-and-breakfast-style accommodation to house them were consequences that a government committed to pursuing an austerity agenda at the expense of the poorest deemed acceptable.

I've made a point throughout this book of calling council homes just that – homes, not the planners' term 'dwellings', still less the bureaucratic term 'units'. However, we now have a state which, while it once promised its citizens security, seems to be offering – and valuing – *insecurity*. One testimony, from a victim of the bedroom tax, can stand here for something more general: 'I felt like I will be kicked out from the house. It's horrible, you know . . . we love this house. We made it how we like, and now it will be a disaster for me to move somewhere else.'[25]

The latest iteration of the regeneration agenda and, in particular, the description of estates as 'brownfield sites', offer a clear demonstration of this new mindset around social housing and its community. This was the language embraced in one of the most influential of recent interventions in the current housing debate, *City Villages*, published by the 'progressive think-tank' the Institute of Public Policy Research in 2015. The pamphlet addressed the housing crisis in London and the South-East and was premised on the need drastically to increase the capital's housing supply. 'Densification' – more units (I'll use the jargon here) occupying less land – was the preferred solution and in the eyes of Andrew Adonis (one can almost see their technocratic gleam), the report's lead author, the means was obvious: the large-scale demolition and subsequent redevelopment of London's council estates:

> Southwark council owns 43 per cent of the land in its borough, mostly council estates. This includes 10,000 garages. Across inner London, councils commonly own 25–30 per cent of the land in their borough. These municipal landholdings translate into a huge number of individual estates. Islington council alone owns about 150 council estates of 50 homes or more . . . on some of the most expensive land in the world.[26]

Of course, the authors offered something more than a rapacious developers' perspective on this twenty-first-century grand project. They talked the language of sustainability, of 'neighbourhoods', of street life and a confident urbanism, but that bottom line kept creeping in. Estates were 'valuable reservoirs of increasingly scarce land in a global city', according to Yolande Barnes, Savills' Director of World Research.[27] And councils which genuinely wanted to build new social housing were quite clear that it could only be achieved through the release of private capital. As Jules Pipe and Philip Glanville (respectively Labour mayor and cabinet member for housing in Hackney) argued:

> Given the squeeze on capital budgets, local authorities in London cannot build homes for social renting without cross-subsidising them by also building private sale properties. In Hackney, delivering shared ownership pays for itself, but to finance a social rent home demands the construction and sale of one and a half private homes.[28]

That may also reflect contemporary wisdom around the desirability of mixed tenure estates but, fundamentally, it's an honest and realistic appraisal of the contemporary state of play. Many will understand that Labour councillors who want to achieve something in office must play this game, but the veto on cost-effective public sector investment is increasingly questioned and the role of social rented housing as a prime means of providing genuinely affordable housing more strongly asserted.

That might be deemed an ideological argument – though this book reminds us how non-ideological the case for council housing has been for most of its lifetime – but the overall case advanced by *City Villages* was flawed in many ways. For one, it simply gets modern social housing estates wrong. It ignores the beneficial renovations and improvements many have already experienced and ignores the fact that, with between one-third and a half of their homes lost to Right to Buy, they are already mixed estates. For another, its sweeping vision catastrophically downplays the sheer, life-changing, sometimes life-threatening, disruption caused by this form of regeneration. It's telling that the report ignores other development options, notably those which might affect middle-class areas and interests. Perhaps they are seen as too difficult when you have working-class homes which are apparently so much more susceptible to some brusque social engineering. As Duncan Bowie, an academic with decades of hands-on housing and planning experience in London, concludes:

> the proposal is ill-informed, not cost-effective in terms of use of public resources, socially divisive, damaging to the social and economic sustainability of London and highly disruptive in terms of the impacts on tens of thousands – possibly hundreds of thousands of lower income Londoners.[29]

We could pass over this episode if it weren't so redolent of a particular worldview with growing acceptance among the political classes. Savills supplied their own report, *Completing London's Streets*, with a more explicit programme of demolishing the 'old blocks of flats' with 'new streets of terraced housing and mid-rise mansion blocks' to the Cabinet Office in January 2016.[30] And a week later David Cameron vowed to 'blitz' poverty by demolishing a hundred of the 'UK's worst sink estates'.[31] To be fair, Cameron acknowledged the 'warm and welcoming homes' to be found on those estates 'but step outside', he continued, 'and you're confronted by concrete slabs dropped from on high, brutal high-rise towers and dark alleyways that are a gift to criminals and drug dealers'. Equally concerning to Cameron was 'how cut-off, self-governing and divorced from the mainstream these communities can become'.[32]

In other words, and contradictorily combining both a blatant disregard for how right-wing policies had helped create the conditions he now decried and an ignorance of the realities which challenged his crude portrayal, he launched into a rehash of every cliché and stereotype – and the tired causal analysis which underpinned them – laid at the door of so-called 'sink estates' since the 1970s. Most commentators concluded that Cameron's mission – 'social turnaround . . . with massive estate regeneration, tenants protected and land unlocked for new housing all over Britain' – was unlikely to be achieved with the paltry £140 million 'pump-priming' investment he promised. Six months later, he resigned as prime minister with history recording as his signature achievement Britain's departure from the European Union. Ten months after that, the man he appointed to oversee this apparently ambitious programme, Michael Heseltine, was himself dismissed by Cameron's successor, Theresa May, for being disobliging about the Brexit process she was now overseeing. We can assume that Cameron's intervention achieved its main object – a few easy headlines – and will go no further or, rather, that it will be folded into the long-running and ongoing programme of estate regeneration and redevelopment of which he seemed strangely unaware.

The 'big ideas' outlined above are really little more than an intellectual gloss on a process well underway and likely to continue. Regeneration is not in itself a bad thing; in many cases (some we have looked at), it's a good thing where estates have been refurbished and improved, new facilities added, lives enriched. Take Broadwater Farm in Tottenham, north London – a Haringey estate begun in 1967 comprising 1,063 homes in twelve precast concrete blocks and towers. In recent years, in the words of an active residents' association, 'huge amounts have been spent on providing concierge suites, new roofs and windows, providing a Community Centre and many other facilities'.[33] Despite that, it was one of the estates unofficially identified in Cameron's hit list but, then, Broadwater Farm has a history.

It was the scene in October 1985 of riots and the tragic killing of PC Keith Blakelock (Winston Silcott and others initially found guilty of his murder were later cleared). Those riots were triggered by the death through heart failure of a black woman, Cynthia Jarrett, during a police raid on her flat near the estate, and came one week after the police shooting and death of another black woman, Cherry Groce, in Brixton. There were riots again in Tottenham in August 2011 after the police shot Mark Duggan, an estate resident, and allegedly mistreated an initially peaceful vigil protesting the killing outside Tottenham Police Station. Five days of looting and violence followed in urban centres across the country. An agonised inquest followed, but one ready response among Conservative politicians such as Iain Duncan Smith was to blame 'ghettoised' council estates.[34] The analysis was reprised by Cameron as he launched his 'blitz' on poverty:

> The riots of 2011 didn't emerge from within terraced streets or low-rise apartment buildings. As spatial analysis of the riots has shown, the rioters came overwhelmingly from these post-war estates. Almost three-quarters of those convicted lived within them. That's not a coincidence.[35]

There was some academic support for this argument in London, at least where there appeared to be a correlation between the location of rioting and the proximity of 'large post-war housing estates', amplified by the fact that a disproportionate number of those convicted came from those estates. Space Syntax argues that such estates created 'over-complex, and as a result, under-used spaces . . . populated by large groups of unsupervised children and teenagers where peer socialisation can occur between them without the supervision of adults' – a sophisticated version of the Defensible Space thesis.[36] It's hard not to see this, however, in part at least, as testimony to the old adage, 'as ye seek, so shall ye find'. Wider, national studies found a broader cross-section of rioters who themselves cited a wide array of causal factors: sheer opportunism was one, the chance of 'shopping for free' as looting was described; an inchoate sense of grievance motivated by the disparities of affluence and poverty was another. But what stood out most was a widespread resentment of police behaviour – 'a lack of respect as well as anger at what was felt to be discriminatory treatment'.[37] These explanations were borne out in a close study of the rioting which took place on the Pendleton Estate in Salford: the riots were a 'response, albeit lacking in a formal political articulation, to perceived injustices that relate to poverty, exclusion and oppressive policing'.[38]

At any rate, the reflex to blame the design of modernist council estates seems simplistic – and too convenient to those politicians seeking not only a scapegoat to blame for social disorder but an opportunity for a little real estate redevelopment. The charge of 'ghettoisation' has greater weight but it contains both a truth – as the preceding pages have demonstrated – and a further simplification. Social housing estates may well be one of the most potent symbols of current inequalities – though their reality is more diverse and complex – but the Brexit vote showed how widely felt are feelings of alienation and exclusion.

Besides, despite the focus on and criticism of large-scale, modernist 1960s estates, taken as archetypical, they are far from the norm. All London estates, in *City Villages* terms, occupy valuable land ripe for densification, even the very best. We noted two such examples in Lambeth in Chapter 6 – Cressingham Gardens and Central Hill – both now threatened with demolition and redevelopment. The architectural and design quality of Cressingham Gardens needs no restatement; its build quality too – some necessary upgrades and continued maintenance for housing now approaching its fifth decade notwithstanding. But, above all, it is a successful and thriving community. In 2013, an independent council-commissioned survey found that 81 per cent of residents wanted to stay in their homes.[39] (Given that the 10 per cent who wished to move wanted either bigger homes or were fearful of the disruption of redevelopment, this represented near-unanimity.) That community has mobilised

powerfully in defence of the estate and has pursued every political and legal means to challenge the council's plans. Currently,
with the High Court rejecting a judicial review of Lambeth's
decision in December 2016, that resistance seems doomed,
though the fight continues. Tenants face the loss of their current
homes and secure tenancies and rent hikes; inadequately
compensated leaseholders wishing to remain on the remodelled
estate need find either £200,000 to buy an equivalent property
or accept some form of shared ownership or rental arrangement.[40] Likewise Central Hill for which, despite widespread
and persistent resident protest, the council reaffirmed its decision to demolish and redevelop in March 2017. In both cases,
residents and housing activists have created alternative plans
which would both save and improve existing homes and allow
for sensitive infill new build.

If you're searching for a single site to study the current
dynamics of social housing, albeit a London version writ large,
the West Hendon Estate in Barnet is as good as any. Even its
current rebranding as Hendon Waterside (it's next to the Welsh
Harp reservoir) might tell you all you need to know, but the
bigger story is worth exploring in a little more detail.

The estate is – or was – a late 1960s system-built mix of one-
bed flats, two-bed maisonettes and three-bed houses; 680 in
total. If you visit it now, you'll see the new private apartments
of the twenty-six-storey Vista point block and some smaller
side-kicks, a large building site, and some remaining run-down
council blocks sliding into an accelerated obsolescence. Some
have already been demolished; the rest await that fate. The
placards on the builders' hoardings promise a concierge service
and fitness centre for the new private residents and a gleaming
artist's impression of the future. For the council tenants and

leaseholders who survive, the present offers only disruption and decline and that future looks desperately uncertain.

It was an estate with problems, those common to many: 'high levels of deprivation' among residents and the design flaws held typical of such designs of the era – 'poorly defined public and private space . . . lack of natural surveillance on public routes' and so on.[41] And back in 2002 the council, then in Labour-Liberal Democrat hands, promised residents (about 700 secure council tenants and 140 leaseholders then) 'the phased redevelopment' of the estate with 'modern homes for all existing residents, set in a new urban environment'.[42] West Hendon needed work; the council claimed an £11.5 million price tag for bringing the estate up to the Decent Homes Standard. Three-quarters of those balloted – accepting the like-for-like pledge of new homes offered – were happy to offer an 'in principle' endorsement. Outline planning permission was granted by the council, now in Conservative control, to the Metropolitan Housing Trust in 2004; a development partnership with Barratt Homes was formed in 2006. Revised master plans and planning applications followed.

Now, the Barratt Homes scheme promises just 543 'affordable' homes of which only 256 are available for social rent. Remaining secure tenants in the council blocks demolished to date have been 'decanted' to a traffic island tower block. Many have left the estate, effectively forced from it by the physical and emotional turmoil of the drawn-out regeneration process. They have been replaced by homeless families without security of tenure and conveniently, therefore, ineligible for any guarantee of in situ rehousing. Leaseholders have been offered paltry compensation and many of these too have opted to relocate. In all, the residents' campaign group, Our West Hendon, estimates that 95 per cent of those originally occupying the estate

The developers' vision of Hendon Waterside

will have been forced out.[43] Meanwhile a two-bed flat in the Hendon Waterside scheme, with the prime views of the Welsh Harp Reservoir once accorded to council tenants, can be yours for £492,000.

The description, the facts and figures, can convey only inadequately the human cost of this ongoing saga. That reality was vividly portrayed by Jackie Coleman, a long-term resident, at a public inquiry into the scheme in January 2015:

> You are displacing a whole community. You make it like you are building for us, but it's for the private sector. It's not fair. When we signed that pledge, it was like for like. All of a sudden I have lost all my neighbours. Yes, it's going to be beautiful, but no-one I know will live there. The social landscape will have changed.[44]

Such regeneration protests have become common in London in recent years. To the west in Hammersmith, lie the West Kensington and Gibbs Green Estates – mixed development estates completed in 1974 and 1961 respectively – whose residents have been campaigning since 2009 against a massive £12 billion redevelopment scheme which proposes to clear and redevelop not only their homes but the Earls Court Exhibition Centres and London Underground's Lillie Bridge depot. Of the 7,500 new flats proposed by principal developers Capco, 760 are intended as replacements for housing lost on the two estates and just 740 further are designated 'affordable', though these – to be rented or sold at 65 per cent market level – are in fact aimed squarely at those on middle incomes.[45] Although a more sympathetic Labour-controlled council was elected in 2014 (returned in part on the back of its commitment to defend the estates), the residents' preferred option remains to secure the estates by transferring their ownership to a resident-controlled community housing association. They too have a 'People's Plan' that would both defend and renovate their existing homes while adding to overall housing stock – in this case, adding 250 new homes for sale on the open market to pay for the estates' upgrades and seventy new social rented homes.[46] It's a recognition of the new economics but an indication that it can be sympathetically applied.

The spate of high-profile housing struggles in recent years testify to the dysfunctionality of the London housing market. Often it's been councils in the firing line – Barnet as we've seen, but most famously in Newham. In 2013 a group of media-friendly 'young mums', evicted from a housing association scheme for the vulnerable homeless in the borough and facing removal by the council to bed-and-breakfast accommodation across the country, occupied Newham's Carpenters Estate, largely emptied as part of a long-running redevelopment scheme. Their slogan 'People Need Homes; These Homes Need People' acquired a powerful resonance; their campaign secured the local rehousing of twenty-nine young mothers and permission to reuse, temporarily at least, four of the estate's empty blocks.

But other housing providers also reflect these powerful local dynamics. The New Era Estate in Hoxton was an anomalous development – interwar four-storey blocks comprising ninety-six flats and twelve retail units, privately built and rented, a more Spartan version of the council schemes of the era. When the estate was sold to the American pension fund manager Westbrook Partners in 2014, residents faced an immediate 17 per cent rise on £600 monthly rents which, to that point, had been broadly equivalent to their social housing equivalents. They were warned to expect further increases – to around £2,400, deemed the market rate for the area. Powerful protests by the community – supported by local resident Russell Brand – eventually saw the estate purchased by Dolphin Living Ltd, a not-for-profit housing association committed to pegging rents to residents' ability to pay.

The Northwold Estate, also in Hackney, is a predominantly interwar LCC scheme – comprising 580 flats (around 140 purchased under Right to Buy) in five five-storey balcony-access blocks and one 1967 addition in similar form, housing around 1,700 people. It was transferred to the Guinness Partnership housing association in 2009 which is planning the demolition of some of the blocks and their replacement by a denser scheme including homes for sale. Reassurances that tenants will receive a like-for-like replacement of their demolished homes and no decrease, even the promise of a net increase, in social housing, are not believed by protesting residents. Lead campaigner Emily Jost articulates their concerns and speaks for many affected by similar proposals:

> the bottom line is we don't want our homes demolished. We're not against change – we know there needs to be refurbishment and improvements because some blocks have been neglected for a really long time. But most of the homes are good homes. Knocking them down will disrupt the community and change the estate forever.[47]

There are perhaps no obvious villains in these various stories (or not always), and in this form it is very much a London phenomenon where population growth and high property values are creating both pressures and incentives to build. Occasionally, there may even be good guys. The ongoing regeneration of the low-rise, 1960s, deck-access blocks of the Bacton Estate in Camden is the scheme most often hailed as exemplary. Genuine consultation by the council and architects with an active and engaged tenants and residents' association is one reason. A first phase – Housing Project of the Year in the 2016 Building Awards – which saw forty-six new council homes (managed in-house by Camden) completed and twenty-one for sale – was another. The overall scheme envisages replacing the ninety-nine council flats (twelve now privately owned) with 293 new homes, including twenty additional council-rented homes. The broad economics remains the same; the good intentions – if fulfilled – of the politicians may make a difference. Upgrading social housing costs money and new social housing requires capital. But the common feature is that, in the new bottom line, estates represent real estate; real estate whose value seems easily captured by clearance and new build, and new build, furthermore, which can provide the new Holy Grail: mixed tenure.

We will end this account with that new build, a small renaissance of council housing – more or less – in a very changed world. One significant factor in this was the reforms announced by Gordon Brown's Labour government in 2009 – enacted in the coalition government's 2011 Localism Act and implemented in 2012 – relating to local authorities' Housing Revenue Accounts (HRAs). Since the 1980s, though nominally ring-fenced (councils were prohibited from cross-subsiding housing or other expenditure through budgetary transfers), central government rules required that local authorities pay a proportion of their housing rental and sales income towards a notional national housing debt.

If that sounds arcane, its impact wasn't. Shelter estimated in 2009 that of the £6.6 billion annual income of local government HRAs, around £1.1 billion was collected by the Treasury. Of the £6.2 billion amassed from Right to Buy sales since 2004, £4.7 billion had gone to the Treasury which redirected it to general spending.[48] Ring-fencing clearly worked only one way. In return for directly taking on an allocated proportion of national housing debt, councils were given full control of their housing stock and the income and expenditures relating to it. Around £28 billion of housing debt was transferred to the 169 local authorities which still owned housing. So long as they paid the allocated debt interest, those councils now retained their rental income in full, had freedom in how to spend it and benefited from increased powers to borrow. In 2012, the Local Government Association estimated that councils might collectively borrow around £3 billion to build 15,000 new homes over the next five years.[49]

That turned out to be optimistic, mitigated by subsequent government policies extending Right to Buy and reducing social housing rents. Within this overall regime some councils are, nevertheless, finding ways of building new council homes; in one account, by March 2017, some 180 local authorities were engaged in some form of housing provision.[50] Needless to say, the vast majority were not using traditional means – monies drawn from central government grants and the Housing Revenue Account – but rather by a bewildering range (twenty-seven were counted in all) of other financial models. The threat that new homes built would be lost to Right to Buy or even by Conservative proposals to force the sale of high-value council homes remains a serious one but, for the time being, means seem to have been found to avert this danger.

The factors behind this are varied. Unfortunately, given the necessarily piecemeal efforts of local councils, sheer demand was not the primary one. Government figures showed 1.8 million households in England alone on local authority social housing waiting lists in 2016. This was actually a fall of almost 700,000 on the 2012 peak – the reduction accounted for not by any upsurge in those being housed but by stringent council efforts to purge their lists.[51] The rising costs of homelessness were one pressing incentive. In 2016 it was estimated that councils across Britain had spent £3.5 billion in the past five years on temporary accommodation for homeless families.[52] One hopes the sheer inhumanity and inadequacy of such accommodation was another. This particular and sharply focused housing crisis led some councils to buy back homes previously sold under Right to Buy. Islington, for example, spent £6.2 million on acquiring twenty-five former council homes sold for £1.2 million and Wakefield, £2.5 million on thirty-five homes sold for £981,000.[53]

By far the largest and most controversial current redevelopment scheme under discussion is the £2 billion Haringey Development Vehicle. Ownership of a large swathe of council-owned land and property – council offices, its commercial portfolio, a care home, library and the Northumberland Park housing estate – will be transferred to a private company owned fifty–fifty by Haringey and the developers Lendlease, an ownership split held to guarantee council control over the process. To the council, which claims to have lost £160 million in funding since 2016 and can borrow only £50 million to build new housing, the imperative to capitalise on its assets and act commercially seemed unavoidable.[54] In backing the scheme, London's Labour mayor, Sadiq Khan, was also clear that 'reductions in government funding, rising land values, and the need for more affordable housing mean that we have to look at solutions that are different to those that may have worked in the past'.[55] The promise, according to Claire Kober, the council's Labour leader, was not only new jobs and 'the modern, high-quality homes that residents deserve' but 'thriving town centres and strong, mixed communities'. To critics, the scheme is little more than 'zombie Blairism' predicated on an apparent belief that 'the best way to relieve an area of poverty is to kick out the poor people who live there'.[56]

Typically, housing is the fulcrum of this dispute. The council pledges 5,000 new homes of which 40 per cent will be 'genuinely affordable'. That term remains somewhat nebulous and hugely contentious. It has also provided current tenants of the Northumberland Estate with an 'absolute guarantee' of a new home on the estate on the same tenure terms and at the same rents. Given that the redevelopment of the estate will be skewed towards larger family homes and that the 'net increase in homes will be skewed towards other tenures', this too is problematic, deliverable only if some tenants choose not to return.[57] Given that the overall project is planned to take up to twenty years, at best the jury is out.

Neighbouring Camden, on the other hand, is able as a result of its high rental income to borrow without a private sector partner. Its current fifteen-year Community Investment Programme aims to provide 3,050 new homes by 2025 across twenty schemes of which around 335 will be for shared owner-ship and 1,650 for private sale. In May 2017, council critics calculated to date that 400 council homes had been demolished and just 278 built; in response, the Labour council reaffirmed its long-term strategy to 'deliver a 50-50 balance between afford-able homes and the private flats that fund them'.[58] Of the latter, the 273 flats built by the council for sale at prices ranging from £450,000 to £685,000 on the regenerated Maiden Lane Estate – 'Scandi-style apartments . . . well-crafted, restrained, crisp and contemporary' with a promised twenty-four-hour concierge service – are the most striking illustration of the entrepreneuri-alism which increasingly shapes local government activities.[59]

Stroud District Council in Gloucestershire, run by a Labour-Liberal Democrat-Green coalition, has found £38 million to invest in new council housing and the refurbishment of existing estates by making interest-only payments on its debts.[60] According to its head of tenant services, they estimate they can build twenty new council homes a year: 'It's not huge numbers but it's a start.'[61] Gateshead Metropolitan Borough is pursuing what is currently the more favoured vehicle – a joint venture partnership with private developers and a local housing associ-ation. Evolution Gateshead, as the consortium is called, proposes to build 2,400 new homes on nineteen sites in the district, their balance between social rented and privately owned remains unclear.

In fairness, we should return to Lambeth, the desecrator of Cressingham Garden and Central Hill. The positive side of the council's agenda is a programme to build 1,000 new council homes in the borough, where there are '21,000 people . . . on the waiting list for social housing, over 1,850 homeless families and 1,300 families in severely overcrowded accommodation'.[62] The means is a Special Purpose Vehicle, Homes for Lambeth: a private but wholly council-owned company which has the benefits of keeping profits in-house (normally this 15–20 per cent margin goes to private developers) and excluding newly built properties from Right to Buy provisions.[63] There remain powerful concerns. The human and financial costs to residents of regenerated estates is the obvious one and the level of the 'social target rents' (Lambeth's term and presumably higher than council rents) of Lambeth's new properties is another.[64]

Southwark's large-scale programme, aiming to build some 11,000 new council homes, has, with the demolition of the Heygate Estate, the wider redevelopment of the Elephant and Castle area, and the proposed demolition of the Aylesbury, been even more controversial. Southwark has chosen to work hand in glove with a range of private developers to further these plans. The dangers of this arrangement – savvy, lawyered-up corporations juxtaposed with poorly resourced local authorities – seem borne out by Southwark's experience of the Heygate scheme where the Australian property giant Lendlease walked away with large (though undisclosed) profits and the council, which had sold the land for the giveaway price of £50 million, ended up with virtually nothing.[65] As the architectural critic, Rowan Moore, concluded:

Southwark Council has been played by developers. It has had its tummy tickled, arm twisted and arse kicked. It has got a poor deal in return for its considerable assets, multiple promises have been broken and violence done to the lives of many who lived there.[66]

Perhaps history will judge Southwark more kindly as its full programme unfolds. In the meantime, it is the council's presence at *Le marché international des professionnels de l'immobilier* – the annual Cannes development fest better known as MIPIM – which symbolises the new nexus of property and profit in which many local authorities now feel compelled to participate.

You'll find a wide range of smaller and less controversial schemes across the country – five new council homes in Shoeburyness built by Southend; new 'homes for social rent' in Berkhamsted, Tring and Hemel Hempstead, as well as a forty-one-bedroom state-of-the-art homeless hostel built by Dacorum Borough Council; twelve houses in Bungay built by Waveney District Council; 274 homes built by the ALMO Nottingham City Homes for the City Council; new council housing in York, Brighton, Bristol, Corby, Wolverhampton, Barnsley, Leeds and so on.

Each of these – and the truly affordable and secure homes developed within larger programmes – is a cause for celebration. They represent a small recalibration and a significant – though inadequate – recognition of the role local government can play in providing the decent homes our people so desperately need.

It seemed in the 2017 general election that that recognition might extend across the major parties. A left-wing Labour Party led by Jeremy Corbyn pledged to suspend Right to Buy and build 'at least 100,000 council and housing association homes a year for genuinely affordable rent or sale'.[67] The

Liberal Democrats promised to 'directly build homes to fill the gap left by the market' with the support of a 'new government-backed British Housing and Infrastructure Development Bank'.[68] And, most surprisingly, even the Conservatives conceded that 'we will never achieve the numbers of new houses we require without the active participation of social and municipal housing providers'. That Damascene conversion was not, however, all it appeared. These were to be 'new fixed-term social houses . . . sold privately after ten to fifteen years with an automatic Right to Buy for tenants' (though with a promise that proceeds would 'be recycled into further homes').[69] Then it turned out that these so-called social homes would be let at so-called 'affordable' rents of up to 80 per cent of the market rate.[70] The precarious minority Conservative government which emerged therefore offers little prospect of any revival of social housing fortunes, still less those of the council housing sector.

In the longer term, there may have been a significant shift in our politics. (Grenfell's role in that remains to be seen.) Against all expectations, Corbyn's Labour, running on a radical anti-austerity agenda, won significant support among a broad electorate. For the first time, the neoliberal dogma which has dominated British government since 1979 seems under threat. Most voters don't think in those terms but many have come to question an economic programme whose prescription for success seemed to rest quite explicitly on the premise that the rich should get richer while the poor get poorer. And they voted in defence of public services reeling from the impact of successive real-term cuts. They voted, in short, for a state which offered succour not pain or perhaps, as Labour claimed, hope not fear. It is time to reclaim the positive role of the state.

In the end, despite those manifesto promises, housing did not play a large part in the 2017 election campaign, but a housing crisis remains in varying forms across the country. And there is a growing and rediscovered acceptance of the role the national and local state can and should play in tackling that crisis. Historically, councils have made an enormous contribution to meeting our housing needs and, in so doing, they have transformed the lives of many millions for the better. Not every new council home was a 'Buckingham Palace' to its new residents, though many were, but to nearly all those who lived in them council housing has provided a decent and secure home. Council housing's record has been much maligned. The form and nature of council housing has been unfairly blamed for problems entrenched in our unequal society and exacerbated by the politics which reflect it. There are indications that public opinion is changing; that, as the failure of the free market to provide good and affordable homes to all those who need them becomes increasingly obvious (the very reason why council housing emerged in the late nineteenth century), many people are revisiting both the past contribution of public housing and its current necessity.

I hope a fuller and more nuanced understanding of both past achievements and current follies may yet shift this politics and allow our municipal dreams to flourish once more.

Acknowledgements

This book was born from a blog started some four years ago to champion the unsung but enormously important pioneering reforms of local government. Over time, as our contemporary housing crisis deepened and its politics grew more fraught, it increasingly focused on council housing as, in the words of the Conservatives' 1951 election manifesto, 'the first of the social services'.

I'd like to thank early supporters of the blog, who include the novelist Linda Grant, historian Helen Rogers of Liverpool John Moores University, historian and activist Ken Worpole, architectural historian Gillian Darley, Michael Edwards of the Bartlett School, and all the good people at SHOUT (Social Housing Under Threat – the Campaign for Social Housing) among whom were Alison Inman, Tim Morton and Tom Murtha. Steve Hilditch of the Red Brick blog on housing policy also spread the word. Their encouragement and interest were a huge boost to my efforts and the success of the blog. Apologies to anyone I've missed out here but every new 'follower', every re-tweet and every supportive comment (as well as some critical ones) helped me write and extend the blog and develop the understanding and knowledge which informs this book.

In this context, I should make a special mention of those past and present residents who have commented on the estates I've written about, all of whom knew them better than me and who, incidentally, in nearly all cases, had positive views of their council homes.

The blog and this book would have been impossible without the expertise of many others. My thanks to the blogger Single Aspect, to Ronnie Hughes for sharing his knowledge of his home city of Liverpool, and to Jane Brake and John Aitken for their hospitality in Salford. The contributions of academic researchers and scholars are too numerous to mention but are recorded in the endnotes. A special thank you to Mark Swenarton (whose essential book, Cook's Camden, came out too late for inclusion in this book) who was personally supportive and helpful.

Much of the detail of the blog and book has depended on the invaluable services of our local history libraries and archives whose work, sadly, is now too often threatened by the swingeing cuts affecting local government provision across the board. A big thank you, in particular, to Malcolm Barr-Hamilton and the staff of my local archives in Tower Hamlets. The RIBA Library, with its welcoming approach to non-affiliated researchers, has also been vital. The British Library hardly needs my personal imprimatur but it's a wonderful resource that should be treasured.

John Grindrod, a lovely man and a fine writer whose books have been a source of inspiration, very generously gave his time and expertise as I set out on the road to publication. My thanks to Nicholas Blincoe for helping me take the next step.

I'm grateful to the team at Verso for making the whole process relatively painless. I'm hugely indebted, in particular, to my editor, Leo Hollis, for his belief in the book and his painstaking, constructively critical reading of earlier drafts. He's made it a much better book.

Finally, I offer my love and gratitude to my wife Michele Grant. She suggested the blog, encouraged the book and has, quite simply, been a rock in my life. As Gillian Darley once remarked, she put the 'dreams' into 'municipal'. This book would not have been possible without her.

Illustration Credits

All attempts were made to contact the original rights holders to obtain their permission for the use of copyrighted material. The publisher apologises for any errors or omissions and would be grateful if notified of any correction to be incorporated in future reprints or editions of this book.

All images, other than those noted below, were taken by the author and remain in his copyright.

Page 36. 'An aerial view of the Becontree Estate, c1930.'

Page 45. 'Barry Parker's plan for the Wythenshawe Estate, Manchester.' Originally published in Dugald MacFadyen, *Sir Ebenezer Howard and the Town Planning Movement* (Manchester University Press, 1933).

Page 71. 'The Town Planning Group County of London Plan poster from Stalag Luft III.' With thanks to Ellie, Katya and Jessica Duffy. © Estate of Phillip Bear.

Page 110. 'Castle Vale Estate, Birmingham, 1968.' Originally published in the *Birmingham Mail*, 26 June 2014.

Page 140. 'The Hulme Crescents, Manchester, as envisaged by Wilson and Womersley.' From City of Manchester, *Hulme 5 Redevelopment: Report on Design by Hugh Wilson and Lewis Womersley* (October 1965).

MUNICIPAL DREAMS

Page 151. 'Byker Wall, exterior facade, Newcastle.' By Bill Toomey. Creatives Commons licence.

Page 180. 'An aerial view of the North Peckham and adjacent estates.' From the website 35percent.org, used with permission.

Page 197. 'The Meadow Well Estate, North Shields, 1990.' With thanks to Steve Conlan. © Steve Conlan <steveconlanphotography. co.ok>.

Notes

Introduction

1   Ben Kentish, 'Number of Government-Funded Social Homes Falls by 97% since Conservatives Took Office', *Independent*, 20 June 2017, independent. co.uk, accessed 26 June 2017.

1. 'How to Provide Housing for the People': Origins

1   'Dwellings of the Poor in Bethnal-Green', *Illustrated London News*, October 1863, 423.

2   Arthur Morrison, *A Child of the Jago* (Duffield and Company, 1906), 1.

3   T.F.T. Baker (ed.), 'Bethnal Green: Building and Social Conditions from 1876 to 1914', in *A History of the County of Middlesex: Volume 11* (Victoria County History, 1998), british-history.ac.uk, accessed 15 January 2016.

4   Charles Dickens, *Hard Times* (Vintage Books, 2009), 1.

5   House of Commons Report from the Select Committee on the Health of Towns, 17 June 1840, viii–ix.

6   Quoted in Jacqueline Roberts, '"A Densely Populated and Unlovely Tract": The Residential Development of Ancoats', *Manchester Region History Review*, vol. VII, 1993, 19.

7   Andrew Mearns, *The Bitter Cry of Outcast London* (James Clarke and Co., 1883), 7 and 12.

8   William Booth, *In Darkest England and the Way Out* (Funk and Wagnalls, 1890), 11–12.

9   Eric Midwinter, *Social Administration in Lancashire, 1830–1860* (Manchester University Press, 1969), 84.

10   From Lord Salisbury, 'Labourers' and Artisans' Dwellings', *National Review*, 2 November 1883, quoted in Neil Kunze, 'Lord Salisbury's Ideas on Housing Reform, 1883–1885', *Canadian Journal of History*, vol. 8, no. 3, December 1973, 252.

11   *Pall Mall Gazette*, 27 October 1883, quoted in Anthony S. Wohl, *The Eternal Slum: Housing and Social Policy in Victorian London* (Transaction Publishers, 2001), 228.

12   Sir Richard Cross, *Nineteenth Century*, vol. 12, August 1882, quoted in Stephen Merrett, *State Housing in Britain* (Routledge & Kegan Paul, 1979), 20.

13   Gloria Clifton, 'Members and Officers of the LCC, 1889–1965', in Andrew Saint (ed.), *Politics and the People of London: The London County Council, 1889–1965* (The Hambledon Press, 1989), 30.

14   John Ruskin, *Modern Painters*, vol. 5 (Estes and Lauriat, 1894), 217.

15   William Morris, 'The Housing of the Poor', *Justice*, 19 July 1884, 4–5.

16   David Gregory Jones, 'Some Early Works of the LCC Architects Department', *AA Journal*, vol. 70, November 1954, 98.

17   Alastair Service, *Edwardian Architecture and its Origins* (Architectural Press, 1975), 31. Fleming is quoted in Deborah E. Weiner, *Architecture and Social Reform in Late-Victorian London* (Manchester University Press, 1994), 233.

18   Quoted in Sarah Wise, *The Blackest Streets: The Life and Death of a Victorian Slum* (Random House, 2013), 261.

19   R. Vladimir Steffel, 'The Boundary Street Estate: An Example of Urban Redevelopment by the London County Council, 1889–1914', *The Town Planning Review*, vol. 47, no. 2, April 1976, 165.

20   Owen Fleming, 'Working-Class Dwellings: The Rebuilding of the Boundary Street Estate'. A paper read before the Royal Institute of British Architects, 2 April 1900 (London Metropolitan Archives, HSG/GEN/2/16).

21   Quoted in Susan Beattie, *A Revolution in London Housing: LCC Housing Architects and Their Work, 1893–1914* (Greater London Council, 1980), 47.

22   Morrison, *A Child of the Jago*, 337.

23   Quoted in Moritz Kaufmann, *The Housing of the Working Classes and of the Poor* (T.C. and E.C. Jack, 1907), 61.

24   Quoted in Stephen W. Job, *Cat's Meat Square: Housing and Public Health in South St Pancras 1810–1910* (Camden History Society, 2012).

25   F.T. Turton, Deputy Surveyor, *Liverpool Exhibition of Housing and Town Planning: Transactions of Conference*, 1914, 117.

26 Raymond Unwin, *Cottage Plans and Common Sense*, Fabian Tract No. 109 (The Fabian Society, 1902), 2.

27 Quoted in Beattie, *A Revolution in London Housing*, 108.

28 Borough of Hammersmith and Fulham, 'Design Guidelines for Old Oak and Wormholt Conservation Area' (1996).

2. 'The World of the Future': The Interwar Period

1 Anthea Masey, 'Spotlight on Putney: A Taste of Country Life in the Capital', *Evening Standard*, 12 July 2011, homesandproperty.co.uk, accessed 7 April 2016.

2 Archibald D. Dawnay (Mayor of Wandsworth), 'A Roehampton Estate', letter to the *Times*, 15 April 1919, 8.

3 A resident quoted in Darrin Bayliss, 'Council Cottages and Community in Interwar Britain: A Study of Class, Culture, Community and Place', thesis, Queen Mary and Westfield College, 1998, 95.

4 Bayliss, 'Council Cottages and Community in Interwar Britain', 90–2.

5 Wandsworth Council, *Dover House Estate Conservation Area Appraisal* (ND), 13.

6 Quoted in Geraint Franklin, *Inner London Schools, 1918–1944: A Thematic Study* (English Heritage, 2009), 107.

7 Quoted in Christopher Middleton, 'A Cultural Feast in Corned Beef City', *Daily Telegraph*, 14 September 2002, telegraph.co.uk, accessed 8 April 2016.

8 Fenner Brockway, *Bermondsey Story: The Life of Alfred Salter* (Allen & Unwin, 1949), 40.

9 Bermondsey Borough Labour Party election address, November 1922, cuttings files, Southwark Local History Library and Archive.

10 J.A. Yelling, *Slums and Redevelopment: Policy and Practice in England, 1918–45, with Particular Reference to London* (Routledge, 2004), 32.

11 Stepney Metropolitan Borough to the Ministry of Health, December 1923, quoted in Simon Pepper and Peter Richmond, 'Stepney and the Politics of High-Rise Housing: Limehouse Fields to John Scurr House, 1925–1937', *London Journal*, vol. 34, no. 1, March 2009, 35.

12 Bayliss, 'Council Cottages and Community in Interwar Britain', 92.

13 Quoted in Andrew Davies and Steven Fielding (eds), *Workers' Worlds. Cultures and Communities in Manchester and Salford, 1880–1939* (Manchester University Press, 1992), 80.

14   Clare Hartwell, Matthew Hyde and Nikolaus Pevsner, *Lancashire: Manchester and the South-East* (Yale University Press, 2004), 490.

15   Davies and Fielding (eds), *Workers' Worlds*, 81.

16   Quoted in John J. Parkinson-Bailey, *Manchester: An Architectural History* (Manchester University Press, 2000), 158.

17   Davies and Fielding (eds), *Workers' Worlds*, 86.

18   Sarah Lyell, 'How the Young Poor Measure Poverty in Britain: Drink, Drugs and their Time in Jail', *New York Times*, 10 March 2007, nytimes.com, accessed 22 January 2016.

19   Pepper and Richmond, 'Stepney and the Politics of High-Rise Housing', 49.

20   Ruth Glass and L.E. White, 'A Warning to Planners: The Story of Honor Oak Estate', *The National House Builder and the Building Digest for the APRR*, 1945.

21   L.E. White, *Tenement Town* (Jason Press, 1946).

22   Quoted in *'A Street Door of Our Own': A Short History of Life on an LCC Estate by Local People from the Honor Oak Estate, London* (Honor Oak Estate Neighbourhood Association, 1977).

23   '2,166 White City Flats: Opening of LCC Estate Today', *Times*, 21 July 1939, 11.

24   Hugh Quigley and Ismay Goldie, *Housing and Slum Clearance in London* (Methuen, 1934), 106.

25   Simon Pepper, 'Ossulston Street: Early LCC Experiments in High-Rise Housing, 1925–29', *The London Journal*, vol. 7, no. 1, 1981, 50.

26   Owen Hatherley, *A Guide to the New Ruins of Great Britain* (Verso, 2011), 336.

27   L.H. Keay, 'Redevelopment in Central Areas in Liverpool', *RIBA Journal*, vol. 46, no. 6, 23 January 1939.

28   Peter Shapeley, *The Politics of Housing: Power, Consumers and Urban Culture* (Manchester University Press, 2007), 61.

29   Nikolaus Pevsner and Enid Radcliffe, *Yorkshire: The West Riding* (Yale University Press, 1967), 337.

30   BBC Leeds, The History of Quarry Hill, comments, bbc.co.uk, accessed 25 February 2016.

31   Quoted in Andrzej Olechnowicz, *Working-Class Housing in England Between the Wars: The Becontree Estate* (Clarendon Press, 1997), 66.

32   A tenants' spokesperson quoted in Quintin Bradley, 'The Birth of the Council Tenants' Movement: A Study of the 1934 Leeds Rent Strike', tenantshistory.leedstenants.org.uk, accessed 26 January 2016.

33   Robert Finnigan, 'Council Housing in Leeds, 1919–1939', in M.J. Daunton (ed.), *Councillors and Tenants: Local Authority Housing in English Cities, 1919–1939* (Leicester University Press, 1984), 117.

34   'Housing Needs: Mr Chamberlain at Birmingham', *Times*, 24 October 1933, 19.

35   Trevor Rowley, *The English Landscape in the Twentieth Century* (A&C Black, 2006), 200.

36   Ruth Durant, *Watling: A Survey of Life on a New Housing Estate* (P.S. King, 1939), 119.

3. 'If Only We Will': Britain Reimagined, 1940–51

1   J. Paton Watson and Patrick Abercrombie, *A Plan for Plymouth* (Underhill [Plymouth] Ltd, 1943), 66.

2   Paton Watson and Abercrombie, *A Plan for Plymouth*, 2.

3   Quoted in Nick Coleman, 'Plymouth: A Pearl on the Seashore', *Independent*, 21 February 2010, independent.co.uk, accessed 4 October 2016.

4   Paton Watson and Abercrombie, *A Plan for Plymouth*, 86.

5   David Kynaston, *Austerity Britain, 1945–1951* (Bloomsbury Publishing, 2010), 25.

6   Peter J. Larkham and Keith D. Lilley, *Planning the 'City of Tomorrow': British Reconstruction Planning, 1939–1952: An Annotated Bibliography* (2005), bcu.ac.uk, accessed 23 May 2016.

7   Frank Mort, 'Fantasies of Metropolitan Life: Planning London in the 1940s', *Journal of British Studies*, vol. 43, no. 1, 2004, 128.

8   Patrick Abercrombie and J.H. Forshaw, *County of London Plan* (Macmillan & Co, 1943), iv.

9   Abercrombie and Forshaw, *County of London Plan*, 20.

10   Peter Willmott and Michael Young, *Family and Kinship in East London* (Routledge, 2013; first published 1957), 97. Debden was anonymised as the 'Greenleigh' estate in the book.

11   Willmott and Young, *Family and Kinship in East London*, 98.

12   Margot Jefferys, 'Londoners in Hertfordshire: The South Oxhey Estate', in Ruth Glass et al., *London: Aspects of Change* (MacGibbon and Key, 1964), 228.

13   Alan Johnson, *Please, Mr Postman* (Corgi Books, 2014), 62–3.

14   Matthew Hollow, 'Utopian Urges: Visions for Reconstruction in Britain, 1940–1950', *Planning Perspectives*, vol. 27, no. 2, 2012, 582.

15 Barlow Report of the Royal Commission on the Distribution of Industrial Population Report (Cmd 6153, HMSO, 1940).

16 New Towns Bill, HC Deb, 8 May 1946, *Hansard*, vol. 422, cc. 1072–184, hansard.millbanksystems.com, accessed 2 June 2016.

17 J.R. and B.L. Hammond, *The Town Labourer* (1917), quoted in David Boyes, 'An Exercise in Gracious Living: The North East New Towns, 1947–1988', PhD thesis, Durham University, 2007, 12.

18 Quoted in Boyes, 'An Exercise in Gracious Living', 19–20.

19 Boyes, 'An Exercise in Gracious Living', 27–8.

20 Boyes, 'An Exercise in Gracious Living', 97.

21 Gary Younge, 'Stevenage', *Granta*, no. 119, Spring 2012, 18.

22 Monica Furlong, 'Harlow: New Town', *Spectator*, 29 September 1960, 11.

23 B.J. Heraud, 'Social Class and the New Towns', *Urban Studies*, vol. 5, no. 1, 1968, 39.

24 Rosemary Wellings (Harlow Development Corporation's social development officer), 'Living in a New Town', *Housing*, vol. 17, no. 7, 1978.

25 Furlong, 'Harlow: New Town', 16.

26 David Smith, 'Poster Churchill Pulped on Show', *Observer*, 30 September 2007, theguardian.com, accessed 28 June 2017.

27 John Allan, 'Lubetkin and Peterlee', in Thomas Deckker (ed.), *Modern City Revisited* (Taylor and Francis, 2005), 108.

28 J.M. Richards, 'Failure of the New Towns', *Architectural Review*, vol. 114, no. 679, 1953, 31.

29 Gordon Cullen, 'Prairie Planning in the New Towns', *Architectural Review*, vol. 114, no. 679, 1953, 34.

30 'Design Problems in New Towns: Result of Building "for all classes"', *Times*, 6 February 1962.

31 Frederick Gibberd, 'The Architecture of New Towns', *Journal of the Royal Society of Arts*, vol. 106, no. 5021, 1958, 343.

32 Jason Cowley, 'Down Town', *Guardian*, 1 August 2002, theguardian.com, accessed 16 November 2016, and Tim Adams, email to author, 15 November 2016.

4. 'The Needs of the People': Council Housing, 1945–56

1 County Borough of Derby, 'The Mackworth Estate' (1959).

2 Mackworth Townswomen's Guild, *Mackworth Estate Jubilee: A Social History* (1980).

3   Kinnock in conversation with Elisabeth Blanchet, 'Photography Exhibition: Elisabeth Blanchet', photofusion.org, accessed 12 May 2016.

4   Quoted in Ros Anderson, 'This Is My Home, My Little Castle', *Guardian*, 28 December 2012, theguardian.com, accessed 12 May 2016.

5   F.W. Deedes (Parliamentary Secretary to the Ministry of Housing and Local Government), quoted in *Hansard*, HC Deb, 15 February 1955, vol. 537, cc. 192–319.

6   Quoted in Alan Murie, 'Housing', in Paul Wilding (ed.), *In Defence of the Welfare State* (Manchester University Press, 1986), 58.

7   Quoted in Alison Ravetz, *Council Housing and Culture: The History of a Social Experiment* (Routledge, 2001), 97 (emphases in original).

8   Quoted in John Burnett, *A Social History of Housing 1815–1970* (Methuen, 1978), 279.

9   Abercrombie and Forshaw, *The County of London Plan*, 78.

10   W. Albert Walker, 'Post-War Housing Development', read at a sessional meeting held at Salford on 14 February 1942; *The Journal of the Royal Society for the Promotion of Health*, vol. 62, 1942, 80.

11   Rowland Nicholas, *The City of Manchester Plan 1945* (published for the Manchester Corporation by Jarrold and Sons, 1945), 4.

12   Quoted in Kynaston, *Austerity Britain, 1945–1951*, 53.

13   Housing Bill, Second Reading: *Hansard*, HC Deb, 16 March 1949, vol. 462, cc. 2121–231.

14   Ian Cox, *The South Bank Exhibition: A Guide to the Story it Tells* (HMSO, 1951).

15   John Westergaard and Ruth Glass, 'A Profile of Lansbury', *The Town Planning Review*, vol. 25, no. 1, 1954, 39.

16   Abercrombie and Forshaw, *The County of London Plan*, 28.

17   Quoted in Elain Harwood, *Twentieth Century Architecture, No. 5, Festival of Britain* (Twentieth Century Society, 2001), 150.

18   Wilson writing in the *Observer*, 20 July 1952, quoted in Nicholas Bullock, *Building the Post-War World: Modern Architecture and Reconstruction in Britain* (Psychology Press, 2002), 105.

19   J.M. Richards, 'Lansbury', *Architectural Review*, vol. 150, no. 660, 1951, 363.

20   Quoted in Hobhouse (ed.), 'The Lansbury Estate: Introduction and the Festival of Britain Exhibition', *Survey of London: Volumes 43 and 44, Poplar, Blackwall and Isle of Dogs* (London County Council, 1994) 213–3.

21   Quoted in John Crace, 'Keys to the Future', *Guardian*, 11 July 2001, theguardian.com, accessed 31 May 2016.

22   Westergaard and Glass, 'A Profile of Lansbury', 34.

23   Westergaard and Glass, 'A Profile of Lansbury', 39.

24   George L.A. Downing, 'Some Aspects of Housing in a Metropolitan Borough', *The Journal of the Royal Society for the Promotion of Health*, vol. 69, no. 5, 1949, 594.

25   Quoted in Harriet Atkinson and Mary Banham, *The Festival of Britain: A Land and its People* (I.B.Tauris, 2012), 185.

26   Frederick Gibberd, 'Housing at Hackney', *Architectural Review*, vol. 106, no. 633, 1949, 146.

27   'Mixed Housing at Hackney', *Times*, 6 September 1949, 2.

28   Peter Foynes, 'The Rise of High-Rise: Post-War Housing in Hackney', *Hackney History*, vol. 1, 1995, 30.

29   Kenneth Powell, 'Powell, Sir (Arnold Joseph) Philip (1921–2003)', *Oxford Dictionary of National Biography* (Oxford University Press, 2007), online edition, September 2013, oxforddnb.com, accessed 10 June 2016.

30   Ian Nairn, *Nairn's London* (Penguin, 2014; originally published 1966), 200.

31   Merrett, *State Housing in Britain*, 320.

32   Conservative general election manifesto, 1951, conservativemanifesto.com, accessed 28 June 2017.

33   Quoted in Chris Hamnett, *Winners and Losers* (Routledge, 2005), 52.

34   Patrick Dunleavy, *The Politics of Mass Housing, 1945–1975: A Study of Corporate Power and Professional Influence in the Welfare State* (Clarendon Press, 1981), 37.

5. 'Get These People Out of the Slums': 1956–68

1   Adam Mornement, *No Longer Notorious: The Revival of Castle Vale, 1993–2005* (Castle Vale Housing Action Trust, 2005), 28, and Helen George, 'New Castle', *Housing* (magazine of CIH), February 2003, 36.

2   Quoted in Miles Glendinning and Stefan Muthesius, *Tower Block: Modern Public Housing in England, Scotland, Wales, and Northern Ireland* (Yale University Press, 1994), 167.

3   Quoted in Phil Ian Jones, 'The Rise and Fall of The Multi-Storey Ideal: Public Sector High-Rise Housing in Britain 1945–2002, with Special Reference to Birmingham', PhD thesis, School of Geography, Earth and Environmental Sciences, University of Birmingham, 2003, 140.

4   The planner David Eversley quoted in Jones, 'The Rise and Fall of the Multi-Storey Ideal', 126.

5   *Birmingham Gazette*, 24 May 1930, quoted in Anthony Sutcliffe, 'A Century of Flats in Birmingham, 1875–1973', *Multi-Storey Living: The British Working Class Experience* (Croom Helm, 1974), 181.

6   Quoted in Stacey Barnfield, 'Sir Herbert Manzoni: The Man Who Changed the Face of Birmingham', *Birmingham Post*, 8 March 2013, birminghampost. co.uk, accessed 28 June 2017.

7   Quoted in Glendinning and Muthesius, *Tower Block*, 179.

8   Quoted in Glendinning and Muthesius, *Tower Block*, 248.

9   Quoted in Mornement, *No Longer Notorious: The Revival of Castle Vale, 1993–2005*, 5.

10   Geoff Bateson, *A History of Castle Vale* (2005), 39, thewordsthething.org.uk, accessed 23 January 2017.

11   Peter Foynes, 'The Rise of High-Rise: Post-War Housing in Hackney', *Hackney History*, vol. 1, 1995, 31. Foynes also provides the quotation which follows from RIBA.

12   Ted Hollamby, interview with Jill Lever, 1997, National Life Story Collection: Architects' Lives, British Library.

13   Quoted in Elain Harwood, 'London County Council Architects (*act. c.*1940–1965)', *Oxford Dictionary of National Biography* (Oxford University Press, 2004), oxforddnb.com, accessed 22 June 2016.

14   Patricia Garside, 'Town Planning in London 1930–1961: A Study of Pressures, Interests and Influences Affecting the Formation of Policy', PhD thesis, London School of Economics and Political Science, 1979, 401–2, and Harwood, 'London County Council Architects (*act. c.*1940–1965)'.

15   Nicolas Bullock, *Building the Post-War World: Modern Architecture and Reconstruction in Britain* (Routledge, 2002), 127.

16   G.E. Kidder Smith, *The New Architecture of Europe: An Illustrated Guidebook and Appraisal* (Meridian Books, 1961), 42.

17   Bridget Cherry and Nikolaus Pevsner, *London 2: South* (Yale University Press, 2002), 689.

18   Sutherland Lyall, 'Banham, (Peter) Reyner (1922–1988)', rev. *Oxford Dictionary of National Biography* (Oxford University Press, 2004), online edition, May 2008, oxforddnb.com, accessed 24 January 2017.

19   Reyner Banham, 'The New Brutalism', *Architectural Review*, December 1955, reprinted online at architectural-review.com, accessed 24 January 2017.

20   Barnabas Calder, *Raw Concrete* (William Heinemann, 2016), 15.

21   Calder, *Raw Concrete*, 14.

22   Nicholas Merthyr Day, 'The Role of the Architect in Post-War State Housing:

A Case Study of the Housing Work of the London County Council 1939–1956', PhD thesis, University of Warwick, 1988, 355.

23   Ivor Smith quoted in Rachel Cooke, 'How I Learnt to Love the Streets in the Sky', *Observer*, 23 November 2008, theguardian.com, accessed 29 June 2016. The following quotations are drawn from the same source.

24   Quoted in Alison Ravetz, *Council Housing and Culture* (Routledge, 2001), 181.

25   Lasdun quoted in John Gold, *The Practice of Modernism: Modern Architects and Urban Transformation, 1954–1972* (Routledge, 2007), 208.

26   Quoted in David Robinson, 'The Tower Block is Back, but This Time as a Des Res', *Daily Express*, 22 July 2000.

27   Quoted in Martin Delgado, 'We Loved Living in our Crumbling Tower Block, Say Residents', *Evening Standard*, 30 April 1993.

28   'An Englishman's Home is his 11-Floor Castle', *Eastern Daily Press*, 1 October 1964.

29   Ministry of Housing and Local Government, *Homes for Today and Tomorrow* (HMSO, London: 1961), 2–3.

30   Quoted in Jamileh Manoochehri, 'Social Policy and Housing: Reflections of Social Values', PhD thesis, University College London, 2009, 228.

31   Secretary of State for Housing and Local Government, White Paper on Housing Policy C. 63 (80), 10 May 1963, 8.

32   Geoffrey Rippon, MP, Minister of Public Building and Works, quoted in Association of Metropolitan Authorities, 'Defects in Housing Part 2: Industrialised and System Built Dwellings of the 1960s and 1970s' (1984), para. 2.45. The following quotation is drawn from the same source, para. 2.43.

33   Quoted in Glendinning and Muthesius, *Tower Block*, 162.

34   Quoted in Kynaston, *Modernity Britain*, 650.

35   Southwark Council Borough Development Department, Aylesbury Development in Use, May 1973.

36   Three long-term residents of the estate quoted in Sarah Helm, 'Lost Souls in the City in the Sky', *New Statesman*, 17 July 2000, and Richard Godwin, 'We Shall Not Be Moved: Residents Give Their Verdict on Life on the Aylesbury Estate', *Evening Standard*, 26 March 2013.

37   Cllr Ian Andrews, quoted in '"Showpiece" Estate is Unfit to Live In, Says Tory Councillor', *South London Press*, 16 October 1970.

38   Andrew Saint and Colin Thom, *Survey of London: Battersea: Pt. 2: Houses and Housing* (Yale University Press, 2013), 176.

39   Dunleavy, *The Politics of Mass Housing, 1945–1975*, 23–5.

40 Glendinning and Muthesius, *Tower Block*, 192.

41 Dunleavy, *The Politics of Mass Housing in Britain, 1945–1975*, 284.

42 'Sharpesville', *Private Eye*, 12 July 1974, quoted in Jones, 'The Rise and Fall of The Multi-Storey Ideal', 170.

43 Quoted in Glendinning and Muthesius, *Tower Block*, 254.

44 Quoted in Tony Cohen, 'Up the Junction in a Tower Block is no Family Life', *South London Press*, 10 November 1976, andrewcunningham43ya-hoocom.blogspot.co.uk, accessed 8 July 2016.

6. 'Anti-Monumental, Anti-Stylistic, and Fit for Ordinary People': 1968–79

1 Interviewed in 'There's No Place Like Hulme', *World in Action*, 10 April 1978, youtube.com, accessed 20 September 2016.

2 City of Manchester, *Hulme 5 Redevelopment: Report on Design by Hugh Wilson and Lewis Womersley*, October 1965, 11.

3 City of Manchester, *Hulme 5 Redevelopment*, 9.

4 City of Manchester, *Hulme 5 Redevelopment*, 8.

5 Rowland Nicholas, *The City of Manchester Plan 1945* (Jarrold and Sons, 1945), 157.

6 Manchester City Council, *A New Community: The Redevelopment of Hulme* (ND, believed to be 1965).

7 A comment from Caroline, dated 15 November 2007, in the Guestbook of the exHulme website, exhulme.co.uk, accessed 17 June 2014.

8 City of Manchester, *Hulme 5 Redevelopment*, 8.

9 'Jungle Estate Report', *Guardian*, 8 November 1973.

10 As described by the architects in *The Smithsons on Housing*, a BBC 2 documentary by B.S. Johnson (1970), available on youtube.com, accessed 26 September 2016.

11 Alison and Peter Smithson, *Ordinariness and Light*, quoted in John Furse, 'The Smithsons at Robin Hood', PhD thesis, University of Sussex, November 1982, 13.

12 *The Smithsons on Housing*.

13 Alison and Peter Smithson, 'Robin Hood Lane: A Housing Scheme for the GLC', in *Ordinariness and Light* (Faber and Faber, 1970), 189.

14 Quoted in Henrietta Billings (Twentieth Century Society), 'Dawson's Heights: The 'Italian' Hill Town in Dulwich', c20society.org.uk, accessed 27 September 2016.

15   Quoted in Tom Cordell, *Utopia London*, utopialondon.com, accessed 27 September 2016.

16   Quoted in James Dunnett, 'World's End: The Pride of Eric Lyons', *Building Design*, 21 November 2008, bdonline.co.uk, accessed 27 September 2016.

17   Henry Herzberg, 'Housing at World's End, Chelsea: Appraisal', *Architects' Journal*, vol. 165, no. 16, 1977, 744.

18   The view of a former long-term resident of the estate offered to me at London Open House 2013.

19   Quoted in Peter Malpass, 'The Other Side of the Wall', *Architects' Journal*, vol. 169, no. 19, 1979, 963.

20   Malpass, 'The Other Side of the Wall', 969.

21   Quoted in Sarah Glynn, 'Good Homes: Lessons in Successful Public Housing from Newcastle's Byker Estate', paper given at the Birkbeck Institute for Social Research, London, 18 November 2011, 1, bbk.ac.uk, accessed 27 September 2016.

22   Quoted in Diana Rowntree, 'Ralph Erskine', *Guardian*, 22 March 2005, theguardian.com, accessed 27 September 2016.

23   Glynn, 'Good Homes: Lessons in Successful Public Housing from Newcastle's Byker Estate', 6.

24   Miles Horsey and Stefan Muthesius, *Provincial Mixed Development, Norwich Council Housing 1955–1973* (Norwich, 1986), 1.

25   Hollamby speaking on 'The Architect's Approach to Architecture' at RIBA, 24 January 1974, quoted in the *Architects' Journal*, vol. 159, no. 6, 1974, 251.

26   Rowan Moore, 'Housing Estates: If They Aren't Broken . . . ', *Observer*, 31 January 2016, theguardian.com, accessed 13 December 2016.

27   Lambeth Borough Council Housing Committee minutes, 20 January 1969 (LBL/22/6).

28   Lionel Esher, *A Broken Wave: The Rebuilding of England, 1940–1980* (Pelican Books, 1983), 161.

29   Cllr Enid Wistrich quoted in Mark Swenarton, 'Reforming the Welfare State: Camden 1965–73', *Footprint: Delft Architecture Theory Journal*, no. 9, Autumn 2011, footprint.tudelft.nl, accessed 19 June 2017.

30   Cook quoted in Fabian Watkinson, *The Most Expensive Council Housing in the World* (Twentieth Century Society, 2001), 3.

31   *Hampstead and Highgate Express*, 20 January 1978.

32   Quoted in Watkinson, *The Most Expensive Council Housing in the World*, 3.

33   'The Branch Bears Fruit', *Hampstead and Highgate Express*, 7 October 1977.

34 Su Rogers, 'Preview: Highgate New Town', *Architectural Review*, vol. 154, no. 919, 1973, 159.

35 Terry Messenger, 'Haven for Hoodlums', *St Pancras Chronicle*, 15 April 1983.

36 Roger Stonehouse, 'Building Study: Housing of Highgate New Town, London N19', *Architects' Journal*, vol. 174, no. 32, 1981, 298.

37 Quoted in Camden Council, 'Press Release HNT Stage 2 got Civic Trust award', 29 November 1983.

38 Quoted in 'Rediscovering the Village in Deptford', *Building Design*, 29 June 2012, bdonline.co.uk, accessed 15 December 2016.

39 Cllr Arthur Wellon quoted in Michael Ewing, 'The Home Truths: A Special Investigation into Housing', *Daily Mirror*, 6 July 1972.

40 Alderman J.H. Dunning JP quoted in Robert Parks, 'Housing Development in Inner London: A Case Study of Hackney', MPhil thesis, University of London, 1975, 194.

41 Council officer Peter Redman in Tony Travers, *London's Boroughs at 50* (Biteback Publishing, 2016), 92.

42 Merrett, *State Housing in Britain*, 145.

43 Figures quoted in NUPE, *Up Against a Brick Wall: The Dead-End in Housing Policy* (Services to Community Action and Tenants, 1978), 20, european-services-strategy.org.uk, accessed 19 December 2016.

44 Figures for Camden and Islington from Michael Passmore, 'The Responses of Labour-Controlled London Local Authorities to Major Changes in Housing Policy, 1971–1983', PhD thesis, King's College London, 71.

45 Paul Watt and Anna Minton, 'London's Housing Crisis and its Activisms: an Introduction', *City*, vol. 20, no. 2, April 2016, 208–9.

46 Shelter, 'Social Housing Factsheet' (2009), 2, england.shelter.org.uk, accessed 20 December 2016.

47 Anne Power, *Hovels to High-Rise: State Housing in Europe since 1850* (Routledge, 1993), 207.

48 The quotation and preceding statistics are drawn from Ian Cole and Robert Furbey, *The Eclipse of Council Housing* (Routledge, 1994), 84.

49 This is dealt with sensitively in Harold Carter, 'Building the Divided City: Race, Class and Social Housing in Southwark, 1945–1995', *The London Journal*, vol. 33, no. 2, 2008, and more controversially in Michael Young, Kate Gavron and Geoff Dench, *The New East End: Kinship, Race and Conflict* (Profile Books, 2011).

7. 'Rolling Back the Frontiers of the State': 1979–91

1   'Britain Belongs to You', Labour Party manifesto, October 1959, politicsresources.net, accessed 7 June 2017.

2   Note from Dan Lucas (Strategy and Research Manager for Nottingham City Homes), 8 December 2015.

3   Martin Crookston, *Garden Suburbs of Tomorrow? A New Future for the Cottage Estates* (Routledge, 2016), 91.

4   UK Government, 'Table 208 House Building: Permanent Dwellings Started, by Tenure and Country', gov.uk, accessed 9 March 2017.

5   For details of legislation, see Alan Murie, 'The Right to Buy: History and Prospect', *History and Policy*, November 2015, historyandpolicy.org, accessed 30 January 2017.

6   Norman Tebbit, Speech to the Conservative Party Conference, 15 October, 1981.

7   Brian Lund, *Housing Problems and Housing Policy* (Longman, 1996), 123.

8   Ian Cole and Robert Furbey, *The Eclipse of Council Housing* (Routledge, 1994), 188–9.

9   Quoted in Brian Milligan, 'Right-to-Buy: Margaret Thatcher's Controversial Gift', *BBC News Online*, 10 April 2013, bbc.co.uk, accessed 31 January 2017.

10   Richard Harris and Peter Larkham (eds), *Changing Suburbs: Foundation, Form and Function* (Routledge, 2003), 68.

11   Reinout Kleinhans and Maarten van Ham, 'Lessons Learned from the Largest Tenure-Mix Operation in the World: Right to Buy in the United Kingdom', *Cityscape: A Journal of Policy Development and Research*, vol. 15, no. 2, 2013, 110.

12   Ray Forrest and Alan Murie, *Selling the Welfare State: The Privatisation of Public Housing* (Routledge, 1991), 11.

13   Figures drawn from Steve Wilcox, *Housing Finance Review 1999/2000* (Joseph Rowntree Foundation, 1999), ukhousingreview.org.uk, accessed 1 February 2017.

14   Quoted in John Stewart and Gerry Stoker (eds), *The Future of Local Government* (Macmillan, 1989), 89.

15   Jane Jacobs, *The Death and Life of Great American Cities* (Vintage Books, 1992), 44–3.

16   Horizon, 'The Writing on the Wall', broadcast on BBC 2, 18 November 1974, available on youtube.com, accessed 8 February 2017.

17   Herzberg, 'Housing at World's End, Chelsea: Appraisal'.

18 Alice Coleman, 'Design Disadvantage in Southwark', *The Dulwich Society Journal*, Summer 2008, dulwichsociety.com, accessed 7 February 2017.

19 Alice Coleman, *Utopia on Trial: Vision and Reality in Planned Housing* (Hilary Shipman, 1985), 22.

20 Valerie Grove, *Sunday Times*, 7 June 1987, cited in Graham Stewart, *Robin Hood Gardens Blackwall Reach* (Wild ReSearch, ND), 15.

21 Charles Jencks, *The New Paradigm in Architecture: The Language of Post-Modernism* (Yale University Press, 2002), 18.

22 'Life at Deck Level', *Southwark Civic News*, July 1968.

23 *Southwark Sparrow*, February 1987.

24 Castle Vale Housing Action Trust, *Castle Vale Masterplan Written Statement*, September 1993.

25 Messenger, 'Haven for Hoodlums'.

26 Bill Hillier, 'City of Alice's Dreams', *Architects' Journal*, vol. 184, no. 28, 1986, 39.

27 One of Coleman's team wrote a fuller treatment of the estate (which she anonymised as 'Omega'). See Frances Reynolds, *The Problem Housing Estate: An Account of Omega and its People* (Gower, 1986).

28 Coleman, *Utopia on Trial*, 6.

29 Anne Power, 'The Development of Unpopular Council Estates and Attempted Remedies, 1895–1984', PhD thesis, London School of Economics, 1985, 276–7.

30 Power, 'The Development of Unpopular Council Estates and Attempted Remedies', 277.

31 Janet Foster and Timothy Hope, *Housing, Community and Crime: The Impact of the Priority Estates Project*, Home Office Research and Planning Unit (HMSO, 1993), 84.

32 Power, *Hovels to High Rise*, 224.

33 Ricardo R. Pinto, 'The Impact of Estate Action on Developments in Council Housing, Management and Effectiveness', PhD thesis, London School of Economics, 1991, 62.

34 Power, *Hovels to High Rise*, 226.

35 Dick Mortimer, 'Breaking the High-Rise Spiral of Decline: One Authority's Campaign of Refurbishment', *Municipal Journal*, 15 May 1987.

36 Carlisle City Council, Riverside Group et al., *Raffles Vision Draft Final Report* (Carlisle, 2003), NP.

37 Wilcox, *Housing Finance Review 1999/2000*, 173.

38 Debra Isaac, 'Rent Fears for the Tenants', *Times*, 14 November 1988.

39   Quoted in Brian Lewis, *New for Old: The Story of the First Housing Action Trust* (Pontefract Press, 1988), 18.

40   Steven Alan Tiesdell, 'The Development and Implementation of Housing Action Trust Policy', PhD thesis, University of Nottingham, 1999, 118–19.

41   Quoted in Phil Ian Jones, 'The Rise and Fall of the Multi-Storey Ideal: Public Sector High-Rise Housing in Britain 1945–2002, with Special Reference to Birmingham', PhD thesis, University of Birmingham, 2003, 219. Emphases in original.

42   Max Wind-Cowie, *Civic Streets: The Big Society in Action* (Demos, 2010), 52, barrowcadbury.org.uk, accessed 15 February 2017.

43   Quoted in Alison Benjamin, 'Putting the Record Straight', *Roof*, November/December 2000, 38.

44   Helen George, 'New Castle', *Housing* (magazine of CIH), February 2003, 36.

8. 'Thrown-Away Places': 1991–7

1   Beatrix Campbell, *Goliath: Britain's Dangerous Places* (Methuen, 1993), 48.

2   Interviewed in *An English Estate*, a Channel Four documentary by Hugh Kelly, broadcast in October 1992, youtube.com, accessed 6 June 2017.

3   Anne Power and Rebecca Tunstall for the Joseph Rowntree Foundation, 'Riots and Violent Disturbances in Thirteen Areas of Britain', *Findings*, *Social Policy Research*, no. 116, 1997, jrf.org.uk, accessed 7 June 2017.

4   Mike Geddes, 'Local Partnership and Social Exclusion in the United Kingdom: A Stake in the Market?' in John Bennington and Mike Geddes (eds), *Local Partnership and Social Exclusion in the European Union: New Forms of Local Social Governance?* (Routledge, 2013), 180.

5   Simin Davoudi and Patsy Healey, 'City Challenge: Sustainable Process or Temporary Gesture?' *Environment and Planning C: Government and Policy*, vol. 13, 1995, 94.

6   Steve Quilley, 'Entrepreneurial Turns: Municipal Socialism and After', in Jamie Peck and Kevin Ward (eds), *City of Revolution: Restructuring Manchester* (Manchester University Press, 2002), 78–80.

7   Gwyndaf Williams, 'City Building: Developing Manchester's Core', in Peck and Ward (eds), *City of Revolution*, 163.

8   Rachel Cooper, Graeme Evans and Christopher Boyko, *Designing Sustainable Cities* (John Wiley & Sons, 2009), 148.

9   Hatherley, *A Guide to the New Ruins of Great Britain*, 129.

10   Lund, *Housing Problems and Housing Policy*, 129.

11   Vikki Miller, 'Peckham Rise', *Building Design*, 8 October 2004, bdonline. co.uk, accessed 22 February 2017.

12   Luna Glücksberg, 'Wasting the Inner-City: Waste, Value and Anthropology on the Estates', PhD thesis, Goldsmiths College, University of London, 2013, 120.

13   Graham Towers, *Shelter is Not Enough: Transforming Multi-Storey Housing* (Policy Press, 2000), 177.

14   Quoted in Matt Weaver, 'Dangerous Structures?' *Building Design*, 15 December 2000, 19.

15   Catherine Bates, a Southwark planning officer, quoted in Ike Ijeh, 'Aylesbury Estate: Taking Back the Streets', 3 August 2012, building.co.uk, accessed 22 February 2017.

16   Jones, 'The Rise and Fall of the Multi-Storey Ideal', 199–200.

17   Jones, 'The Rise and Fall of the Multi-Storey Ideal', 203.

18   Quoted in 'Over £4m Funding to Benefit Southwark and Newham LBC Estates', *Local Government Chronicle*, 27 February 1998.

19   Nick Triggle and Lucy Gooding, 'We Have Been Left Up Dawson Creek', *South London Press*, 14 September 2001.

20   Tony Blair, Speech to the Labour Conference, October 1996, prnewswire. co.uk, accessed 24 February 2017.

21   Steve Wilcox, *Housing Finance Review 1999/2000*, 136 and 139.

22   Madeline McKenna, 'The Development of Suburban Council Housing Estates in Liverpool between the Wars', PhD thesis, University of Liverpool, 1986, vol. 2, 480 and 448.

23   Quoted in Mornement, *No Longer Notorious: The Revival of Castle Vale, 1993–2005*, 2, crp-ltd.co.uk, accessed 7 March 2017.

24   Tony Parker, *People of Providence: A Housing Estate and Some of its Inhabitants* (Hutchinson, 1983), 26.

25   Quoted in Les Back, *New Ethnicities and Urban Culture: Racisms and Multi-culture in Young Lives* (Routledge, 1996), 33.

26   Back, *New Ethnicities and Urban Culture*, 41.

27   Jennifer Maureen Lowe, 'Social Justice and Localities: The Allocation of Council Housing in Tower Hamlets', PhD thesis, Queen Mary College, University of London, 2004, 169.

28   Rachael Clegg, 'Peace of Mind and Happiness on Sheffield's Manor', *Star*, 20 July 2012, thestar.co.uk, accessed 24 February 2017.

29   Interviewed in 'On the Manor, Sheffield', 1986, emphases in original, available on youtube.com, accessed 24 February 2017.

30   Michael Ball and Paul J. Maginn, 'The Contradictions of Urban Policy: The Case of the Single Regeneration Budget in London', *Environment and Planning C: Government and Policy*, vol. 22, 2004, 739.

9. 'A Different Kind of Community': 1997-2010

1   Quoted in Ben Campkin, *Remaking London: Decline and Regeneration in Urban Culture* (I.B.Tauris, 2013), 97. Research has shown, however, that the commonly deployed trope of three workless generations is very largely an urban myth.

2   Office of the Deputy Prime Minister, *Sustainable Communities: People, Places and Prosperity*, 2005, 65.

3   Madanipour, Cars and Allen quoted in Dave Adamson, *The Impact of Devolution: Area-Based Regeneration Policies in the UK* (Joseph Rowntree Foundation, January 2010), 9, jrf.org.uk, accessed 14 March 2017.

4   Adamson, *The Impact of Devolution: Area-Based Regeneration Policies in the UK*, 9–10.

5   'Report of the Social Exclusion Unit: A New Commitment to Neighbourhood Renewal National Strategy Action Plan', Cabinet Office, January 2001, 8, neighbourhood.statistics.gov.uk, accessed 14 March 2017.

6   Aylesbury Tenants and Leaseholders First website, aylesburytenantsfirst.org.uk, accessed 14 March 2017.

7   Christopher Beanland, 'Channel 4's Aylesbury Estate Ident Gets a Revamp – Starring the Residents', *Guardian*, 14 March 2014, theguardian.com, accessed 15 March 2017.

8   Loretta Lees, 'The Urban Injustices of New Labour's "New Urban Renewal": The Case of the Aylesbury Estate in London', *Antipode*, vol. 46, no. 4, 2014, 923–4.

9   Southwark Council, Aylesbury Area Action Plan, January 2010, 179.

10   David Blackman, '"Where Did it All Go Wrong?" in Regeneration', *Inside Housing*, 22 February 2002, insidehousing.co.uk, accessed 15 March 2017.

11   Southwark Council, *Southwark Affordable Rent Product Study July 2015*, 5–6, and London's Poverty Profile: Southwark, londonspovertyprofile.org.uk, accessed 17 March 2017.

12   Colin Marrs, 'Javid Rejects Aylesbury Estate CPO as Breach of Human Rights', *Architects' Journal*, 19 September 2016, architectsjournal.co.uk, accessed 8 June 2017.

13 Heygate was Home, 'Broken Promises', heygatewashome.org, accessed 8 June 2017.

14 Jon Kirk, 'Welcome to the Aylesbury Estate – Once So Grim its Residents Dubbed it a Hell-Hole', *The People*, 24 June 2007.

15 Cited in Karl Murray, 'Understanding the Impact of the Economic Down Turn on BAME Communities: A Case Study of the Aylesbury Estate in the London Borough of Southwark', Black Training and Enterprise Group, June 2012, 11, bteg.co.uk, accessed 22 March 2017.

16 Murray, 'Understanding the Impact of the Economic Down Turn on BAME Communities: A Case Study of the Aylesbury Estate', 12.

17 Centre for Regional Economic and Social Research, Sheffield Hallam University, 'The New Deal for Communities Experience: A Final Assessment' (Department of Communities and Local Government, March 2010), 6, extra.shu.ac.uk, accessed 23 March 2017.

18 Centre for Regional Economic and Social Research, 'The New Deal for Communities Experience: A Final Assessment', 40.

19 See Paul Watt, 'Housing Stock Transfers, Regeneration and State-Led Gentrification in London', *Urban Policy and Research*, vol. 27, no. 3, 2009.

20 Gene Robertson, 'Labour's Legacy', *Inside Housing*, 7 May 2010, insidehousing.co.uk, accessed 24 March 2017.

21 London Borough of Tower Hamlets, Housing Evidence Base, June 2016, 86, towerhamlets.gov.uk, accessed 27 March 2017.

22 Jennifer Maureen Lowe, 'Social Justice and Localities: The Allocation of Council Housing in Tower Hamlets', PhD thesis, Queen Mary College, University of London, March 2004, 150–2.

23 Tower Hamlets Fairness Commission, 'Who Lives in Tower Hamlets? Where Do They Live?' Communities and Housing Evidence Pack (ND), 13–14, towerhamlets.gov.uk, accessed 27 March 2017.

24 Mark Leftly, 'Charm Offensive', building.co.uk, no. 48, 2005, accessed 27 March 2017.

25 Tenant Participation Advisory Service, Office of the Deputy Prime Minister, 'Arms Length Management Organisations', Factsheet 2003, 4, housingcare.org, accessed 28 March 2017.

26 Carl Brown, 'Council Takes ALMO Services Back In House', *Inside Housing*, 17 May 2011, insidehousing.co.uk, accessed 28 March 2017.

27 Jules Birch, 'Up in Arms: Are We Facing the Death of the Almo?' *Guardian*, 3 November 2011.

28 Rachel Newton, with Rebecca Tunstall, 'Lessons for Localism: Tenants'

Self-Management' (Urban Forum, ND), 13, york.ac.uk, accessed 29 March 2017.

29   Quoted in John Seddon, *Systems Thinking in the Public Sector: The Failure of the Reform Regime . . . and a Manifesto for a Better Way* (Triarchy Press, 2008), 16.

30   Quoted in Thomas Ellerton, 'Exploring the Impact of New Labour Urban Regeneration Policy at the Local Scale: The Implications of an Approach to "Joining-Up" on the Coordination of Urban Regeneration', PhD thesis, University of Sheffield, April 2014, 63.

31   J.P. Smith, *Low Hill: Study of a Wolverhampton Housing Estate* (Wolverhampton Young Volunteers, 1971).

32   Sheffield City Council, *Wybourn, Arbourthorne, Manor Park Master Plan* (2005).

33   Phil Griffin, 'On the Terraces', *Building Design Magazine Supplement*, no. 8, special issue, bdonline.co.uk, 15 June 2007.

34   Philip Leather and Brendan Nevin, 'The Housing Market Renewal Programme: Origins, Outcomes and the Effectiveness of Public Policy Interventions in a Volatile Market', *Urban Studies*, vol. 50, no. 5, 871.

35   Hatherley, *A Guide to the New Ruins of Great Britain*, xvii.

36   Stuart Hodkinson, 'The Private Finance Initiative in English Council Housing Regeneration: A Privatisation too Far?' *Housing Studies*, vol. 26, no. 6, 2011, 914.

37   *Salford City Partnership Creating a New Pendleton: Benefits Realisation Plan* (July 2009), 7, partnersinsalford.org, accessed 31 March 2017.

38   Pendleton Together, *An Ideal for Living* (ND), pendletonway.co.uk, accessed 31 March 2017.

39   Luke Cross, 'Together Closes Salford PFI with £82.6m Two-Tranche Bond', *Social Housing*, 4 October 2013, socialhousing.co.uk, accessed 31 March 2017.

40   Stuart Hodkinson, *Council Housing Regeneration and the Private Finance Initiative: An Overview* (ND), defendcouncilhousing.org.uk, accessed 31 March 2017.

41   National Audit Office, *PFI in Housing*, June 2010, 5–9, nao.org.uk, accessed 31 March 2017.

42   Cathy Davis, *Finance for Housing: An Introduction* (Policy Press, 2013), 14.

43   National Audit Office, *The Decent Homes Programme*, January 2010, 12, nao.org.uk, accessed 3 April 2017.

44   National Audit Office, *The Decent Homes Programme*, 6 and 19.

45   Koos Couvée, 'Woodberry Down in Hackney: How "Regeneration" is

Tearing Up Another East London Community', *The Multicultural Politic* (28 June 2012), tmponline.org.

46   Rachael Clegg, 'Welcome to the Modern Manor, Sheffield', *The Star*, 31 July 2012, thestar.co.uk, accessed 3 April 2017.

47   The Riverside Group, Carlisle Housing Association, Carlisle City Council, Lovell, Ainsley Gommon Architecture and Urban Design, *Raffles Vision: Draft Final Report* (ND). It's worth noting the joint authorship as an indication of the interests involved.

48   Julian Whittle, '£100,000 for a New Home as Rundown Estate Goes Posh', *News and Star*, 8 October 2003; Deborah Kuiper, 'Raffles: The Trendy New Place to Live', *News and Star*, 14 September 2006; Chris Story, '£30m Investment Leaves Carlisle Estate's Bad Old Days in Past', *Cumberland News*, 6 September 2013.

49   'Raffles: From Riots to Show Homes in 10 Years', *Cumberland News*, 6 September 2013.

50   Riverside, 'Work Starts on £5 Million Affordable Housing Scheme Raffles', 16 June 2014, riverside.org.uk, accessed 6 March 2015.

51   'Who Built More Council Houses – Margaret Thatcher or New Labour?' *Full Fact*, 12 November 2013, fullfact.org, accessed 4 April 2017.

52   Robertson, 'Labour's Legacy', *Inside Housing*, 7 May 2010, insidehousing. co.uk, accessed 19 June 2017.

53   Kate Barker, *Review of Housing Supply: Final Report* (HM Treasury, March 2004), 139, news.bbc.co.uk, accessed 4 April 2017.

54   Office of the Deputy Prime Minister, *Sustainable Communities: Homes for All* (2005), 33–4 and 41.

55   John Hills, *Ends and Means: The Future Roles of Social Housing in England* (CASE Report 34, February 2007), 1, eprints.lse.ac.uk, accessed 4 April 2017.

10. 'People Need Homes; These Homes Need People': 2010 to the Present

1   Simon Jenkins, 'The Lesson from Grenfell is Simple: Stop Building Residential Towers', *Guardian*, 15 June 2017, theguardian.com, accessed 21 June 2017.

2   Grenfell Action Group, 'Playing with Fire', grenfellactiongroup.wordpress. com, accessed 20 June 2017.

3   Toby Helm, Jamie Doward and Michael Savage, 'Revealed: The Tower Block Fire Warnings that Ministers Ignored', *Guardian*, 17 June 2017, theguardian.com, accessed 20 June 2017.

4   Deon Lombard, 'Architects Like Me Know Grenfell Tower Fire Was an Avoidable Tragedy', *Guardian*, 17 June 2017, theguardian.com, accessed 20 June 2017.

5   Suzanne Fitzpatrick and Beth Watts, 'Competing Visions, Security of Tenure and the Welfarisation of English Social Housing', *Housing Studies*, 20 February 2017, 3, tandfonline.com, accessed 27 April 2017.

6   'The Regulatory Framework for Social Housing in England from April 2010', quoted in Elizabeth Parkin and Wendy Wilson, House of Commons Library, 'Social Housing: The End of "Lifetime" Tenancies in England?' Briefing Paper Number 07173, 27 May 2016, 8.

7   Grant Shapps, Minister of Housing and Local Government, Written Statement to Parliament: Localism Bill and Social Housing, 9 December 2010, gov.uk, accessed 28 April 2017.

8   Fitzpatrick and Watts, 'Competing Visions, Security of Tenure and the Welfarisation of English Social Housing', 7–10.

9   A Department for Communities and Local Government spokesman quoted in Toby Helm, "Pay to Stay" Trap will Force Working Families Out of Council Homes', *Observer*, 6 February 2016, theguardian.com, accessed 2 May 2017.

10   Tim Ross, 'Council Houses Go to Professionals Earning £100,000', *Daily Telegraph*, 16 February 2014, telegraph.co.uk, accessed 2 May 2017.

11   Cited in Helm, "Pay to Stay" Trap will Force Working Families Out of Council Homes'.

12   Patrick Collinson, 'Right to Buy: How Will it Work?' *Guardian*, 14 April 2015, theguardian.com, accessed 3 May 2017.

13   Shelter, *The Forced Council Home Sell-Off*, September 2015, 12, england.shelter.org.uk, accessed 3 May 2017.

14   Fifty-five per cent of the federation's 584 members voted in favour of the voluntary scheme, 39 per cent abstained and 6 per cent opposed. Henry Zeffman, 'Right-to-Buy Deal Backed by Only 55% of Housing Associations', *Guardian*, 17 October 2015, theguardian.com, accessed 3 May 2017.

15   Peter Apps, 'First Tenants Purchase Homes under Right to Buy Pilots', *Inside Housing*, 10 September 2016, insidehousing.co.uk.

16   Shelter, *Starter Homes: Will They Be Affordable?* August 2015, 3, england.shelter.org.uk, accessed 3 May 2017.

17   Quoted in Simon Hattenstone, 'Nick Clegg: "I Did Not Cater for the Tories' Brazen Ruthlessness"', *Guardian*, 3 September 2016, theguardian.com, accessed 12 June 2017.

18   Department for Communities and Local Government, *English Housing*

Survey: Headline Report, 2015–16, March 2017, 1–2, gov.uk, accessed 3 May 2017.

19 Cited in Damien Gayle, 'Private Landlords Get £9.3bn in Housing Benefit from Taxpayer, Says Report', *Guardian,* 20 August 2016, theguardian.com, accessed 3 May 2017.

20 SHOUT, the Campaign for Social Housing, *Affordable, Flourishing, Fair: A Manifesto to Save and Extend Social Rented Housing,* June 2014, 14, cloudfront.net, accessed 3 May 2017.

21 Pete Apps, 'Financial Impacts of Bedroom Tax Mitigated but Tenants Struggle"', *Inside Housing,* 8 January 2015, insidehousing.co.uk, accessed 4 May 2017.

22 Quoted in S. Moffatt, S. Lawson, R. Patterson, E. Holding, et al., 'A Qualitative Study of the Impact of the UK "Bedroom Tax"', *Journal of Public Health,* vol. 38, no. 2, 2016, 119–200, academic.oup.com, accessed 5 May 2017.

23 Kathryn Hopkins, 'Social Housing Builder Genesis Blames Rent Cut as it Slashes Affordable Homes', *Times,* 29 October 2015, thetimes.co.uk, accessed 7 May 2017.

24 Patrick Butler, 'Benefit Cap Will Hit 116,000 of Poorest Families, Say Experts', *Guardian,* 1 November 2016, theguardian.com, accessed 5 May 2017, and Jenny Pennington, 'The Benefit Cap: This Changes Everything', *Shelter Policy Blog,* 20 July 2015, blog.shelter.org.uk, accessed 5 May 2017.

25 Moffatt, Lawson, Patterson, Holding, et al., 'A Qualitative Study of the Impact of the UK "Bedroom Tax"', 202.

26 Andrew Adonis and Bill Davies (eds), *City Villages: More Homes, Better Communities* (IPPR, March 2015), 9, ippr.org, accessed 8 May 2017.

27 Yolande Barnes, 'A City Village Approach to Regenerating Housing Estates', in Adonis and Davies (eds), *City Villages,* 56.

28 Jules Pipe and Philip Glanville, 'Hackney City Villages', in Adonis and Davies (eds), *City Villages,* 82.

29 Duncan Bowie, 'City Villages – The Wrong Solution to London's Housing Crisis', *Red Brick,* 12 January 2016, redbrickblog.wordpress.com, accessed 8 May 2017.

30 Savills Research Report to Cabinet Office, *Completing London's Streets: How the Regeneration and Intensification of Housing Estates Could Increase London's Supply of Homes and Benefit Residents,* January 2016, 5, pdf.euro.savills.co.uk, accessed 8 May 2017.

31 Caroline Davies, 'David Cameron Vows to "Blitz" Poverty by Demolishing UK's Worst Sink Estates', *Guardian,* 10 January 2016, theguardian.com, accessed 8 May 2017.

32   David Cameron, *Estate Regeneration*, 10 January 2016, gov.uk, accessed 8 May 2017.

33   *Haringey Council's Local Plan Consultation: Response by Broadwater Farm Residents' Association* (24 March 2015), 7, haringey.gov.uk, accessed 9 May 2017.

34   Iain Duncan Smith, 'We Cannot Arrest Our Way Out of These Riots', *Times*, 15 September 2011, thetimes.co.uk, accessed 9 May 2017.

35   Cameron, *Estate Regeneration*.

36   Space Syntax, *2011 London Riots Location Analysis: Proximity to Town Centres and Large Post-War Housing Estates* (2011), image.guardian.co.uk, accessed 9 May 2017.

37   *Reading the Riots: Investigating England's Summer of Disorder* (*Guardian* and the London School of Economics, 2011), 4, eprints.lse.ac.uk, accessed 9 May 2017.

38   Bob Jeffery and Waqas Tufail, '"The Riots Were Where the Police Were": Deconstructing the Pendleton Riot', *Contention: The Multidisciplinary Journal of Social Protest*, vol. 2, no. 2, October 2016, 53, shura.shu.ac.uk, accessed 9 March 2017.

39   Social Life, *Cressingham Gardens Estate*, October 2013, social-life.co, accessed 10 May 2017.

40   Save Cressingham Gardens, *Petition: Stop Mott MacDonald Profiting from Community Destruction*, 6 May 2017, savecressingham.wordpress.com, accessed 10 May 2017.

41   Barnet Council, 'West Hendon Estate, West Hendon, London NW9: Application Summary', 17 December 2014, barnet.moderngov.co.uk, accessed 13 June 2017.

42   Dave Hill, 'Jasmin Parsons and the Troubled Tale of the West Hendon Estate', *Guardian*, 4 November 2015, theguardian.com, accessed 13 June 2017.

43   Chris Godfrey, 'How Council Promises Have Fallen Away, Leaving the West Hendon Estate in Dire Straits', *New Statesman*, 28 January 2015, newstatesman.com, accessed 10 May 2017.

44   James Caven, '"You Are Displacing a Whole Community": Public Inquiry into West Hendon Estate Starts', *Hendon and Finchley Times*, 20 January 2015, times-series.co.uk, accessed 13 June 2017.

45   Dave Hill, 'Earls Court Regeneration: Reviews and Uncertainties', *Guardian*, 3 October 2016, theguardian.com, accessed 10 May 2017.

46   West Ken and Gibbs Green – The People's Estates, 'Residents Launch People's Plan for Improvements and New Homes Without Demolition', 21 July 2016, westkengibbsgreen.wordpress.com, accessed 10 May 2017.

47 Sam Gelder, 'Northwold Estate Campaigners Fight Developers over Demolition of Housing Blocks', *Hackney Gazette*, 30 November 2016, hackneygazette.co.uk, accessed 11 May 2017.

48 Shelter, *Shelter's Response to the CLG's Consultation – Reform of Council Housing Finance*, October 2009, 6, england.shelter.org.uk, accessed 12 May 2017.

49 Price Waterhouse Cooper, *HRA Reform: One Year On*, July 2013, 2, pwc.co.uk, accessed 12 May 2017.

50 Janice Morphet, 'Is Austerity the Mother of Invention? How Local Authorities are Providing Housing Again', *LSE British Politics and Policy*, blogs.lse.ac.uk, accessed 11 May 2017.

51 UK Government, 'Table 600: Numbers of Households on Local Authorities' Housing Waiting Lists, by District, England, from 1997', gov.uk, accessed 11 May 2017.

52 Michael Buchanan and Sophie Woodcock, 'Councils Spent £3.5bn on Temporary Housing in Last Five Years', *BBC News*, 17 November 2016, bbc.co.uk, accessed 11 May 2017.

53 Alex Homer, 'Town Halls Buy Back Right-to-Buy Homes', *BBC News*, 3 May 2017, bbc.co.uk, accessed 11 May 2017.

54 Haringey Council, 'Haringey's Development Partnership – A New Approach to Regeneration', 11 November 2015, haringey.gov.uk, accessed 13 June 2017.

55 Dave Hill, 'Q&A: Haringey Leader Claire Kober on Borough's "Development Vehicle" Plans', 28 February 2017, onlondon.co.uk, accessed 13 June 2017.

56 Aditya Chakrabortty, 'Lives Torn Apart and Assets Lost: This is What a Labour Privatisation Would Mean', *Guardian*, 19 January 2017, theguardian.com, accessed 13 June 2017.

57 Shelter, 'Can Haringey's Housing Development Vehicle Provide a Case Study in Joint Ventures?' 24 February 2017, blog.shelter.org.uk, accessed 13 June 2017.

58 Frankie Crossley, 'Council Responds to Claims that Camden Community Investment Programme is Failing to Build Enough Social Housing', *Ham & High*, 9 May 2017, hamhigh.co.uk, accessed 12 May 2017.

59 David Spittles, 'It's a Game Changer: Camden is First Council to Build Homes to Sell', *Evening Standard Homes and Property*, 19 November 2014, homesandproperty.co.uk, accessed 12 May 2017.

60 Stroud District Council, *Housing Strategy 2015–2019*, March 2015, 6, stroud.gov.uk, accessed 12 May 2017.

61   Quoted in Mark Wilding. 'Councils Use Financial Freedoms to Invest in New Affordable Homes', *Guardian*, 14 May 2012, theguardian.com, accessed 17 June 2017.

62   Cllr Matthew Bennett (Cabinet member for Housing), 'Homes for Lambeth', *Lambeth Council Estate Regeneration*, 2 October 2016, estateregeneration. lambeth.gov.uk, accessed 12 June 2017.

63   Mark Lawrence, 'Lambeth Council to Build "More and Better Homes"', *24Housing*, 13 October 2015, 24housing.co.uk, accessed 12 May 2017.

64   Lambeth United Housing Coop, 'Lambeth's New Houses – A Poor Effort Built on Misery', lambethunitedhousingco-op.org.uk, accessed 12 May 2017.

65   35% Campaign, 'No Profit for Southwark: The True Value of the Heygate Regeneration', 11 May 2016, 35percent.org, accessed 12 May 2017.

66   Rowan Moore, *Slow Burn City: London in the Twenty-First Century* (Pan Macmillan, 2016), 213.

67   The Labour Party 2017 Manifesto, 'Secure Homes for All', labour.org.uk, accessed 12 June 2017.

68   The Liberal Democrat 2017 Manifesto, 'Building More and Better Homes', libdems.org.uk, accessed 12 June 2017.

69   The Conservative Party 2017 Manifesto, 'Homes for All', conservatives.com, accessed 12 June 2017.

70   Sophie Barnes, 'Barwell: New Homes for "Social Rent" Will Be Let at Affordable Rent Levels', *Inside Housing*, 2 June 2017, insidehousing.co.uk, accessed 12 June 2017.

Index

Abercrombie, Patrick, 61–2, 63, 65, 70, 72, 73, 77, 95, 99, 104, 113, 141
Addison, Christopher, 35, 41–2, 58
Adonis, Andrew, 269
affordable homes, 2, 34, 58, 251, 265, 270, 286, 288
    Carlisle, 247
    Conservative Party, 262, 264, 287
    demand for, 6, 248–9
    Labour Party, 286
    Liverpool, 231
    London, 224–6, 246, 278, 283
    National Rent Rebate Scheme, 167
    Salford, 242
Alexandra Road Estate, 158, 159
ALMO (Arms-Length Management Organisation), 234, 235, 236, 238, 244, 246, 286
Alsop, Will, 221, 227
Alton Estate, 117–20
architects, 120, 133, 178
    Battersea, 131
    Bermondsey, 38
    Birmingham, 108, 109, 135, 207
    Boundary Estate, 20
    Camden, 158, 159, 161

    Kensington and Chelsea, 148
    Lambeth, 116, 154, 155, 156
    LCC, 36, 51, 70, 97, 105, 117, 154, 155
    Norwich, 152, 153
    Old Oak Estate, 25
    Sheffield, 140
    Southwark, 209
Architectural Association, 20, 83, 104
Architectural Review (magazine), 82, 100, 119, 148
Armstrong, Hilary, 209
Arts and Craft movement, 7, 9, 19, 21, 28
Arts Council, 65
Art Workers' Guild, 20, 25
asbestos, 92, 188, 245
Asquith, Herbert, 28
Association of Metropolitan Authorities (AMA), 128, 129
Attwood, Charles, 156
austerity, 2, 41, 88, 255, 268, 287
Aylesbury Estate, 129–30, 154, 178, 206, 219–23, 225, 226, 229, 285

Back, Les, 214

Bacton Estate, 280
Banham, Reyner, 119
Bank of England, 249
Barbican, 120
Barker, Kate, 249
Barlow, Montague, 77
Barlow Report. *See* Report of the
    Barlow Commission on
    Distribution of Industrial
    Population
Barnes, Yolande, 269
Barnet, 260, 275, 278
Barnett, Henrietta, 27
Barnett, Samuel, 27
Barwell, Gavin, 261
Bath, 69, 139
Becontree Estate, 33, 36, 37, 41
Benn, John, 18
Benson, Gordon, 159
Berkeley Homes, 245
Bethnal Green, 8, 20, 98, 122, 123, 232
Bevan, Nye, 93–4, 96–7, 106, 144, 228
Beveridge, William, 68, 69, 72, 78
Birmingham, 54, 57–8, 108–14, 134–5,
    193, 198
  architects, 108, 109, 135, 207
  Castle Vale Estate, 108–10, 181, 194,
    195
  Handsworth, 197, 198
  Lee Bank Estate, 207, 208
  slums, 208, 211
BISF (British Iron and Steel
    Federation), 83
Black, John, 191, 192
Blackbird Leys Estate, 179, 183, 198
Blair, Tony, 210, 219, 220, 222, 231,
    248
Boer War, 18
Booth, Charles, 9
Booth, William, 12

Boundary Estate, 8, 19, 20, 21, 22, 24,
    29, 59
Bowie, Duncan, 270
Brand, Russell, 279
Brexit, 263, 272, 274
Bristol, 62, 286
British Architect (magazine), 22
British Housing and Infrastructure
    Development Bank, 287
British Library, 23, 51, 100
Broadwater Farm, 272
Broken Britain, 46, 47
Brooke, Peter, 125
Brown, George, 135
Brown, Gordon, 248, 249, 281
Brown, Neave, 158, 159
Brutalism, 119, 120, 121, 122, 145, 159
Bryants, 135
Buchanan, Colin, 140
Builder, The (magazine), 13–14
Burman, Charles, 110
Burns, John, 18, 28–30
Burns, Wilfred, 133, 149

Cadbury-Brown, H.T., 148
Caffrey, Joe, 197
Cambridge, 56, 263
Cameron, David, 46, 264, 271, 272, 273
Campbell, Beatrix, 197
Canterbury, Archbishop of, 25
Cardiff, 198
Carlisle, 58, 188, 246, 247
Carlyle, Thomas, 10
Catford, 91–2
CEMA (Committee for the
    Encouragement of Music and
    the Arts), 65
Centre 8, 108, 110
Chamberlain, Joseph, 109
Chamberlain, Neville, 41, 57

Chamberlain Act, 41, 42
Chance, Steve, 206
Channel Four, 222
Chartism, 10
children, 82, 95, 100, 101, 179, 185, 225,
    266, 268
    estates, 49, 55, 75–6, 78, 86, 95–6,
        100, 125, 143, 149, 160, 162,
        273
    playgrounds, 62
    schools, 43, 70, 86, 197
    suburbs, 53
Christian socialists, 27, 56
Churchill, Winston, 61, 68, 81, 104,
    170
CIAM (*Congrès internationaux
    d'architecture moderne*), 82, 83
City Challenge, 198–9, 201, 207
City Villages (pamphlet), 268, 270, 274
Civic Trust, 104, 163
Clapham, Sidney, 125
Clarke, C.W., 80
Clay Cross, 164, 167
Clegg, Nick, 264
Coleman, Alice, 148, 179–84, 188
Coleman, Jackie, 277–8
Commission for Racial Equality, 216
Committee on the Appearance of
    Housing Estates (1948), 94–5
Commons Select Committee on the
    Health of Towns (1840), 10
Communist Party, 154
conservatism, 29, 167, 184, 194
Conservative Party, 5, 17, 48, 89, 105,
    127, 217, 220, 287
    austerity, 41
    Churchill, 68, 170
    coalition, 258
    councils, 104, 131, 159, 189, 282
    Housing Committee, 157

housing standards, 58
LCC, 39, 52–3
Local Government Association, 261
Metropolitan Housing Trust, 276
national government, 60, 85, 93,
    97
New Towns, 113
Right to Buy, 262, 282
spending, 248
Starter Homes, 264
Cook, Sydney, 158, 160
Copenhagen, 131
Corbyn, Jeremy, 286, 287
corporations, housing, 13, 24, 37, 53,
    78, 79, 80, 81, 109, 111, 168,
    201, 230
cottage suburbs, 29, 59, 152, 188, 196.
    See also suburbs
    interwar period, 65, 67, 75, 162, 216,
        238
    working-class housing, 30, 40, 120
Cotton, Archie, 154
Cowley, Jason, 85
Crawley, 77, 108, 109
Creation Trust, 227
Cressingham Gardens, 156, 157, 274,
    285
crime, 89, 122, 143, 146, 149, 178, 181,
    182, 194, 222, 226, 227
    juveniles, 183
    rates, 114, 179, 197, 202, 214, 223,
        247
Crooks, Will, 18
Crow, Bob, 260
Cruddas Park, 133, 134
Cullen, Gordon, 82
Culpin, Ewart G., 38–9, 40
Cumberland News (newspaper), 247
Czechoslovakia, 154

Dagenham, 33, 53
Dawson's Heights, 146–8, 209
Debden, 73, 74
Decent Homes Programme, 244, 245, 246, 276
defensible space, 178, 181–2, 184, 188, 200, 222, 273
demolition, 14, 97, 102, 149, 154, 164, 193, 221, 224, 239, 241, 242, 245, 275, 276
  Camden Estate, 204
  Carlisle, 247
  Charlecote Tower, 208
  critics of, 284
  Hulme Crescents, 201
  London, 271
  Longleat Tower, 208
  North Peckham, 204
  Raffles, 246
  slums, 17, 21
  Sumner Estate, 203
  tenants, 280
densification, 30, 157, 268, 274
Department for Communities and Local Government, 245
Department of the Environment, 189
Department of Work and Pensions, 55, 268
Derby, 86–9, 164, 170
Dickens, Charles, 10
disabled people, 157, 245, 260, 266
Doddington Estate, 131, 133
Dolphin Living Ltd, 279
Doncaster, 62
Dover House Estate, 31, 33, 37, 42, 47
Drake, Francis, 63
Dudley Committee, 94, 95
Duncan, William Henry, 10, 11, 13
Duncan Smith, Iain, 273
Dunning JP, J.H., 164

Durant, Ruth, 59
Durham, 69, 77, 78

Easington, 78, 80
elderly, 37, 88, 102, 107, 119, 157, 212
Engels, Frederick, 10
English Heritage, 147, 151, 159
ERCF (Estates Renewal Challenge Fund), 206–10
Erskine, Ralph, 149–51
Escombe, Jane, 23
Esher, Lionel, 157
Essex, 33, 75
Estate Action schemes, 187, 188, 192, 207, 229–30, 246
Europe, 51, 53, 54, 130, 151, 168, 171, 184
European Union, 271
Evening Standard (newspaper), 31
Excalibur Estate, 91–2
Exchequer, 58, 93, 106, 261, 267

Fabianism, 18, 28, 150
Faraday Housing Association, 221
Faraday Community School, 227
fascism, 42–3, 67, 213
Felton, Monica, 81
Fergusson, Adam, 164
Festival of Britain, 97, 98, 99, 103
fire safety, 1–2, 252–5
First World War, 18, 30, 33–4, 56
Fitzpatrick, Suzanne, 259
Five Estates, 202, 203, 205, 212, 221
Fleming, Owen, 20–22
Flint, Alderman, 88–9
Forrest, George Topham, 51–2
Forshaw, J.H., 70, 95
Forsyth, Alan, 159
free market, 2, 13, 17, 34, 58, 166, 172, 183, 248, 258, 288

garden cities, 26, 37, 85
garden suburbs, 25, 27, 28, 64
Geddes, Eric, 41
General Improvement Areas, 137, 163
general needs, 48, 58, 88, 97, 106, 144,
    166, 256, 257
    General Needs subsidy, 107,
    260
Genesis Housing Association, 246, 267
George, Lloyd, 31, 34, 41
Germany, 18, 54, 61
Gibberd, Frederick, 82–4, 99, 102, 103,
    115
Glanville, Philip, 269
Glasgow, 34
GLC (Greater London Council), 213
Glendinning, Miles, 132–3
Glynn, Sarah, 152
Goldfinger, Ernő, 70–71, 232
Gorvin, Diane, 37
Gould, Jeremy, 64
Grade II listed buildings, 8, 91, 125,
    151, 159, 232
Great Depression, 59, 66, 77, 256
Great War. *See* First World War
Greenwood, Anthony, 126
Grenfell Action Group, 254
Grenfell Tower, 1–6, 252–5, 263, 287
Guinness Partnership, 279

Hansard (report), 25
Harcourt, William, 17
Haringey Development Vehicle, 283
Harloe, Michael, 166
Harlow, 77, 80, 82, 83, 84, 85, 105
Hatherley, Owen, 53, 201
HATs (Housing Action Trusts), 189,
    192–5, 198, 200, 207
Heath, Edward, 167
Hendon Waterside scheme, 275, 277

Heseltine, Michael, 195, 198, 171–2
Hill, Octavia, 14–15
Hills, John, 249–50
Hobhouse, Arthur, 18
Hogarth, William, 28
Hollamby, Ted, 116, 154–7
Hollow, Matthew, 76
homelessness, 228, 276, 278, 282, 286
Housing Act, 16, 28–9, 41, 42, 47, 58,
    96, 97, 106, 114, 137, 166, 170,
    176
    1935, 48, 69
    1974, 163, 167
    Housing (Temporary
        Accommodation) Act (1944),
        91
Housing Action Areas, 137, 163, 167
Housing and Planning Bill (2015),
    260
Housing and Town Planning Act, 28,
    35
housing associations, 192, 202, 224,
    235, 245, 250, 258–63, 267
    complaints against, 210
    loans, 177
    New Labour, 248
    partnerships, 201, 203
    subsidies, 168
    Tower Hamlets, 231
Housing Benefit, 175, 257, 265, 266,
    267
Housing Finance Act (1972), 167
Housing (Financial and Miscellaneous
    Provisions) Act (1946), 93
Housing (Homeless Persons) Act
    (1977), 143, 215, 257
Housing Manual, 95, 99
Housing of the Working Classes Act
    (1890), 16–17
Housing Subsidies Act (1956), 107

Housing Survey, 111, 265
Howard, Ebenezer, 25, 26, 59, 66, 76, 80
HRAs (Housing Revenue Accounts), 281
Hull, 191–3
Hulme Crescents, 139–41, 201

Illustrated London News (newspaper), 9
Income Support, 143, 188
industrialism, 10, 19, 67, 109, 128, 131, 132, 137, 142
Industrial Revolution, 10, 11, 216
International Club, 19
Ireland, 213

Jackson, Herbert, 113
Jackson, W.T., 42–4
Jacobs, Jane, 178
Javid, Sajid, 225
Jencks, Charles, 180
Jenkinson, Charles, 54, 56
Jespersen system, 129, 131
Jews, 41, 124
Joseph, Keith, 134
Jost, Emily, 280

Karl Marx-Hof, 43, 55
Keay, Lancelot, 53–4
Keeling House, 122, 123, 124–5
Kensington and Chelsea, Borough of, 6, 148, 253–4, 263
Kent, 23, 75
Kent, William, 139
Keynesianism, 66
Kinnock, Neil, 92

Labour Party, 5, 39, 59, 68, 97, 126, 143, 201, 209. *See also* New Labour, 269–70, 276

1945 victory, 67, 68–9, 86
Bevan, Nye, 94
Corbyn, Jeremy, 286, 287
councils, 93, 113, 132, 158, 164, 206, 207, 260
Decent Homes Programme, 244
Derby, 87, 88
early years of, 34, 42, 50
elections, 127
home ownership, 249
Housing Act, 47, 58, 163
housing schemes, 40
Independent Labour Party, 38, 56
Kinnock, Neil, 92
Leeds, 57
policy, 40
Laings, 129, 131, 132, 133
Land Acquisition Act (1946), 69
Lansbury Estate, 98, 100, 101, 117
Lasdun, Denys, 122, 123, 125
Latham, Arthur, 71, 242
LCC, *See* London County Council
Le Corbusier, 54, 81, 100, 119, 154–5
Lee, Peter, 80
Leeds, 54–7, 263, 286
Lendlease, 226, 283, 285
Letchworth, 25, 26, 44
Liberal Democrat Party, 174, 224, 258, 264, 276, 284, 287
Liverpool, 30, 53, 5, 197, 216, 230
housing conditions, 10–12, 13, 23, 239–40
Labouring Classes Dwellings Act (1866), 13, 14
Norris Green Estate, 53–4, 174, 212, 229, 230
Public Health Act (1848), 13
Sanitary Act (1842), 12–13
Toxteth, 197, 198
Vauxhall, 13

Livett, R.A.H., 55, 56
Living Well Trust, 247
Localism Act (2011), 258, 281
London, 14, 59, 154, 206, 225, 226, 268, 270
  Battersea, 29, 131, 132
  Bermondsey, 37–40
  Bethnal Green, 8, 20, 122, 123, 232
  Bow, 20, 232
  Brixton, 155, 197, 198, 272
  Camden, 52, 157–63, 165, 173–4, 181–2, 263, 280, 284
  Clapham, 51, 125
  Covent Garden, 164
  Docks, 37, 101
  East End, 20, 40, 74, 98, 231, 232
  Euston, 51, 164
  Hackney, 20, 93, 103, 114–15, 164, 216, 235, 246, 269–70
    Northwold Estate, 279
    Priority Estates Programme, 186
    Somerford Grove, 102–3
    Trelawney Estate, 115, 129
    Woodberry Down, 245
  Hammersmith, 24, 278
  Hampstead, 25, 27, 28, 158–60
  Haringey, 272, 283
  Highgate, 81, 160, 162
  Hoxton, 279
  Lambeth, 116, 154, 155, 156, 186, 274–5, 285
  Lewisham, 49, 164, 186, 213, 214
  Pimlico, 104
  Poplar, 20, 56, 73, 98, 99, 144, 145, 231–3
  protests, 278
  riots, 272, 273
  slums, 9
  Shoreditch, 7, 19, 98
  South Bank, 97, 98
  Southwark, 37, 165, 179, 205, 206, 227, 269, 285–6
    architects, 130
    Aylesbury, 129, 154, 178, 219, 223–6
    Brandon Estate, 212
    Dawson's Heights, 146, 147, 209
    Heygate Estate, 154, 225, 285
    Lakanal House, 254–5
    North Peckham Estate, 180–81, 188–90, 202–5, 221
    Peckham Partnership, 203, 204
  Spitalfields, 14
  Stepney, 20, 40, 41, 73, 98, 99
  St Pancras, 23, 158
  Tower Hamlets, 124, 165, 179, 180, 215, 231, 232, 234
  Wandsworth, 93, 105, 118–19, 131, 132, 160
  Westminster, 104, 263
  Whitechapel, 20
  White City, 51
  Woolwich, 114
London County Council (LCC), 17, 28–9, 47, 50, 51, 114, 279
  architects, 36, 51, 70, 97, 105, 116, 117, 154, 155
  Architect's Department, 20, 100, 116, 117, 154
  elections, 18
  finance, 52–3
  Housing of the Working Classes Branch, 20
  New Towns, 77–8
  Reconstruction Group, 99
  tenement blocks, 38
LPS (Large Panel System), 129, 136, 142
Lubetkin, Berthold, 81–2

Luftwaffe, 72, 112
Lynn, Jack, 120, 121
Lyons, Eric, 148

Macintosh, Kate, 147
Mackworth Estate, 86–91, 94, 170
Macmillan, Harold, 88, 101, 105–6,
    107, 126, 257
Major, John, 157, 195, 198, 241, 248
Manchester
    council homes, 30, 58, 139
    Hulme Crescents, 139–42, 143, 144,
        190, 200–202
    Jackson, W.T., 42–4
    regeneration, 230
    slums, 11, 43, 141
    Wythenshawe Estate, 42–6, 53, 96,
        258
Manzoni, Herbert, 108, 109, 111, 112
Marxist Socialist League, 19
Massey, Doreen, 258
Matthew, Robert, 117
May, Theresa, 272
Meadow Well Estate, 196, 197, 199,
    200, 202
Mearns, Andrew, 12
middle class, 9, 20, 27, 46, 93, 175, 182,
    223, 228, 253, 270
    Boundary Estate, 22
    Camden, 165
    Derby, 88
    Highgate, 81
    Islington, 165
    MIRAS, 217
    New Towns, 80
    planners, 65
    racism, 214
    slum clearance, 10–12, 15, 50
    suburbs, 13, 190
    Westminster, 104

MIPIM (*Le marché international des
    professionnels de l'immobilier*),
    286
MIRAS (Mortgage Interest Relief at
    Source), 173, 217
mixed communities, 4, 190, 223, 225,
    228, 241, 249, 250, 283
Modern Architecture Research
    (MARS), 83
modernist architecture, 51, 54, 81, 83,
    97, 112, 118, 121, 163, 181–2,
    204, 274
monumentalism, 43, 85, 119, 156
Moore, Rowan, 156, 285–6
Mornement, Adam, 114
Morris, William, 19–20, 21, 27, 65
Morrison, Arthur, 9–10, 22
Moya, Hidalgo, 104
Muthesius, Stefan, 132–3

Nairn, Ian, 105
National Coal Board, 81–2
National Health Service, 68, 90, 173
National Housing Federation, 263, 266
National Living Wage, 264
National Rent Rebate Scheme, 167,
    257
National Review (magazine), 15
National Theatre, 122
NDC (New Deal for Communities),
    220, 226–8
neoliberalism, 2, 3, 67, 241, 251, 287
Newcastle, 133–4, 149, 151, 152, 196
    Byker, 149–52
New Era Estate, 279
Newham, 136, 278–9
New Humanism, 103, 119
New Labour, 211, 217, 219, 223, 235,
    236, 248, 251
    Blair, 248

ERCF, 208, 210,
housing transfers, 177, 228–9
regeneration, 184, 202, 241, 244
social exclusion, 202, 217–18, 221
Newman, Oscar, 178–9, 180
New Right, 171–2, 184
News and Star (newspaper), 247
Newton Aycliffe, 77–9
New Towns, 26, 40, 73, 76, 77, 78, 80, 82, 85, 126
New Towns Act (1946), 77
New York, 178
New York Times (newspaper), 46
No-Fines houses, 89, 90. *See also* Wimpey homes
Norfolk, 152, 153
North Hull Estate, 191–2
North Kensington, 1, 4
North Peckham Estate, 180–81, 188–90, 202–5, 221
Peckham Partnership, 203, 204
North Shields, 196–7
Norwich, 58, 125, 152, 153, 171
Nottingham, 170, 235, 286

Old Oak Estate, 24, 27–9, 32
Osborn, F.J., 76, 80
Osborne, George, 261, 264, 267
Ossulston Estate, 51, 52
Oxford, 27, 69, 179, 183, 198

Pacifist Service Unit, 50
Pall Mall Gazette (newspaper), 16
Paris, 56, 63, 131
Parker, Barry, 26, 27, 44, 45
Parker, Tony, 212
Parker Morris, 126–7, 222
Paton Watson, James, 62, 65
Peabody Trust, 14, 124
Pennine Housing 2000, 246

People (magazine), 226
Pepys Estate, 212–13
Percival, David, 152
Peterlee, 77–82
Pevsner, Nikolaus, 43, 55, 118
PFI (Private Finance Initiative), 224, 241–4, 246
Pipe, Jules, 269
Plan for Plymouth (Abercrombie/ Paton Watson), 62, 65, 71, 72–3, 95
Plymouth, 61, 62, 63, 64, 73
police, 75, 183, 196, 197, 200, 272, 273, 274
Poor Law, 57, 175
Poulson, John, 133, 134
poverty, 17, 19, 38, 182, 184, 189, 198, 216, 217, 228, 237, 271, 273, 274, 283
Powell, Philip, 104
prefabricated homes, 89, 91–2, 128
problem estates, 3, 143, 195, 220, 223
protests, 190, 196, 208, 278, 279
Public Sector Borrowing Requirement, 177, 210
Public Works Loans Board, 14, 93, 243

Quakerism, 43, 150
Quarry Hill Estate, 54–6

racism, 166, 212–16
Radburn, New Jersey, 95
Radburn design housing, 95, 102, 109, 140
redevelopment areas, 48, 69, 114, 137, 207
Reed, William, 135–6
regeneration, 2, 185, 195, 198, 201, 202, 225, 231, 270, 276, 280, 284, 285

Aylesbury, 221, 226
Conservatives, 187
displacement, 228
estates, 4, 184, 210, 224, 268, 271,
    272
Five Estates, 203
Grenfell Tower, 254
Hackney, 245
Inpartnership, 230
New Labour, 241
North Peckham, 189, 205
Pendleton, 242, 243
protests against, 278
Raffles, 247
Willowbrook Estate, 203–4
Reith Commission, 69, 77, 81
renovation, 1, 253–4, 270, 278
Report of the Barlow Commission on
    Distribution of Industrial
    Population (1940), 66, 76–7
residualisation, 144, 152, 166, 211, 217,
    257
RIBA (Royal Institute of British
    Architects), 115, 117, 131, 157
Richards, J.M., 82, 100
Right to Buy, 170, 173, 174, 224, 231,
    257, 258, 263, 270, 279, 285,
    287
  Boundary Estate, 8
  Conservative Party, 169, 261–2
  Corbyn, Jeremy, 286
  inequality, 175
  introduction of, 5
  Labour Party, 127
  legislation, 171, 228, 282
  residualisation, 211
  sales, 281
Riley, W.E., 25
riots, 183, 196, 198, 272–4
RMT, 260

Roberts, Allan, 139
Robin Hood Gardens, 144, 145, 180
Rochdale, 137, 236
Rogers, Su, 161–2
Ronan Point, 136, 137, 142, 147
Rotherham, 27, 235
Ruskin, John, 15, 19, 27
Russia, 34, 81

Salford, 96, 129, 240, 241, 242, 246, 274
Salisbury, Lord, 15–16
Salix Homes, 246
Salter, Ada, 37, 38, 56
Salter, Alfred, 37–40, 56
Salter, Joyce, 37, 56
Salvation Army, 12
Samuel Lewis Housing Trust, 209
Sandys, Duncan, 107
Scandinavian architecture, 103, 115,
    118, 136
Scotland, 53, 262
Scunthorpe, 90
Second World War, 26, 45, 48, 60, 61,
    62, 77, 90, 92–5, 98, 256

Shapps, Grant, 259
shared ownership, 204, 208, 230, 239,
    242, 262, 264, 267, 275
Sharp, Thomas, 69
Sheffield, 30, 62, 120, 140, 216, 235,
    239, 246
  Park Hill, 120–22, 140, 240
Shelter, 263, 264, 281
Sheppard Fidler, A.G., 108, 109, 110,
    111, 112, 135, 207
Silkin, Lewis, 54, 77, 78, 79, 81
Simon, Ernest, 42, 44, 46
Simon, Shena, 42
slums, 2, 47, 130. See also slum clearance
  Birmingham, 208

conditions in, 59, 77, 127
working-class, 46, 59, 256
slum clearance, 15, 90, 94, 107, 115, 198
Birmingham, 111
Camden, 160, 163, 165
Conservative Party, 166
Housing Act, 47, 48
Labour Party, 40, 47, 58
Leeds, 54–5
Lewisham, 50
Liverpool, 24
Norwich, 58
Old Nichol, 9–10, 12, 14, 22
Plymouth, 64
Smith, Duncan, 273
Smith, Ivor, 120, 121
Smith, T. Dan, 133–4, 149
Smithson, Alison and Peter, 145, 146, 151,
Social Darwinism, 18, 184
social exclusion, 202, 217–18, 221
socialism, 43, 67, 81, 104, 143, 159–60, 201
anti-socialism, 58
Christian socialists, 27, 56
socialists, 17, 18, 19, 20, 28, 40, 65, 164
social security, 68, 220, 225, 257–8, 265
Society for the Protection of Ancient Buildings, 19–20
Somerford Grove, 102, 103, 115
Soviet constructivism, 81
Soviet Union, 67, 154
Space Syntax, 273
Spanish Armada, 63
Special Areas Act (1934), 66
Sporle, Sidney, 132, 133, 136
squatters' movement, 90
SRB (Single Regeneration Budget), 202–3, 206, 246

Stalag Luft III, 71
Stepney, 20, 40, 41, 73, 98, 99
Stevenage, 76, 79–80
Stonehouse, Roger, 163
suburbia, 13, 53, 57, 110, 111, 116, 125, 163, 190, 205. *See also* cottage suburbs
surveillance, 178, 180, 200, 276
Swales, Ken, 247
Sweden, 150

Tábori, Peter, 160
Taut, Bruno, 54
Taylor, Nicholas, 164
Tayler and Green, 152
Tebbit, Norman, 173
Telegraph (newspaper), 260
Tenants' Choice, 176, 209
Thatcher, Margaret, 167, 173, 184, 195, 197–8
aspirational working class, 210, 262
Housing Act (1970), 170
Right to Buy, 5, 169, 171, 174
Thatcherism, 183, 184, 201, 219
Thresh, John, 11
Times (newspaper), 51, 103
TMOs (Tenant Management Organisations), 175, 236, 238, 254
Town Planning and Housing and Public, 54, 77
Townswomen's Guild, 89, 90
Toynbee Hall, 20, 27
Trippier, David, 190, 191, 192
Tudor Walters Report, 35, 41, 112

unemployment, 66, 173, 182, 183, 197, 198, 200, 214, 216, 220, 227, 228, 238, 246
Unwin, Raymond, 26–8, 35, 44, 59

urbanisation, 11, 25, 67
urbanism, 82, 100, 201, 269
utopianism, 22, 66, 67, 76, 85, 90, 161,
    163, 183

vandalism, 124, 132, 149, 162, 179, 181,
    182, 185
Vienna, 42, 43, 51, 54

Waddington, Derek, 193
Wales, 58, 132, 171, 262
Walker, Cyril, 116–17
Wates, 89, 131, 132
Watton, Harry, 113
Watts, Beth, 259
Webb, Sidney, 18
Welfare Reform and Work Act (2016),
    267
Welfare State, 64, 68, 88, 90, 119–20,
    127, 184
    Scandinavia, 100
welfarisation, 257, 258, 260
Welsh Harp Reservoir, 275, 277
Westbrook Partners, 279
West Hendon Estate, 275, 276

Wheatley, John, 39, 42
Wheeler, E.P., 51
White, Len, 50
Whittington Estate, 160–62, 173–4,
    181–2
Willmott, Peter, 74
Willowbrook Estate, 188, 203–4
Wilson, Harold, 128
Wilson, Hugh, 139, 140, 142

Wilson, Sandy, 100, 116, 117, 128,
Wimpey homes, 89, 90, 132, 133–4,
    207
Winter, John, 159
women, 43–4, 96, 143
Womersley, J. Lewis, 120–21, 139, 140,
    142
Woodrow, Taylor, 132, 136
working class, 4, 52, 54, 59, 65, 68, 121,
    122, 144, 145, 165, 173, 184,
    199, 214
  aspirational working class, 47, 210
  better-off working class, 3, 22, 27,
    29, 47, 58, 174, 256
  Boundary Estate, 8
  children, 75
  cottage suburbs, 30, 40
  Dover House Estate, 31
  housing, 14, 15, 17, 22, 93–4, 97,
    120, 124, 232, 270
  Labour Party, 129
  Newcastle, 133
  Plymouth, 64
  poor working class, 47, 58
  rehousing, 28
  terraced housing, 23, 74
  women, 96
World's End Estate, 148, 149, 179
World War 1, 30, 31, 33, 34, 35
World War 2, 67

Yorke, F.R.S., 83
Yorkshire, 27, 133, 193
Young, Michael, 74
Younge, Gary, 79–80